Privacy and Crir

Daniel Marshall • Terry Thomas

Privacy and Criminal Justice

palgrave
macmillan

Daniel Marshall
School of Law
Liverpool John Moores University
Liverpool, UK

Terry Thomas
School of Social Sciences
Leeds Beckett University
Leeds, UK

ISBN 978-3-319-87901-7   ISBN 978-3-319-64912-2   (eBook)
https://doi.org/10.1007/978-3-319-64912-2

Cover illustration: Fatima Jamada

Printed on acid-free paper

This Palgrave Macmillan imprint is published by Springer Nature
The registered company is Springer International Publishing AG
The registered company address is: Gewerbestrasse 11, 6330 Cham, Switzerland

To Sandy

Preface

What is privacy? To what extent should individual privacy be dismissed in the interests of crime prevention and investigation? Who benefits from this intrusion of privacy? How often do the benefits from preventing crime or criminal behaviour exceed this intrusion of individual privacy? Is individual privacy dead? In a rapidly evolving technological world, can information ever be private? Who owns this (private) information and how is it used? These are some of the important challenges facing criminal justice policymakers today. Responding to them is no easy task, but answers are needed to ensure that the criminal justice system maintains the integrity of individuals who encounter it.

This book grew out of the news stories of undercover police officers and the 2016 arguments for and against a new Investigatory Powers Act for the UK. It attempts to build on the work of surveillance studies and the need for agencies of the state to keep a watchful eye on certain people and even whole categories of people. The authors attempt to do this by taking the concept of 'privacy' as a starting point rather than the means of surveillance and examine how that concept is realised and potentially intruded upon in contemporary society. At the same time, it recognises current needs to combat serious crime and terrorism and the various ways of doing this. In doing so, the book critically examines legislative developments and technological developments that have been made that facilitate the agencies of surveillance and also examines other parts of the criminal justice system where issues of privacy and privacy information are relevant. The book is intended to be a source book for readers who wish to go further into the subject.

We would like to acknowledge the help of various people who have assisted our understanding of this subject area over the years, including Bill Hebenton, Steve Wright, Steve Lister, Eva Kemecsei, Colin Webster, Laura Bui, Per-Olof Wikström and Loraine Gelsthorpe.

Liverpool, UK   Daniel Marshall

Leeds, UK   Terry Thomas

Contents

1 Introduction   1

2 A Brief History of Privacy   13

3 Police (1): Interventions   39

4 Police (2): Techniques of Investigation   71

5 Police (3): Data Collection and Retention   101

6 Photographs, CCTVs and Other Cameras   127

7 The 'Open' Court   153

8 Punishment and Privacy   183

9 Counterterrorism   215

10   Rehabilitation After Punishment   239

11   Conclusions   263

Bibliography   269

Index   317

Abbreviations List

AAMR	Alcohol Abstinence and Monitoring Requirement
ACPO	Association of Chief Police Officers
AIT	Advanced Imaging Technology
AMHP	Approved Mental Health Professional
ANPR	Automatic Number Plate Recognition
APP	Authorised Professional Practice
ASBO	Anti-Social Behaviour Order
ATR	Automated Target Recognition
BBW	Big Brother Watch
BME	Black or Minority Ethnic
BOF	Back Office Facility
BOSS	Body Orifice Security Scanner
BWV	Body Worn Video
CCDC	Covert Communications Data Capture
CCRC	Criminal Cases Review Commission
CCTV	Closed Circuit Television
CHIS	Covert Human Intelligence Sources
CID	Criminal Investigation Department
CNA	Certified Normal Accommodation
CONTEST	Counter Terrorism Strategy
CPS	Crown Prosecution Service
CRB	Criminal Records Bureau
CRC	Community Rehabilitation Company

CRO	Criminal Records Office
CSOD	Child Sex Offender Disclosure
CSP	Communications Service Providers
DBS	Disclosure and Banning Service
DNA	Deoxyribonucleic Acid
DRIPA	Data Retention and Investigatory Powers Act
DSOU	Don't Spy on Us
DST	Dedicated Search Teams
DVLA	Driver and Vehicle Licensing Agency
ECHR	European Court of Human Rights
ECJ	European Court of Justice
EGT	Evidence Gathering Teams
FGM	Female Genital Mutilation
FIB	Force Intelligence Bureau
FIT	Forward Intelligence Teams
FRT	Facial Recognition Technology
GCHQ	Government Communications Headquarters
GMP	Greater Manchester Police
GPMS	Government Protective Marking Scheme
GPS	Global Positioning System
GRC	Gender Recognition Certificate
HDC	Home Detention Curfew
HMIC	HM Inspectorate of Constabulary
HOLMES	Home Office Large Major Enquiry System
IAO	Investigation Anonymity Orders
ICC	Interception of Communications Commissioner
ICO	Information Commissioners Office
ICR	Internet Connection Records
IMSI	International Mobile Subscriber Identity
IPCC	Independent Police Complaints Commissioner
IPT	Investigatory Powers Tribunal
ISC	Intelligence and Security Committee
LASIE	Large Scale Information Exploitation
LSS	Local Security Strategy
MAPPA	Multi-Agency Public Protection Agency
MARAC	Multi-Agency Risk Assessment Conferences
MASH	Multi-Agency Safeguarding Hubs
MBU	Mother and Baby Unit

MDT	Mandatory Drug Testing
MHA	Mental Health Act
MIB	Motor Insurance Bureau
MIDAS	Mobile Identification at Scene
MIS	Mercury Information System
MOPI	Management of Police Information
MPS	Metropolitan Police Service
NADC	National ANPR Data Centre
NAPO	National Association of Probation Officers
NCA	National Crime Agency
NDEU	National Domestic Extremism Unit
NDNAD	National DNA Database
NIM	National Intelligence Model
NOMS	National Offender Management Service
NPCC	National Police Chief's Council
NPIA	National Policing Improvement Agency
NPOIU	National Public Order Intelligence Unit
NPS	National Probation Service
NPS	New Psychoactive Substances
NSA	National Security Agency
NSF	National Security Framework
OCJR	Office for Criminal Justice Reform
PACE	Police and Criminal Evidence Act 1984
PCSO	Police Community Support Officer
PHOENIX	Police Home Office Extended Names Index
PIA	Privacy Impact Assessment
PIN	Personal Identification Number
PNC	Police National Computer
PND	Police National Database
PPI	Public Interest Immunity
PSDB	Police Scientific Development Branch
PSI	Prison Service Instructions
PSO	Prison Service Order
RIPA	Regulation of investigatory Powers Act
RUSI	Royal United Services Institute
SAR	Suspicious Activity Report
SCC	Surveillance Camera Commissioner
SCR	Serious Case Review

SDS	Special Demonstration Squad/Special Duties Squad
SHPO	Sexual Harm Prevention Order
SIAC	Special Immigration Appeals Commission
SOS	Special Operations Squad
SRO	Sexual Risk Order
TPIM	Terrorism Prevention and Investigation Measures
UAV	Unmanned Ariel Vehicles
VODS	Vehicle Online Descriptive Search
VOI	Vehicle of Interest

List of Tables

Table 3.1   Types of stop and search (McCandless et al. 2016: 6)   42
Table 10.1 The 2012 review of the Rehabilitation of
            Offenders Act 1974   242

1

Introduction

Over the summer of 2016, the British press reported the story of a man in North Yorkshire who had been made subject to a court order that banned him from having sex with anyone unless he told the police about it 24 hours in advance. He then had to provide the police with details of the proposed partner. News of this order first broke in January 2016 when an interim Sexual Risk Order (SRO) was applied for by the North Yorkshire police; the man was not named (BBC News 2016a). In July 2016, a district judge ruled that his name could be revealed (BBC News 2016b). On 22 September 2016, the 24-hour notice condition was replaced by the phrase 'as soon as is reasonably practicable' (Finnigan 2016).

The question posed was how the British police were being allowed to demand 24-hour notice of two UK citizens who had decided to have sex. The man subject to the order had no previous convictions. To what extent was the criminal justice system of 2016 being allowed to invade the privacy of citizens in the interests of 'public protection' or 'crime prevention'?

There has been a good deal of other public comments in recent years about police interventions and the activities of other criminal justice

© The Author(s) 2017
D. Marshall, T. Thomas, *Privacy and Criminal Justice*,
https://doi.org/10.1007/978-3-319-64912-2_1

agencies that appear to be overly invasive of citizen's privacy. Examples include:

- Police powers to stop and search people in the streets and the ethics of 'full' or strip searches in police custodial areas and in prisons.
- The use of undercover police officers infiltrating protest groups to the extent of forming personal relationships and fathering children by the group members.
- The police and security services' use of phone tapping and the need for a new Investigatory Powers Act (IPA), immediately renamed the 'snoopers charter' by the press.
- The collection of personal information on such arrangements as the Police National Database (PND)
- The registration of sex offenders, terrorists and domestic extremists.
- The press revelations from Edward Snowden that the security services in the UK and the USA have the capacity to monitor millions of e-mails and other digital exchanges.
- The collection of DNA samples for a national biometric database.
- The steady spread of Closed Circuit Television (CCTV) cameras watching public spaces and the Automatic Number Plate Recognition (ANPR) cameras covering our roads. This list could be extended.

Privacy can also be invaded by other agencies and by other individuals; the criminal law may offer individuals some protection from these invasions. The purpose of this book, however, is to take privacy as a starting point and to examine all those areas of police and criminal justice work in a systematic and critical way and to consider the ways in which the privacy of people can appear to be infringed by these state agencies. It looks at policing and investigative techniques involving surveillance and the degree to which privacy intrudes upon the procedures of a trial. Are these interventions proportionate and necessary for purposes of crime prevention or investigation? It looks at the privacy accorded to people completing sentences of the court. Are some invasions of privacy put in place solely because they have become technologically possible? Does the prisoner hold on to his or her rights to privacy?

Many of these 'invasions of privacy' may be necessary for the prevention and investigation of crime to uphold the principles of criminal justice in the UK. We would not wish to solely paint a picture of a dystopian Orwellian world where 'Big Brother' is always watching our every move. We do want to examine the advancing of technology and especially information technology together with that technology's merging into what might be called a 'culture of surveillance' that sometimes overlooks privacy. As one UK Information Commissioner once warned us, we may even be sleepwalking into a 'surveillance society' where we take for granted being filmed everyday by four million CCTV cameras.

Whatever the stated rationale for these multiple interventions, we have started by stepping back and looking at the wider concept of privacy and just what privacy means in contemporary Britain. Do we have a coherent idea of what privacy is in the twenty-first century? Or is privacy—as some would suggest—'dead' these days, not least when it comes to crime reduction activities which should always take precedence over privacy—or should they?

Privacy

A problem that besets anyone writing about privacy is that of actually defining what privacy means. Most people have a rough idea of what they mean by privacy, and they usually know when their privacy has been intruded upon or even 'invaded'. In this sense, privacy takes on a personal meaning regarding spatial areas around a person where that space may be taken up and trespassed on. Most people want at least some privacy and an area of life that they can retreat into that they would regard as 'private'; privacy is said to be a psychological need, a social need and sometimes even a legal right. Some people will inevitably like more privacy than other people, and the drawing of hard-and-fast lines around privacy to show where it begins and ends for everyone is a difficult task.

'Privacy' is often contrasted with the 'public' area of life—the 'public' life being the world that is entered into when you leave your home and take to the streets or the world of employment or if you are intent on taking up a more 'public profile' in terms of a level of community or political engagement with the world. Much of our current interest in privacy has been around figures regarded as being in the public eye because they are high-profile sportsmen, show-business 'stars', politicians or members of the royal family. How much privacy are they entitled to? For example, are they entitled to take out injunctions to secure their privacy and stop press reporting of their alleged indiscretions? But the study of surveillance in contemporary society now engages us all, whether public figures or just the person in the crowd.

In the USA, in the last days of the nineteenth century, two lawyers put forward the idea that privacy was so important that it might be something that should be enshrined in law. Samuel Warren and Louis Brandeis writing in the *Harvard Law Review* described privacy as 'the right to be let alone' and the right to privacy as an example of how the common law can grow to take account of changing circumstances (Warren and Brandeis 1890).

We may have ideas about the 'essence' and 'value' of privacy, but in the UK, we have no legal definition in statutory law or common law even though some laws make references and aside to it in their provisions. The Mental Health Act 1983, for example, requires anyone being considered for a compulsory admission to a psychiatric hospital to be examined by a doctor 'in private' (s24 (1)). But the Act offers no definition of 'in private'.

Trying to pin down a more exact legalistic definition of what privacy is, is somewhat harder. Some legal cases specifically refer to the absence of a legal definition of privacy in the UK and the need for such a definition (see, e.g., *Kaye v Robertson [1991] FSR 62*).

Case Study

The lack of a UK law protecting privacy was considered in the case of *Kaye v Robertson*. Gordon Kaye was a well-known television actor who had been involved in a car crash suffering head injuries. While recovering from surgery, two *Sunday Sport* journalists went into his hospital dressed as medical staff to take photographs of him. Lawyers acting on behalf of Mr Kaye obtained an injunction to prevent publication of the photos, and the newspaper appealed against the injunctions. Mr Justice Eady ruled against the newspaper and bemoaned the lack of a law of privacy; he declared his belief that there was 'a serious gap in the jurisprudence of any civilised society, if such a gross intrusion could happen without redress'., (*Kaye v Robertson [1991] FSR 62*).

Definitions of privacy have been attempted in non-legal forums but again with little success. In the UK, the Younger Report on privacy declared that 'everyone needs some privacy ... [but]...the effects ... vary from person to person' (Younger Report 1972: para.105); the Lindop Committee agreed (Lindop Report 1978: para.2.01). The Calcutt Report on press intrusions into privacy tried again but became resigned to the fact that there was 'little possibility of producing a precise or exhaustive definition of privacy' (Calcutt Report 1990: para.3.4).

The Younger Committee pointed to the preferred way in which English law seeks to protect its citizens, based on the civil liberty principle that that which is not prohibited is therefore permitted. The law, in matters of privacy as well as other aspects of life, emphasises only the need to keep within acceptable limits and to draw what we might call negative boundaries around certain actions.

David Feldman has written of:

The combination of the idea of a right to be respected as a moral agent with the idea of social spheres of decision-making within which people or groups are entitled to regard themselves as free from outside coercion are, I suggest, of the essence off the notion of privacy as a civil liberty. (Feldman 1994)

And, more recently, privacy was said to be indispensable:

Privacy protects a set of deeply significant values that no society can do without; it is about the lines, boundaries and relationships we draw between and among ourselves, communities and institutions. Rather than an empty ideal or state, attitudes towards privacy tell us much about those fundamental relationships; what people think and expect of their neighbours, their fellow citizens and their government. (RUSI 2015: para.2.15)

Definitions of privacy have been put forward in international declarations and conventions that have been endorsed by the UK. Two of these followed on from the atrocities of the Second World War. The United Nations Universal Declaration of Human Rights made it clear that 'no one shall be subjected to arbitrary interference with his privacy, family, home or correspondence' (UN 1948: Article 12), and the Council of

Europe's European Convention on Human Rights (ECHR) made a similar statement in its Article 8 that 'everyone has the right to respect for his private and family life, his home and his correspondence' (CoE 1950: Article 8). Article 8 can be legally tested insofar as the Human Rights Act 1998 brought the Convention into UK law and alleged violations can be heard in the UK Courts as well as the European Court of Human Rights in Strasbourg.

The Convention does allow the state and public authorities to interfere with an individual's Article 8 right to privacy if the interference has an obvious legal justification. Among other reasons, this could be because the interference is necessary to protect national security for the prevention of crime. In addition to having a clear legal justification, the amount of interference with the right must be proportionate to the end result achieved and only go as far as is required to achieve that result. Article 8 has been the subject of discussion by the European Court of Human Rights, and a working definition has slowly evolved. Many of these cases are considered later in this volume. For present purposes, we might note the European Court comments on trying to interpret Article 8:

> As the court has had previous occasion to remark, the concept of 'private life' is a broad term not susceptible to exhaustive definition. It covers the physical and psychological integrity of a person. ... It can sometimes embrace aspects of an individual's physical and social identity. ... Elements such as, for example, gender identification, name and sexual orientation and sexual life fall within the personal sphere protected by Article 8. ... Article 8 also protects a right to personal development, and the right to establish and develop relationships with other human beings and the outside world. (*Pretty v United Kingdom (2002) 35 EHRR 1*, para 61)

Information Privacy

Another way forward is to consider not physical or spatial privacy but information privacy. Information privacy accepts that people create 'personal information' in the form of letters, telephone calls and e-mails where they expect a degree of privacy to be accorded with that information. Various other agencies may in the course of their duties collate and maintain records containing personal data in the form of police files or databases, medical files, social security files, social work files and even journalistic files. As long as this information can be 'attached' to an identifiable person, we may call it 'personal information'. Personal information is a lot easier to define than the more generalised idea of privacy. When it is held on computers we may call it personal data and in turn recognise its need to be subject to forms of 'data protection' to maintain its privacy.

Raymond Wacks thought the study of information privacy was more useful than looking just at personal or spatial privacy and what it might mean:

> Instead of pursuing the false god of 'privacy', attention should be paid to identifying what specific interests of the individual we think the law ought to protect. And it is submitted that at the core of the preoccupation with the right to privacy is the protection against the misuse of personal, sensitive information. (Wacks 1989: 10)

Information privacy is sometimes referred to as relating to 'confidential' information or as information that should be 'protected' which in turn gives us the idea of 'data protection'.

Information privacy is still not easy to draw a clear boundary around and retains an element of a negotiable status. An individual's personal address may well be seen as a piece of personal information but it becomes more private if someone is threatening to come around and put their windows through and equally less private if someone wants to send them a cheque for £10,000. The personal information itself—the address—remains a constant, but its status becomes negotiable given the context that surrounds it.

But just how easy is it for law enforcement officials to get hold of this personal information? As we shall see there is a long history of private letters being opened by representatives of the British state going back to the fourteenth century. The advent of digital information on the internet has considerably increased the volume of personal information that is now available online:

> Put together all the data and so-called meta-data from our emails, mobile phone calls, online searches, other data sending equipment such as your smart fridge and central heating meter as well as tiny radio frequency indicator chips in things we use, not to mention facial recognition analysis of footage from CCTV cameras and photos posted on line and an observer can know far more about us than does an ornithologist following a flock of electronically tagged birds. We are all tagged pigeons now. (Garton Ash 2016a: 283)

In the USA, Scott McNealy, the then Chief Executive Officer of Sun Microsystems, has suggested that there is so much information available online and in the digital form that there is no such thing as privacy anymore; he has often been misquoted as saying 'Privacy is dead – get over it'. His actual words were:

> 'You have zero privacy anyway', Scott McNealy told a group of reporters and analysts Monday night at an event to launch his company's new Jini technology. 'Get over it'. (Sprenger 1999)

Mark Zuckerberg, the American programmer, internet entrepreneur and the Chief Executive Officer and co-founder of the social networking website Facebook, has also declared that privacy is a limited concept in the digital age (Van Buskirk 2010).

In this book, we attempt to measure the concepts of privacy and information privacy solely against the processes of the criminal justice system. We have taken this system to include policing, court work, probation and prison service work and other allied matters.

We should repeat that without a firm definition and boundary line, privacy and information privacy remain something that is constantly negotiable within the criminal justice context that surrounds it. When it comes to weighing this privacy against such terms as 'the prevention of disorder or crime' and law enforcement and security, privacy is often described as something to be 'balanced', and we may all have to give up some privacy to enable the police and others to perform their roles.

Any such balancing would need to be done in a proportionate and justifiable manner:

> While we recognise privacy concerns about bulk interception, we do not subscribe to the point of view that it is acceptable to let some terrorist attacks happen in order to uphold the individual right to privacy – nor do we believe that the vast majority of the British public would. (House of Commons 2015a: 36)

We should also note that despite the difficulties of pinning down privacy and defining it, the importance accorded with privacy by the people of the UK remains significant.

One report using opinion poll data since 2013 and in-depth studies on public attitudes towards privacy and surveillance found the British public to be more averse to bulk data collection than the government. Other surveillance technologies were considered to be useful to security agencies but targeted technologies were more acceptable than blanket surveillance; some technologies were considered to be compromising human rights and liable to abuse by security agencies. People under the age of 60 were more concerned than older people (Bakir et al. 2015: 4–5).

Another report undertaken by Big Brother Watch (BBW) and ComRes involved 10,354 interviews across 9 countries (the UK, Germany, France, Spain, India, Japan, South Korea, Brazil and Australia), and the key findings were:

- Three-quarters (79%) globally say that they are concerned about their privacy online.
- Two-fifths (41%) of consumers surveyed globally say that consumers are being harmed by big companies gathering large amounts of personal data for internal use.

Globally, 79% of people said they were concerned about their personal privacy online, with India (94%), Brazil (90%) and Spain (90%) showing the highest level of concern. In the UK, the figure was 68% while Germany, which has one of the strongest data protection laws of any country, was the only country where a majority (56%) say they are unconcerned about their privacy online (BBW 2013).

All societies draw their own privacy line between that which is acceptable behaviour in public and that which is better kept to the private spheres of life. The private spheres of life could mean within the family or within certain organisational constraints of privacy guided by professional codes or such concepts as 'commercial confidentiality' or 'financial confidentiality'.

Privacy is also seen as an important part of a democratic society. Privacy gives people space to think about their government and be able to question that government. Totalitarian states are characterised by their opposition to 'privacy' and to allowing any alternative discussions to take place about their government. At the extremes in Nazi Germany, it was held that 'the only person who is still a private individual in Germany is somebody who is asleep' while Lenin in the USSR declared 'we recognise nothing private. Our morality is totally subordinate to the interests of the class struggle of the proletariat' (both cited in Lyon 1994: 185–6).

Present Approaches

This book opens in Chap. 2 with a brief history of privacy. This history focuses on component parts of the early criminal justice systems as we know them to show how our present systems have evolved. Thereafter, the book considers the idea of the criminal justice system as a 'system' with an input at one end and an 'output' at the other.

Chapter 3 follows the alleged adult offender during his or her first contacts with the police and the police activities involved in ascertaining identity and investigating the alleged crime. Such police activities include 'stop and search' techniques, arrest and detention and the matching of photographs, fingerprints, DNA samples and so on. The law and practice of 'strip searching' or 'full searching' is also examined as well as the searching of premises.

Chapter 4 looks at the use of specific police interventions in the investigation of crime such as letter and telephone interceptions and the legal constraints and accountability arrangements that are in place. We consider the various laws from the Regulation of Investigatory Powers Act 2000 (RIPA) to the IPA 2016 that seek to take the police further into the realms of knowing about a citizen's e-mails and internet use. The use of undercover police officers and informers is also discussed in this chapter.

Chapter 5 moves on to consider general surveillance in the name of crime prevention and looks at the collation of personal information that is maintained by the police in such arrangements as the Police National Computer (PNC), PND and more specialised databases such as that known as a Violent and Sexual Offender Register (ViSOR) that covers sex offenders and other potentially 'dangerous' people. This personal information includes criminal records, fingerprints, DNA samples and photographs as well as generalised police information in the form of intelligence.

Chapter 6 outlines the phenomenon of CCTV that covers so much of our public space to watch people and vehicles in our cities and towns. The regulation of these cameras has been somewhat late into the field, and meanwhile, some four million cameras are said to have been installed. Cameras have also appeared inside both private and public buildings and are now making their presence known in the form of 'body worn videos (BWVs)' on the uniforms of police officers and other workers in public roles.

In the courts, the rules on privacy are examined in Chap. 7 in the form of 'reporting' rights and restrictions and the idea of the open court for 'fair' trials. The US arrangements for TV cameras in court that are not replicated here in the UK. The special case of the youth court and its reporting restrictions, 'special measures' to protect the 'vulnerable' and 'intimidated' witnesses called to court and the videoing of children's testimony to avoid them having to appear in court.

Continuing with the idea of a 'system', we come to the punishment end of the criminal justice system. The rights to privacy in prison are outlined in Chap. 8 including such areas as searches, mandatory drug testing, the interception of letters and phone calls as well as the general problem of overcrowding in prisons and the effect that has on privacy. There are also particular problems of prison officers leaking information to the press about 'celebrity' prisoners and the searching of people visiting prisons to see relatives. Non-custodial punishments raise questions of visibility and privacy in terms of such policies as offenders completing community orders in public spaces wearing orange bibs with identifying labels on the back saying 'Community Payback' and the wearing of electronic tags to monitor a person's whereabouts.

Chapter 9 examines UK counterterrorism. In doing so, it attempts to balance the privacy of the terrorist—or alleged terrorist—against the safety and security of the general public. At the end of the criminal justice system, we have the rehabilitation of offenders to consider in Chap. 10. Rehabilitation here is taken to cover the resettlement of people back into the civic society they left before their punishment started. The Rehabilitation of Offenders Act 1974, for example, allows certain convictions to be considered 'spent' or 'forgotten' after given periods of time but the storage and maintenance of criminal records by the police and the various uses that may be made of them remain. Some ex-prisoners require greater degrees of anonymity accorded to them as do some ex-witnesses.

In Chap. 11, we draw some general conclusions on our subject matter.

2

A Brief History of Privacy

Introduction

This chapter is a selective brief history of privacy, drawing attention to relevant elements of the early criminal justice system and how some of these elements still have a resonance today. There will inevitably be gaps and omissions in our chronology, but reading is recommended for those who wish to make a more in-depth study of the subject of privacy and the early criminal justice system.

Early Days

The history of privacy has often overlooked the middle ages as an age when people did not really understand what privacy was all about. People mostly lived in small rural towns where everyone knew each other and most communication between people was of a face-to-face nature. Within a household, families shared rooms and the idea that people could withdraw into their own private space was a limited one.

Privacy was certainly recognised in terms of laws against trespass, burglary and housebreaking, with the latter two being at one time capital

© The Author(s) 2017
D. Marshall, T. Thomas, *Privacy and Criminal Justice*,
https://doi.org/10.1007/978-3-319-64912-2_2

offences. The middle ages gave us other crimes such as 'eavesdropping' whereby people were prosecuted for listening in to private conversations from under the eaves of a house.

David Vincent suggests that this early picture of the middle ages was not quite as simple as we might think and people could and would find privacy and private spaces. One way of doing this was to leave their homes and go out into the fields or the countryside where they could talk to others more freely, without fear of being overheard. Vincent also notes the evolution of more private forms of spirituality and prayer that did not require the public processes of the organised church and allowed people to withdraw into their own quiet space for meditation and prayer and the development of literacy and writing amongst the better educated, and in the form of letters, creating yet another new form of private area enjoyed by people (Vincent 2016: 20–26).

The history of state interception of letters in the UK can be traced back to the fourteenth century. A Royal Writ of December 1324 reminded port officials of their duty to find all suspect letters from overseas:

> To make diligent scrutiny of all persons passing from parts beyond the seas to England… to stop all letters concerning which sinister suspicions might arise' and to send these to the King 'with utmost speed. (cited by Porter 1989: 10)

Another Act of 1350 was the Statute of Labourers which required all towns and villages to build stocks for the punishment of offenders. Public humiliation was built into this punishment rather than any private suffering being inflicted behind closed doors. The local populace were also invited to throw rotten vegetables—or worse—at the known offenders. More severe public punishments, including whipping and even executions, were also carried out in this public manner.

The last public hanging was in 1868 (see below) but only after a long history of executions in public. The demise of the public element appears to be because of the rowdiness of the crowds that gathered. Their temperament could be moved in either a negative way if they disagreed with the sentence being carried out or a positive way if they agreed with the decision. Today we still use the word 'gala'—corrupted from the word 'gallows'—for any festive open air bank holiday or special occasion.

The Tudors to the Early Hanoverians

The Tudors (1485–1603) in government developed their own sophisticated systems of spies and surveillance. Here was a world of plots and treason, deception and secret agents, codes and cyphers. Mostly this was to protect Elizabeth 1 and her Protestant government against Catholic plots both at home and abroad. It has been described as the birth of the state as we know it, and Sir Francis Walsingham, Elizabeth's chief secretary of state from 1573 until his death in 1590, 'should be regarded as the true father of the British secret state' (Porter 1989: 12–13). One spy from this era was described by a contemporary as:

[having] authority from the royal council to break into all men's houses as he will and to search all places, which he does diligently, wherever there is a gleam of hope of booty. (Alford 2012: 100)

The Tudors recognised the value of 'registers' to keep tracks on people. The religious divide of the time between Protestants and Catholics led to a law of 1593 requiring all Catholics as dissenters to sign the recusants register held by the local minister and constable of the borough so that their whereabouts were always known to the authorities (Kent 1986: 34). Elizabeth I's Protestant Archbishop of Canterbury Matthew Parker (1559–1575) was known for his zealous use of search warrants in order to recover religious works from the private libraries of collectors. Parker salvaged medieval manuscripts dispersed at the dissolution of the monasteries to try to preserve anything related to Anglo-Saxon England that was evidence of an ancient English-speaking church independent of Rome. The Archbishop is said to have coined the name 'Nosy Parker' that was subsequently attributed to anyone keen to invade other people's privacy.

Vincent outlines how the growth of new forms of privacy was itself construed as somewhat of a risk to the governance of the country. The household might be seen as a stabilising facet of society after the Civil War (1642–1651) but at the same time what was going on behind its closed doors? An Englishman's house might be his castle as the lawyer and politician Sir Edward Coke had pronounced in 1628 in *The Institutes of the Laws of England* but that did not stop people from thinking that 'its private nature was itself a threat to the collective wellbeing, fomenting or concealing spiritual, sexual or physical misconduct' (Vincent 2016: 35). What was arguably emerging was a division between a public and a private realm of life.

The 1660 Post Office Act acknowledged how a new public national service carried private personal information around the country. Letters constituted a new private world but it was a world that the government retained a right to intervene in and a right to intercept and open private letters in the name of national security. The 1740 Post Office Act forbade the opening of letters save under warrant. More difficulties arose later regarding the interception of correspondence in 1844 when the Mazzini 'affair' revealed that the Home Secretary was authorising the opening of letters in the name of the national security of other countries (for more on this, see Chap. 4).

At this time, the authorities were made aware of the need to accurately identify those who transgressed against them. One system involved the branding of offenders with a hot iron in order that courts in particular would know if a person was a second- or third-time offender. The brand might be V for vagabond, T for thief or even M for manslaughter (Stephen 1973: 271–4). Branding was no doubt painful but it was not a punishment; it was a form of record keeping and was carried out on a part of the body that could be covered. The 1699 Shoplifting Act did allow for branding on the cheek but this was not a popular practice (McLynn 1989: 281)

In the early 1700s (Porter 1989), the organised poaching of deer and other animals from the king's land raised another issue of identity. This poaching was carried out by gangs in the south of England who wore black masks and black gloves or who blacked up their faces to avoid identification. They were known simply as 'the Blacks' and according to historians:

> Poaching has always been endemic in any forest area, and has no doubt been coeval with the forest's existence. 'Blacking' or disguise had long been used by poachers ... [and] severe laws supplemented by rewards offered to informers, inevitably engendered a conspiratorial secrecy among the poachers. (Thompson 1977: 57–8)

In response, the government passed the Black Act 1723 to outlaw this behaviour.

In 1791, the philosopher Jeremy Bentham published his idea of prison design in the form of the 'panopticon'. Bentham's design involved guards watching prisoners, managers watching guards and a governor of the prison watching everyone. Nobody would be able to see their 'watcher' or to know if they were being watched at any given time; the 'ruling image … was the idea of the eye of the state – impartial, humane and vigilant – holding the 'deviant' in the thrall of its omniscient gaze' (Ignatieff 1978: 113). The perfect 'panopticon' prison was never actually built even though elements of Bentham's work were taken up and the word 'panopticon' itself was to go down in history as a byword for sophisticated surveillance whether inside prisons or outside (ibid.: 109–113; see e.g. Lyon 2006).

The 1790s–1820s were troubled times for the government. Industrial troubles and direct collective action as well as political demonstrations were widespread and no doubt were taken up from the model of the 1789 French Revolution. For present purposes, we might note the activities of one group of people in the north of England in the years 1811–1812 who became known as the Luddites.

Luddites have gone down in history as mindless people unwilling to accept 'progress' by smashing the newly invented mechanised weaving frames that were putting them out of work. Historians have revealed that the Luddites were far from mindless. They were skilled weaving men who resented the disastrous decline being caused to their living standards. They were supported by their local communities who saw only unskilled men and children being drafted into the new mills and poor-quality cloth coming out. Some of the frame breaking that took place was carefully calculated to only reduce the mills' capacity to impact on the skilled workers' incomes, and some frames could be left untouched during a raid (Thompson 1968: 598–659).

The Combination Act of 1799 had made trade unions and collective bargaining illegal and the 1812 Frame Breaking Act specifically made frame breaking a capital offence. Luddites responded by acting in a secretive and disciplined fashion that the authorities found hard to contain. Their allegiance was to the mythical 'General Ludd' and they allocated themselves individual numbers rather than using names for their activities.

Groups of men moved silently at night with blackened faces along back-roads and paths unfamiliar to the militia sent from London to confront them. Spies and informers previously used only against foreign enemies were now once again turned on the home population:

> In order to penetrate these forms, the authorities were prompted to employ spies and informers on a scale unknown in any other period… The informer was paid by piece-rate; the more alarmist his information, the more lucrative his trade. Fabricated information might be eagerly accepted by the authorities who propagated the myth. (Ibid. 1968: 529)

Some men were known to have been punished based on fabricated evidence and the whole episode has left us with the concept of 'framing' innocent people with false allegations and evidence (ibid.: 645).

The use of the military against the local people was thought of as difficult and clumsy. After the military had killed 15 people and injured hundreds of others in 1819 during demonstrations at St Peter's Field in Manchester, efforts were renewed to find an alternative form of force. The incident was named as the 'Peterloo massacre' after the Waterloo victory over the French in 1815; the alternative new form of force was to be the formation of the police force. The first mainland police force was formed in London in 1829, and by the 1850s, police forces were in place across the country. The British public did not take kindly to what they saw as the 'imposition' of a police force, comparing it unfavourably to the centralised French system of policing, which they argued was based on 'spying'—the *mouchards*—by the central government:

> The police of France say some is admirable. Then go to France and enjoy it, be the reply of every freeborn Briton. (pamphlet 1812 cited in Palmer 1988: 165)

The government sought to confront this sense of 'imposition' of a police force by veering away from the centralised French system of policing to the so-called Anglo-Saxon model of policing. This was a model based on decentralised police forces for small populations of cities and towns. Some 200 forces were created and overseen by local Watch

Committees whereby local communities felt they had some control over this new agency.

The Victorians

Victorian times were marked by the rapid expansion of towns and cities through the British industrial revolution and the creation of an urbanised population and mass communication. The hostility towards the police slowly reduced and a gradual acceptance of policing as a part of civic society was established. The introduction of Criminal Investigation Departments (CIDs) in 1878 caused some renewed resentment especially with its officers now designated as detectives wearing plain clothes—and therefore becoming 'invisible'; but even they eventually found their place in Victorian thinking.

The Victorians had also to adjust their policing and other policies to account for wider changes in penal policy. Earlier systems of punishment, for example, had been based on simple principles of 'exclusion' whereby offenders were removed from society by either being transported to Australia and other colonies or being executed. By the mid-1850s, both transportation and hanging as forms of 'exclusion' were in decline as punishments and there was a need to rethink ways of dealing with offenders. Prison sentences now became the main form of punishment after which offenders returned to the community in new policies of 'rehabilitation' and 'inclusion', replacing that of 'exclusion'.

These new policies introduced new forms of tracking ex-prisoners once they were released. The police needed this information to deal with persistent offenders, and the courts to know the previous convictions of an offender to help them decide the new sentence. Previously, the police had only rudimentary forms of literally just standing and watching the prisoners at exercise in order to have a mental record of who they were when back in the community. More efficient systems were proposed and as an editorial in *The Times* put it:

> …much of new crime is committed by old criminals. If the system was to be continued there should be an efficient system of registration by

which the police would know where the different criminals were located. ('The Home Secretary and Crime in the Metropolis', *The Times*, 4 February 1869)

The 1869 Habitual Criminals Act established a national criminal record collection to assist the police and the courts. Forces across the country had to submit convictions and sentences to the Home Office in London who in turn would make the information available to local forces. In 1913, this collection was passed from the Home Office to be coordinated by the Criminal Record Office (CRO) at Scotland Yard and is today held on the PNC (Thomas 2007: Chap. 5).

The establishing of a national collection of criminal records was one thing but the accompanying problem was knowing if the correct person had been identified to whom the conviction and sentence record applied. This was solved by the discovery of the fingerprint as a unique record of every individual (Beavan 2001). In England and Wales, the 1891 Penal Servitude Act first provided for the measuring, photographing and fingerprinting of convicted prisoners. Those on remand could only be fingerprinted on the issue of a warrant from a magistrate, and if they were not subsequently convicted of an offence, their fingerprints were to be destroyed. A national fingerprint repository was started to be added to the files held by the new CRO.

The Criminal Justice Act of 1948 allowed the police to fingerprint suspects before conviction but the requirement to destroy fingerprint records if the person was acquitted remained until the Criminal Justice Act 1967 removed that requirement. Police were still frustrated, by the continuing requirement to gain the authority of a magistrate to take the fingerprints, but this too was removed by the Police and Criminal Evidence Act 1984. Today, all fingerprint information is held digitally on the computerised fingerprint database known as IDENT 1 (see Chap. 5).

The policing of terrorism, which in Victorian times was committed mostly by Irish separatists, required liaison between the police and the country's security services to form what has been called 'the vigilant state' (Porter 1987). The police formed their own Special Irish Branch in 1883, which later became known as the Special Branch and which continues to this day (Bunyan 1977; Wilson and Adams 2006). The

Metropolitan Police Special Branch was merged with its Anti-Terrorism Branch to form a new department called Counter Terrorism Command in October 2006.

Other forms of 'official' entry into the private household were more for purposes of child health and welfare. The 1853 Vaccination Extension Act, which required all children to be registered, and the 1889 Prevention of Cruelty to, and Protection of, Children Act were concerned with the physical safety of children. The 1870 Education Act required all children to be registered by their parents as attending elementary school for the first forms of state education.

This was also the age of the great philanthropists like Lord Shaftesbury and Dr Barnardo again concerned mostly with the welfare of children. One of the lesser known Victorian charities was the Charity Organisation Society (COS), which is remembered today for its introduction of expansive case files kept on the individuals it was working with. These files held detailed accounts of the lives of people and whether or not they actually 'deserved' help. The COS model of record keeping was seen as the template for modern-day social work ('case work') and probation officer files (Fido 1977).

At the same time as building case files, the embryonic social work profession also promoted the need for discussions between the professional and the client to be private and confidential conversations. The belief was that working relationships had to be built on trust if they were going to achieve any change in attitude and behaviour and that trust in turn came from confidential transactions with clients. Offering a confidential service was seen as a critical part of the professional's ethical code.

After the Victorians

In the last days of the Victorians, two US lawyers put forward the idea that privacy was so important that it might be something that could be enshrined in law as a right. Louis Brandeis and Samuel Warren drew attention to the potential for 'recent inventions and business methods' to undermine the autonomy of individuals, and made the case for the legal protection not just of privacy in its traditional sense but what they called

'the more general right of the individual to be let alone'. They were refer-
ring more to the intrusions of the press and businesses than to those of the
criminal justice system; Warren, in particular, as an established local public
figure, had been subject to intrusive press activities (Warren and Brandeis
1890). The idea of a 'right to privacy' did not take hold in the UK with its
preferred culture of civil liberties rather than a culture of rights.

At this time, it was legal for anyone to take photographs in a court of
law. This practice was deemed unacceptable and a law passed in 1925 to
make it illegal. During the parliamentary discussions on the Criminal
Justice Bill, an example was given on why this new law was needed:

> There was a dreadful case some time ago, in which a photograph was taken
> at the Old Bailey of a Judge passing sentence of death. That photograph
> was published – a most shocking thing to have taken, or to have published,
> dreadful for the Judge, dreadful for everybody concerned in the case. Of
> course, the Judge knew nothing of it, could not do anything to prevent it,
> and could not punish the person who had done it. (*Hansard House of Lords
> 26 Feb 1924 col 313*)

In 1933, the Children and Young Persons Act of that year introduced
the idea of the juvenile court to separate children and young people from
adults. This court would be held in private and the public would not be
allowed in. The press could attend but they could not report names,
addresses or schools which might allow the children in court to be identified. The idea was that children and young people should have the right
to privacy in order to grow up and to grow away from their youthful
indiscretions. These arrangements have remained in place and today the
youth court (successor to the juvenile court) operates to the same laws.

Legal attempts to define private premises and public places were also
made in the 1930s. The Public Order Act 1936 designed to help the policing of fascist rallies in the UK came up with the following definitions:

> 'Private premises' means premises to which the public have access (whether
> on payment or otherwise) only by permission of the owner, occupier, or
> lessee of the premises;

'Public meeting' includes any meeting in a public place and any meeting which the public or any section thereof are permitted to attend, whether on payment or otherwise;

'Public place' means any highway, public park or garden, any sea beach, and any public bridge, road, lane, footway, square, court, alley or passage, whether a thoroughfare or not; and includes any open space to which, for the time being, the public have or are permitted to have access, whether on payment or otherwise. (Public Order Act 1936 s9 (1))

In the Second World War, identity (ID) cards were introduced for all citizens as a wartime security measure under the Wartime National Registration Scheme (National Registration Act 1939). The ID cards were left operative after the War ended in 1945 and continued into the 1950s. It only fell into disuse when challenged in the courts as being an invasion of privacy and no longer necessary; the law was duly repealed (*Willcock v Muckle [1952] 1 KB 367*; see also Dovey 1986). The use of ID cards as a possible crime prevention measure returned in the form of the Identity Cards Act 2006, but the act was never implemented (see Chap. 5).

Modern Times

A major influence on thinking about privacy came after the Second World War in the form of George Orwell's novel *Nineteen Eighty-Four*. Building on the totalitarian experiences we now had of wartime Germany and Russia under the Soviet Union, Orwell presented a vision of a society where privacy no longer existed because an all-encompassing government referred to as 'Big Brother' had sight of everyone all the time and 'Big Brother is Watching You' became the all too familiar slogan still used today. It was an electronic version of Bentham's panopticon. The term 'Orwellian' passed into the language as a synonym for any dystopian form of police-state activities; Orwell had, of course, taken the precaution of writing under a pseudonym to protect his own privacy (Orwell 1949).

Orwell said he had taken his inspiration for his writing from another futuristic novel written by Yevgeny Zamyatin in 1924. Zamyatin was a Russian who had experienced the Soviet transformation of his country and in the novel *We* had made reference to the houses of the future being made of glass that everyone was now required to live in and where there was no privacy at all:

> We live in broad daylight within these walls that seem to have been fashioned out of bright air, always on view. We have nothing to hide from one another. Besides, this makes it easier for the Guardians to carry out their burdensome, noble task … Maybe it was the strange opaque dwellings of the ancients that gave rise to their pitiful cellular psychology. 'My [*sic*] home is my castle!' Brilliant, right? (Zamyatin 1993: 19)

Experiences in the Second World War lay behind other more overtly political statements about the importance of privacy. As noted in our 'Introduction', the UN's *Universal Declaration of Human Rights* made it clear that 'no one shall be subjected to arbitrary interference with his privacy, family, home or correspondence' (UN 1948: Article 12), and the Council of Europe's *European Convention on Human Rights* made a similar statement in its Article 8 part 1:

> 1. Everyone has the right to respect for his private and family life, his home and his correspondence. (CoE 1950: Article 8)

Article 8 was a heavily qualified right in the sense that its part 2 went on to say:

> 2. There shall be no interference by a public authority with the exercise of this right except such as is in accordance with the law and is necessary in a democratic society in the interests of *national security, public safety* or the economic well-being of the country, *for the prevention of disorder or crime*, for the protection of health or morals, or for the protection of the rights and freedoms of others (ibid. – emphasis added).

The police clearly had an opening in Article 8 part 2 to avoid the strict tenet of the right to privacy but Article 8 remains the nearest we have to a right of privacy in the UK. Today the Convention has been brought into domestic law by the Human Rights Act 1998 and can be tested in the British courts. The UK has been the subject of a number of hearings before the European Court of Human Rights and its own courts where its criminal justice proceedings have been said to 'engage' Article 8 and even to 'not be compatible' with it, and some of these cases will be considered in this book.

The *European Convention on Human Rights* Article 6 had further implications for privacy in its declaration that when on trial in a criminal court, 'everyone is entitled to a fair and public hearing' where 'judgement shall be pronounced publicly'. But again, there was a qualification that allowed for the press and public to be excluded from all or part of the trial:

> in the interests of morals, public order, or national security in a democratic society, where the interests of juveniles, or the protection of the private life of the parties so require, or to the extent strictly necessary in the opinion of the court in special circumstances where publicity would prejudice the interests. (CoE 1950: Article 6 (1))

These restrictions on press reporting will also be considered later in this volume.

The EU's own Charter of Fundamental Rights of the European Union would later declare similar rights:

Article 7 Respect for private and family life
  Everyone has the right to respect for his or her private and family life, home and communications.
  Article 8 Protection of personal data

1. Everyone has the right to the protection of personal data concerning him or her.
2. Such data must be processed fairly for specified purposes and on the basis of the consent of the person concerned or some other legitimate basis laid down by law. Everyone has the right of access to data which has been collected concerning him or her, and the right to have it rectified. (EU 2000)

The rights guaranteed in Article 7 correspond to those guaranteed by Article 8 of the European Convention of Human Rights. To take account of developments in technology, the word 'correspondence' has been replaced by 'communications'.

The UN produced further statements on how privacy for children and young people should be protected in the UN Convention on the Rights of the Child 1989:

1. No child shall be subjected to arbitrary or unlawful interference with his or her privacy, family, or correspondence, nor to unlawful attacks on his or her honour and reputation.
2. The child has the right to the protection of the law against such interference or attacks. (UN 1989: Article 16)

The same Convention reaffirming that children in a criminal court should be able:

To have his or her privacy fully respected at all stages of the proceedings. (UN 1989: Article 40 (2 b vii)

The importance of privacy was taken up in the USA through writers such as Alan Westin (1967), James Rule (1973) and later Penn Kimball (1983), making the case for the better protection of privacy especially in relation to government-held files on citizens. The emphasis was on information privacy with an eye to the growing amounts of records being held for official purposes; according to Rule, this was leading to people existing in two worlds:

Any member of a modern, highly 'developed' society is apt to feel that he inhabits two worlds at once. One is the ordinary social world or events, people, relationships and so on as they impinge directly on experience. The other is a 'paper world' of formal documentation which serves to verify, sanction and generally substantiate the former experiential reality. (Rule 1973: 13)

The Americans had been transfixed by the 1972 activities that became known as the 'Watergate' affair. Attempts had been made by agencies of the Republican Party to intercept communications of the Democratic

Party to assist them in fighting the next US elections. Telephone intercepts had been laid in the Watergate complex in Washington DC where the Democrats had established their electoral office. The line of accountability for this invasion of privacy was tracked back to the President himself. The book and the film that followed placed the whole affair firmly in the public domain (Bernstein and Woodward 1974).

At the same time in the UK, concerns were being expressed about intrusions on privacy (see e.g. Justice 1970) and a formal government report on the subject was commissioned. The Younger Report focussed solely on the private sector and had nothing to say on the public sector or criminal justice agencies but it did reaffirm the importance of 'privacy [as] a basic need, essential to the development and maintenance both of a free society and stable personality' (Younger Report 1972: para.113).

Others at the time were directly critical of public authorities, who might intrude upon privacy. Drug use lay behind other concerns about contemporary policing and privacy in the 1970s. The Misuse of Drugs Act 1971 had given police the right to stop, search and detain people in the street on the suspicion that they were in possession of drugs. This so-called sus law was later repealed but problems of 'stop and search' by the police have continued to this day (see Chap. 3).

Attention was also drawn to the fact that the police were increasingly using cameras in public spaces. Durham police, for example, in autumn 1970 had installed a secret camera to take photographs of people arriving at Durham Magistrates Court for the hearing of a drugs case. The chair of the Bench gave assurances that the police would destroy all the pictures taken and added that '[the police] gave me good reasons why the photographs had been taken but I am not prepared to disclose these' (Madgwick and Smythe 1974: 43).

In 1972, the police launched the PNC that caused ripples of concern about police records becoming more extensive and more quickly retrieved. Some saw the PNC as yet another invasion of privacy while others wondered just how accurate their records were going to be (Campbell and Connor 1986: Chap. 8). Similar ripples would be caused when the PNC was upgraded in 1991 (Watts 1991; for more on this see Chap. 5).

The West Mercia police started experimenting with helicopters as a form of policing in 1971. The chief constable said the helicopter would:

> ...add a new dimension to policing. If you are 500 feet up you have an enormously large view of what is happening on the ground not only in the streets *but in private gardens and things like that.* (quoted in Madgwick and Smythe 1974: 45 emphasis in original)

Today, policing by helicopter is an accepted part of modern policing and experiments have been started to provide policing by drones (BBC News 2015a).

1975–2000

The government had followed up the Younger Report on privacy with the Lindop Report (1978) which focussed solely on the safeguarding of personal information held on computers. It had little to say that was new but was in any event soon overtaken by developments in Europe. The Council of Europe produced detailed guidance on how member states of the Council—including the UK—should start to introduce data protection laws to safeguard the privacy of information held on computer; the guidance contained eight data protection principles comparable to the Americans' 'fair information practices' (CoE 1981).

This was followed up by the UK's first Data Protection Act 1984, which reproduced the eight principles in its Schedule 1. The act also required all 'controllers' of computers processing personal information to be registered with the newly formed data protection registrar who would report annually to parliament on his or her work and developments in matters of information privacy.

The eight principles required, for example, all personal data to be processed, fairly and lawfully, and to be held only for specified purposes. It followed that the data was considered confidential and not to be disclosed for any non-specified purposes. The data was to be kept accurate and up to date and not held for any longer than was necessary for the purpose in question. Anyone who was the subject of data held by a data user was entitled to know under what provisions information was held through the subject-access provisions (Data Protection Act 1984 Schedule 1).

The 1984 Act also allowed the Home Secretary to pass regulations stating that certain personal information could be designated as 'particularly sensitive'; this included:

(a) the racial origin of the data subject;
(b) his political opinions or religious or other beliefs;
(c) his physical or mental health or his sexual life; or
(d) his criminal convictions. (Data Protection Act 1984 s2(3))

The subsequent Data Protection Act 1998 s.2 confirmed this power to regulate what it now called 'sensitive personal data' but no Home Secretary has ever made such regulations under either this law or its 1998 successor.

The Data Protection Act 1984 also contained provisions that allowed anyone who was the subject of information held on a registered computer to have access to that information. Other acts allowing 'subject access' to local authority records (Access to Personal Files Act 1987) and to medical records (Access to Health Records Act 1990) soon followed; both are now replaced by the 1998 Data Protection Act.

Some statutory laws at this time did make passing references to 'privacy' but never really elaborated on how privacy was to be defined. The Wolfenden Report that had recommended new laws to decriminalise homosexual acts had suggested it be for acts in private but had made no attempt to define 'private' (Wolfenden Report 1957: para.64). During the parliamentary debate on the subsequent Sexual Offenders Bill, attempts were made by lobbyists to define 'private' as anywhere that was not in 'public', but these attempts were in vain. A much more restricted definition was eventually decided upon whereby any homosexual act would not be regarded as 'private', 'when more than two persons take part or are present' (Sexual Offences Act 1967 s. 1(2); see also Grey 1992: 103–4 and 116). The European Courts later declared this to be a violation of Article 8 of the European Convention (*A.D.T. v. the United Kingdom (application no. 35765/97) judgment Strasbourg 31 July 2000*; see also Dyer 2000); the wording was removed by the Sexual Offences Act 2003.

All other sexual activity in a public place whether heterosexual behaviour or same-sex behaviour was—and still is—dealt with by the common law. The offence of 'outraging public decency' consists of performing any indecent activity in such a place or way that more than one member of the public may witness it and be 'outraged' by it. An attempt was made to amend the Sexual Offences Bill going through the House of Lords in 2003 to make sex in a public place a criminal offence. Lady Saltoun of Abernethy argued strongly against such a move:

> It seems to me to be a very restrictive injunction worthy of the Government in nasty nanny mode and determined to interfere in every area of people's private lives ... to prohibit sexual activity ... outside a building at all seems almost unbelievably puritanical and worthy only of the most bigoted ayatollah or the very nastiest nanny killjoy. (*Hansard House of Lords Debates 19 May 2003: Col. 583*)

The amendment was withdrawn.
In the leading case of *Hamilton*, the court of appeal has ruled that:

> ... if the offence of outraging public decency were to be proved, it was necessary to prove two elements. (i) The act was of such a lewd character as to outrage public decency; this element constituted the nature of the act which had to be proved before the offence could be established; (ii) it took place in a public place and must have been capable of being seen by two or more persons who were actually present, even if they had not actually seen it. (*R v Hamilton [2007] EWCA Crim 2062, [2008] QB 224 para 21 (CA)*)

The Law Commission has subsequently revisited the law but felt it should remain as it is other than being moved from common law to statutory law (Law Commission 2010: para. 6.8; the annual number of prosecutions using the law was put at 300–400 per year (ibid.: para.4.36). New technology has recently entered the 'sex in public' debate when it allows people to watch pornographic films on devices like phones that can be used on public transport; are fellow travellers likely to be 'outraged'? (BBC News 2017a).

The 1984–1985 miner's strike led to further allegations against the security services using telephone taps to monitor the National Union of Mineworkers (NUM):

> Arthur Scargill and Mick McGahey, two of the three NUM national officials during the strike, had been under comprehensive surveillance for many years … every single NUM branch and lodge secretary had his phone monitored. So did the entire national and union leaderships, as well as sympathetic trade unionists and support group activists all over the country. (Milne 2004: 341–343)

Milnes allegations have since been contested (see Chap. 4), but the police were particularly concerned to know where mobile teams of pickets known as 'flying pickets' were being deployed to. The NUM were said to test this out by arranging fictitious meeting places by telephone for the pickets to meet up and then watched as no one but the police turned up (Fitzgerald and Leopold 1987).

During a 1984 trial involving James Malone, who had allegedly handled stolen property, it became clear that the prosecution had intercepted his telephone conversations on the authority of the Secretary of State's warrant. When this was challenged in court, it was revealed that no English law had been breached. Malone took his case to the European Court in Strasbourg who held that his right to respect for private life under Article 8 had been violated (*Malone v UK (1984)* 7 EHRR 14). The interception of a telephone call had already been held to fall within the definition of both 'private life' and 'correspondence' in Article 8 (1) (*Klass v Germany (1978) 2 EHRR 214*). This anomaly had to be corrected with a new law and led to the Interception of Communications Act 1985.

The Interception of Communications Act 1985 was mainly about breaking up the British Telecommunications (BT) monopoly on telephone services and allowing other private companies to provide services. Section 94 of the act, however, allowed the government (i.e. any Secretary of State) to 'direct' a company to act 'in the interests of national security' (s94 (1)). This was generally held to be the interception of telephone calls.

Thirty years later in 2015 and in response to a parliamentary question, Prime Minister David Cameron asked the Interception of Communications Commissioner (ICC) to review the use of section 94. The ICC felt unable to help because of the lack of records:

> There does not appear to be a comprehensive central record of the directions that have been issued by the various Secretaries of State. My office is therefore not yet in a position to be able to say confidently that we have been notified of all directions. (ICC 2015: para. 4.4)

In the aftermath of the miner's strike, attempts were made to tighten the law on public order. The 1986 Public Order Act defined riots and affray in both private and public areas (Public Order Act 1986 s. 1 (5)). Once again, the word 'private' is not defined but private dwelling places (homes) were excluded from the definition.

As for the security services, at this time, former MI5 Officer Peter Wright, in his book *Spycatcher*, famously described the cavalier outlook to 'privacy' the services held:

> And we did have fun. We bugged and burgled our way across London at the state's behest, while pompous bowler-hatted civil servants in Whitehall pretended to look the other way. (Wright 1987: 54)

On the information privacy front, new police databases continued to appear. In 1990, the PNC was given a substantial upgrade to improve its capacity and efficiency and the world's first National DNA Database (NDNAD) was established in 1995 to assist the police to identify people from samples taken at scenes of crime (Home Office 1995a). The database was built up over the years from DNA taken from all arrestees. This process continued until there were complaints made to the courts by people who had been arrested but not charged; they objected to their DNA samples being collated by the police when they were innocent people. The case went to the European Court of Human Rights where the government lost their case (*S and Marper v United Kingdom [2008] ECHR 1581*); the significance of this ruling is picked up again in Chaps. 3, 5 and 9).

The European Commission in Brussels had by now intervened again over matters of information privacy and data protection. The 1981 Council of Europe guidance on data protection was considered outdated and the EU now produced its own Directive on the subject (EU Directive 1995) which in turn led to an upgrading of the UK law with the new Data Protection Act 1998.

The role of the press and other forms of media were increasingly being questioned at this time about their role in intruding upon privacy. Much of this debate was about the privacy of celebrities and sports stars and their rights to not have their private lives discussed in the press. New forms of cameras with long-distance lens could invade all sorts of private spaces, and the term 'paparazzi' had become synonymous with cameramen and women who would follow the stars anywhere to get a good picture (Calcutt Report 1990); the word 'paparazzi' had been derived from the intrusive Italian photographer named 'Paparazzo' in the 1960 Fellini film *La Dolce Vita*.

2000 Onwards

RIPA attempted to give new clarity to law enforcement rights to target individuals for reasons of surveillance. What surprised many observers was the additional sections of the act giving rights of directed surveillance to all sorts of authorities not usually thought of as law enforcement bodies including the health service and local authorities. Local authorities, for example, had secret cameras trained on families who said they lived in a certain school catchment area which was doubted by the council (Shepherd 2010). See Chap. 4 for more on RIPA.

At this time, much of the debate and arguments about privacy were now couched in terms of privacy as balanced against freedom of expression with the latter being represented by the press. A number of legal cases on privacy were heard before the courts involving sports stars and celebrities trying to limit press disclosures of their behaviour; many of them were using the Article 8 of the European Convention—the right to privacy— that had recently been incorporated into UK law through the Human Rights Act 1998. The cases involved, for example, the model Naomi

Campbell (*Campbell v Mirror Group Newspaper [2004] UKHL 22*) and film star Michael Douglas (*Douglas v Hello! Ltd. [2007] UKHL 21*). Campbell wanted remedy for published pictures of her leaving a drug dependency unit and Douglas wanted remedy for a magazine getting unauthorised pictures of his wedding.

The expressed fear was that having had no law on privacy for years in the UK, a 'judge-made' new law was now being created by the 'back door' using Article 8. A parliamentary committee examined the developments but confirmed that in their view this was not the case:

> We disagree with criticisms that privacy law has been 'judge made' and does not have parliamentary authority; it has evolved from the Human Rights Act 1998. (House of Lords/House of Commons 2012: para.41)

Another unnamed celebrity alleged to be involved in sexual indiscretions was successful in getting a 'super injunction' to prevent publication of his name (*PJS v News Group Newspapers Ltd. [2016] EWCA Civ 100*). The order made covered only England, Wales and Northern Ireland. This meant their name was freely available in Scotland, the Republic of Ireland and numerous other countries. The ease of access brought about by the internet made something of a mockery of the court order.

The House of Commons Home Affairs Committee had made its own enquiry into the relationship between the media and privacy in 2003 and took a critical look at the relationship between the press and the police. They expressed concern that Rebekah Wade, the then editor of the *News of the World*, was happy to tell them that her newspaper had paid the police for information and both she and the editor of the *The Sun* would do so again if it was in 'public interest'. The Committee were not critical of this position:

> … it appears clear that, when they feel it is demanded by the 'public interest', the editors of *The Sun* and *The News of the World* remain ready to make payments to the police in exchange for information. As far as we are aware this practice is illegal for both parties and there is no public interest defence that a jury could legitimately take into account. (House of Commons 2003: para.92)

Some of these themes would later be picked up by the Leveson Committee of Inquiry that reported in November 2012 (Leveson Report 2012).

The murder of two girls in Soham, Cambridgeshire, in the summer of 2000 led to another development in police-held information. After the conviction of Ian Huntley for the two murders, it came to light that he had been known to the police for a series of allegations of sexual offending in another part of the country. The resulting Bichard Inquiry into what had gone wrong recommended a new computerised system of holding soft information (Bichard Report 2004: Recommendation One). It took some time to create this database but it was duly launched on 7 May 2010 and named as the PND) (see Chap. 5 for more on this development).

In party political terms, the Labour Party in government (1997–2010) had appeared to prioritise the storage and exchange of personal information over worries about data protection and privacy. Laws were passed to facilitate personal information exchange between criminal justice agencies and local authorities (Crime and Disorder Act 1998 s115), and on the question of building up the DNA database, Prime Minister Tony Blair believed 'the civil liberties argument is completely misplaced' (quoted in Watt 2000). In his widely reported 're-balancing the system' speech, Blair declared that 'many of our criminal justice IT systems are still in the dark ages'; in the future, there would be 'a major investment in IT right across the system – in the courts, CPS and police – to enable them all to communicate effectively' (Blair 2002).

On the wider front, New Labour went on to espouse its vision of yet more information sharing:

> … to deliver the best possible support to people in need. We can only do this with the right information about people's circumstances. We are determined that information sharing helps us better target support to the most disadvantaged in our society… [t]hat is why Government is committed to more information sharing between public sector organisations and service providers. This statement sets out our vision for better, more customer-focused services supported by greater information sharing which will protect and support individuals and society as a whole. (HMG 2006b: 2)

Much of the government's 'vision' concerned fighting crime and ensuring the protection of the public. Within the criminal justice system, Home Secretary Jacqui Smith told parliament that:

> [a] huge programme of work is already under way to strengthen information handling within policing and the broader criminal justice system, but we need to recognise the need to join up even more the focus on public protection. (*Hansard House of Commons 16 July 2008 Col.25-6WS*)

In an interview with *The Times* in August 2004, the first Information Commissioner Richard Thomas warned that the UK risked 'sleepwalking into a surveillance society' due to the government plans for an increasing number of digital databases:

> My anxiety is that we don't sleepwalk into a surveillance society where much more information is collected about people, accessible to far more people shared across many more boundaries than British society would feel comfortable with. (quoted in Ford 2004)

Two years later, following the enactment of the Identity Cards Act 2006, the Commissioner gave another interview in which he said that his fears had become a reality (BBC News 2006). The 2006 Identity Cards Act was never implemented and nor was the children's database which would have put every child in the country on a national database in the interests of child protection.

Both the House of Commons (2008) and the House of Lords (2009) followed up these warnings from the Information Commissioner's Office (ICO) with investigations of their own. The House of Lords in their report declared that surveillance was a fact of life:

> Surveillance is an inescapable part of life in the UK. Every time we make a telephone call, send an email, browse the internet, or even walk down our local high street our actions may be monitored and recorded. To respond to crime, combat the threat of terrorism, and improve administrative efficiency successive UK governments have constructed one of the most extensive and technologically advanced surveillance systems in the world. (House of Lords 2009: para.1)

A report from the Rowntree Trust looked at 46 of the UK's public databases and concluded that 11 of them should be closed down because of insufficient regulatory regimes (Anderson et al. 2009) and:

> Only six of the 46 systems, including those for fingerprinting, get a 'green light' for being effective, proportionate, necessary and established – with a legal basis to guarantee against privacy intrusions. But even some of these databases have operational problems. (Travis 2009)

The change of government in 2010 and the creation of the Coalition government made up of the Conservatives and the Liberal Democrats brought forward statements suggesting a change of direction:

> The Government believes that the British state has become too authoritarian, and that over the past decade it has abused and eroded fundamental human freedoms and historic civil liberties. We need to restore the rights of individuals in the face of encroaching state power, in keeping with Britain's tradition of freedom and fairness. (HMG 2010a: 6)

In June 2013, the *Guardian* in the UK and the *Washington Post* in America ran stories based on information leaked by the American Edward Snowden a former CIA employee. These revealed the existence (since publicly confirmed) of two vast data-gathering projects in the USA. The first known as *Prism*, which collected information directly from technology companies, including Google, Facebook, YouTube and Skype (Jeffreys-Jones 2017: 207), and the other named *Tempora*, under which the UK's government communications headquarters (GCHQ) had been collecting data from the fibre-optic cables of BT, Vodaphone and other companies carrying internet traffic in and out of the UK (ibid.: 208ff). Stories followed that Angela Merkel, the German chancellor, had had her personal phone tapped. The UK government (in accordance with long-standing policy) neither confirmed nor denied *Tempora's* existence. But this has not stopped some intensive scrutiny by statutory oversight bodies and others.

Shortly after the Snowden revelations, the House of Commons Intelligence and Security Committee issued an early statement concluding that allegations that GCHQ had acted illegally by accessing the content of private communications via the *Prism* programme were 'unfounded'. It also conducted an inquiry into the intelligence agencies' intrusive capabilities which were reported in March 2015. This concluded that the existing legal framework governing these capabilities was unnecessarily complicated and recommended that it be replaced with a new act of parliament (House of Commons 2015a).

3

Police (1): Interventions

Introduction

This chapter addresses police interventions and privacy. Intervention is taken to mean any contact police may have with the public. It is necessary for the police to negotiate and sometimes intrude upon personal and information privacy; however, at times, this negotiation or intrusion can contravene the rights of individuals and in some cases break the law. The chapter reviews police intervention processes, highlighting the key legal tenets governing the police and the practical implication of these laws. Case examples highlight the complexities of these processes and the impact of these police interventions on privacy.

Concerns in this area had come from two critical reports. Consolidation of the law had been recommended by the 1981 Royal Commission on Criminal Procedure (Philips Report 1981: para.3.10) and endorsed by the Scarman Report after the 1981 riots and disorders in Brixton and other inner city areas:

> the power of stop and search is necessary to combat street crime. The state of the law is, however, a mess, as the Royal Commission on Criminal Procedure has shown. I respectfully agree with the Commission's proposals

© The Author(s) 2017
D. Marshall, T. Thomas, *Privacy and Criminal Justice*,
https://doi.org/10.1007/978-3-319-64912-2_3

for the rationalization of the law and for certain additional safeguards.
(Scarman Report 1982: para.8.58)

The Police and Criminal Evidence Act 1984 (PACE) was intended to
restore confidence in the criminal justice system and especially in police
face-to-face contacts with members of the public.

PACE made provisions for Codes of Practice regulating the stop and
search, arrest, detention, investigation, identification and interviewing of
detainees; these are drawn up by the Home Office. Originally there were
just four codes covering these areas but they have grown incrementally
over the years and there are now eight codes, lettered from A to H (see
Home Office 2016a):

A: searching a person or vehicle
B: searching premises and seizing property
C: the detention, treatment and questioning of suspects
D: identification methods
E: audio recording of police interviews
F: visual recording of police interviews
G: powers of arrest
H: the detention,, treatment and questioning of suspects related to acts
of terrorism

Stop and Question: Police Powers

A police officer does not require any statutory power to talk to any individual he or she chooses without detaining the person (see Home Office
2015a: para.2.11). An officer can stop a person in a public place at any
time and ask them what they are doing and to 'account for themselves'
(such as, their actions and behaviours, where they are going, etc.) without
the need to record such incidents (ibid.: para.4.12). A police officer does
not always have to be wearing uniform when questioning someone but
must show their warrant card.

The person questioned does not have to answer any questions the
police officer asks. At common law, there is no legal duty to provide the

police with information or otherwise to assist them with their inquiries (see *Rice v Connolly [1966]*). It is, however, said to be a civic duty to assist the police. This is outlined in PACE Code A which states that citizens have a 'civic rather than a legal duty' to 'help police officers to prevent crime and discover offenders' and that such encounters should be with the cooperation of the person concerned (Home Office 2015a: 18–19 Notes for Guidance 1).

The code further states that without prior reasonable grounds for suspecting a person 'is in possession of an item for which there is an existing power to search' (ibid.: 12, 2.29) or if there ceases to be reasonable grounds, no search may take place. 'In the absence of any other lawful power to detain, the person is free to leave at will and must be so informed' (ibid.: 8, 2.10) 'and cannot be compelled to remain with the officer' (ibid.: 19 Notes for Guidance 1).

This creates the problem that the act of a police officer stopping a member of the public to ask questions or to search them is a form of (temporary) detention (see, e.g., Bowling and Phillips 2007). This police intervention can unnecessarily intrude upon the personal privacy of any citizen in a public space. While the person has the right to leave at any time, this remains a discretionary, non-statutory intrusion upon the privacy of the individual. As Bowling and Phillips point out, although PACE distinguishes between power of arrest and of detention for the purposes of a search, 'both amount to a deprivation of liberty consistent with the notion of a detention' (ibid.: 940). There has been some debate over what constitutes 'deprivation of liberty' and 'restriction of movement' (see, e.g., *R (Gillan) v Commissioner of Police for the Metropolis* [2006]), but the act of stopping and questioning an individual in a public space does amount to an intrusion upon that individual's privacy.

Stop and Search: Police Powers

PACE covers the main police powers to stop and question or search people in the street; however, there are over 20 other statutory powers of search within law (HMIC 2013a). In addition to PACE, the Misuse of

Drugs Act 1971 and section 60 of the Criminal Justice and Public Order Act 1994 are the three main Acts of the Parliament which contain police powers to use stop and search. Within PACE, there are many legislative articles which provide the police with such powers (see Table 3.1 and PACE Code A (Home Office 2015a: Annex A)).

Before the search, the police officer must tell the person their name and police station, what they expect to find, the reason they want to search or why they are legally allowed to search. The person concerned is told they can have a record of the search and if this is not possible at the time, how they can get a copy (Gov.uk 2015a).

Directly detecting offences through stop and search is relatively rare. Of the 539,788 stop and searches that took place in England and Wales

Table 3.1 Types of stop and search (McCandless et al. 2016: 6)

	Act	Reason/offence targeted	Reasonable suspicion required?
Section 1	The Police and Criminal Evidence Act 1984 (PACE)	Stolen property	Yes
		Offensive weapons	Yes
		Going equipped for stealing	Yes
		Going equipped for criminal damage[a]	Yes
Section 23	Misuse of Drugs Act 1971	Drugs	Yes
Section 43	Terrorism Act 2000	Terrorism	Yes
Section 44[b]	Terrorism Act 2000	Terrorism	No—not required in and around specific protected areas/places
Section 47	Firearms Act 1968	Firearms	Yes
Section 60	Criminal Justice and Public Order Act 1994	Anticipated violence	No
Section 139	Criminal Justice Act 2003	Offensive weapons—schools	Yes
Section 163	Road Traffic Act 2003	Stops of vehicles	No (for stop) Yes (for search)

[a]Searches for articles intended to commit criminal damage were added to the S1 PACE categories in the 2003 Criminal Justice Act
[b]S44 searches were scrapped in July 2010 following a European Court of Human Rights ruling that they were illegal

in 2014/2015 under section 1 of PACE, only 14% resulted in an arrest (Home Office 2015b). In *Foka v. Turkey*, the European Court of Human Rights held that 'any search effected by the authorities on a person interferes with his or her private life'.

The power to stop and search is an *investigative* power for crime prevention or detection (Bowling and Phillips 2007), when the police 'have reasonable suspicion that a crime has been, or is about to be committed' (Choongh 1998: 624). Police officers have powers to stop and search any person if they have *reasonable grounds for suspicion* that they are carrying illegal drugs, a weapon, stolen property or something which could be used to commit a crime, for example, a crowbar. A person can only be stopped and searched *without reasonable grounds* if it has been approved by a senior police officer. This can happen if it is suspected that serious violence could take place (Criminal Justice and Public Order Act 1994 s.60) if the person is carrying a weapon or has used one or the person is in a specific location or area (Gov.UK 2015a).

Reasonable grounds for suspicion is not defined in the PACE Codes of Practice (see Home Office 2015a) but it is made clear that these grounds must be objective and cannot be established based on personal factors:

> Reasonable suspicion can never be supported on the basis of personal factors. This means that unless the police have information or intelligence which provides a description of a person suspected of carrying an article for which there is a power to stop and search, the following cannot be used, alone or in combination with each other, or in combination with any other factor, as the reason for stopping and searching any individual, including any vehicle which they are driving or are being carried in:

> (a) A person's physical appearance with regard, for example, to any of the 'relevant protected characteristics' set out in the Equality Act 2010, section 149, which are age, disability, gender reassignment, pregnancy and maternity, race, religion or belief, sex and sexual orientation … or the fact that the person is known to have a previous conviction; and

> (b) Generalisations or stereotypical images that certain groups or categories of people are more likely to be involved in criminal activity. (ibid.: 2.2B p6)

and:

> Reasonable grounds for suspicion should normally be linked to accurate and current intelligence or information, relating to articles for which there is a power to stop and search, being carried by individuals or being in vehicles in any locality. (ibid.: 2.4 p7)

The Terrorism Act 2000 s.44 provided one of the most intrusive powers allowing police to stop and search any person or vehicle in a designated area without having to show reasonable suspicion. An assistant chief constable or someone of similar rank or above could designate an area where these searches could take place at any time they considered it 'expedient for the prevention of acts of terrorism' (Terrorism Act 2000, s.44(3)). Thousands of people have been stopped under s.44, but not one has been convicted of a terrorism offence (Liberty 2016a).

These 'suspicionless' stops ceased in July 2010 following a European Court of Human Rights ruling that they were illegal. In *Gillan and Quinton v UK [2013]*, the Court ruled that section 44 violated Article 8 of the ECHR to respect for private life because the power is so broad that it failed to provide safeguards against its misapplication. Furthermore, the Metropolitan Police Commissioner conceded that the exercise of the power under section 44 amounted to an interference with the individual's Article 8 rights, and the Court of Appeal described it as 'an extremely wide power to intrude on the privacy of the members of the public' (*Gillan and Quinton V. the United Kingdom (Application no. 4158/05) Judgment, 12 January, Strasbourg*) (the use of the Terrorism Act is returned to in Chap. 9).

Section 60 of the Criminal Justice and Public Order Act 1994 is similar to section 44 of the Terrorism Act 2000, in that it is authorised by a senior police officer—inspector or above—and a police officer does not require suspicion in individual cases, based upon a belief that:

(a) incidents involving serious violence may take place in any locality in his police area and that it is expedient to give an authorisation under this section to prevent their occurrence

(b) if persons are carrying dangerous instruments or offensive weapons in any locality in his police area without good reason, he may give an authorisation that the powers conferred by this section are to be exercisable at any place within that locality for a specified period not exceeding 24 hours (Criminal Justice and Public Order Act 1994, s.60(1)).

In May 2012, the use of section 60 stops was challenged in the High Court by Ann Juliette Roberts (*Roberts, R v The Commissioner of the Metropolitan Police [2012]*). In September 2010, Ms Roberts became involved in an argument with police after a ticket inspector on a bus discovered that there were insufficient funds on her Oyster payment card to pay her fare. The police officer called to the scene said he believed Ms Roberts might have been carrying a knife, and she was subjected to search under section 60—which was in place in the Haringey area because of gangland violence involving the use of weapons. Ms Roberts was restrained face down on the floor and handcuffed after she refused to be searched. No weapons were found and she received a police caution, which was later quashed. The High Court rejected Roberts' claim that the powers to search without reasonable suspicion were incompatible with the ECHR, Articles 5 and 8. In February 2014, Ms Roberts appealed the judgement in the Court of Appeal; this appeal was dismissed (*Roberts, R v The Commissioner of Police of the Metropolis & Ors [2014]*).

The use of stop and search powers has attracted much criticism. For example, a Metropolitan Police Report found that guidelines underlying stop and searches were vague and in practice required increased police officer discretion (Fitzgerald 1999). Several other UK-based studies have highlighted the damaging impact of stop and search powers on relations between the police and the Black community (see, e.g., Bowling and Phillips 2007; Van Bueren and Woolley 2010; Quinton 2015). The latest Home Office statistics on stop and search for England and Wales (April 2014–March 2015) show those who considered themselves to be from the Black or Minority Ethnic (BME) groups were around twice as likely to be stopped and searched than those who considered themselves to be White, and those who are from Black (or Black British) ethnicities are four times more likely to be stopped than those who are White (Home Office 2015b: para.4.9).

In practice, with no consistent legal basis, stop and search powers are commonly utilised by police officers simply to gain intelligence on people and for the broader purposes of social control (Bowling and Phillips 2007; Ellis 2010). Quinton found that the police practice of stop and search was even at odds with the law. Decision-making was found to be subjective and based upon generalisations and stereotypes, with many stop and search decisions based on weak grounds which are possibly unlawful. Quinton suggested that police use of stop and search is not effectively regulated by the law and this increases the likelihood of police officer subjectivity and bias of any decision to stop and search an individual or group of people and unwarranted intrusion of personal privacy by police officers (Quinton 2011). As the late Bernie Grant MP declared, '[t]he right to walk the streets is a fundamental one, and one that is quite rightly jealously guarded' (NACRO 2002).

In 2013, Her Majesty's Inspectorate of Constabulary (HMIC) published a report which examined 2338 stop and search records and found that 27% did not contain reasonable grounds to search people (HMIC 2013a). A public consultation on stop and search was launched by the then Home Secretary, Theresa May, in July 2013. The government put forward 13 proposals (see Home Office 2014a), including: (a) making clear what constitutes 'reasonable grounds for suspicion', (b) commissioning the College of Policing to review training for stop and search (which began in September 2015, see College of Policing 2015a) and (c) the introduction of the 'Best use of Stop and Search Scheme' (Home Office 2014b) which aimed to improve transparency, community involvement and support intelligence-led policing.

In 2016, HMIC reported that 15% of stops were carried out without recording 'reasonable grounds', despite the majority being authorised by a supervisor (HMIC 2016a). Many of these stops may have been unlawful, which supports the findings of Quinton (2011).

It can be concluded from the legislative framework that the police have numerous powers available to them to intrude upon the privacy of individuals or groups. The use of these powers has been shown to be exercised inconsistently by police officers and in some cases deemed unlawful.

The improper use of this police intervention is tantamount to using 'coercive force that infringes on the rights of citizens such as privacy, personal liberty and freedom of association in a variety of situations' (Bowling and Phillips 2007: 941).

The searches themselves may be categorised by varying levels of intensity from a simple removal of outer clothing through to strip-searching and intimate searches.

Removal of Clothing

A police officer can ask someone to take off their coat, jacket or gloves. There is no power to require a person to remove any other clothing in public, except under section 60AA of the Criminal Justice and Public Order Act 1994 (which empowers a constable to require a person to remove any item worn to conceal identity).

If the officer wants someone to remove more than a coat, jacket and gloves, he or she must be the same sex as the person being searched. An officer may place his or her hand inside the pockets of the outer clothing or feel round the inside of collars, socks and shoes if this is reasonably necessary in the circumstances to look for the object of the search or to remove and examine any item reasonably suspected to be the object of the search (Home Office 2015a: para.3.5).

Strip Searches

A strip search involves the removal of more than a person's outer clothing and can only be conducted with reasonable grounds to suspect if a person is carrying a prohibited article, such as a weapon or drugs. The search must be performed by a police officer of the same sex and not in the presence of anyone of the opposite sex, unless the person being searched requests it, and it must take place out of public view (Home Office 2015a: para.3.6).

Searches which expose intimate body parts cannot be performed as a routine extension of a less thorough search and must be carried out at a nearby police station or a suitable nearby location out of public view which is not a police vehicle. These searches must conform 'with paragraph 11 of Annex A to Code C except that an intimate search mentioned in paragraph 11(f) of Annex A to Code C may not be authorised or carried out under any stop and search powers' (ibid.: para: 3.7).

There have been many cases which highlight the intrusive nature of strip searching. In 2011, Anna Gavenciakova won her civil action case against Dorset police for unlawful detention, during which she was subjected to a strip search (Bailey 2011). In March 2011, a 22-year-old woman was arrested and 'forcibly strip-searched by five male officers and left naked in a cell while a camera broadcast the images into the custody suite'. The woman complained to the Independent Police Complaints Commission (IPCC) who found that London's Metropolitan Police had breached PACE 1984 codes and subsequently required the police to pay the woman £37,000 in damages (IPCC 2013; Laville 2015).

The Guardian newspaper used Freedom of Information requests in March 2014 to reveal that 4638 children aged 10–16 had been strip-searched by the Metropolitan Police between April 2008 and December 2013 (Clarke 2014). Twice as many children had been strip searched in 2013 compared to 2008. In 44% of cases, no 'appropriate adult' was present (an 'appropriate adult' is a parent, guardian, social worker or any responsible person over 18 who safeguards the welfare and rights, and ensures the effective participation, of children and vulnerable adults detained or interviewed by police (Home Office 2017a: para.1.7)), and 49.6% of children searched were released without charge (CRAE 2014). There was particular concern that the police were not following safeguards in PACE 1984 codes for children being 'stripped for their own protection'.

In February 2015, the Court of Appeal ruled that children and vulnerable detainees being 'stripped for their own protection' must have an 'appropriate adult' present, except in exceptional circumstances. The case they were ruling on involved a 14-year-old girl who had a history of mental illness and had been a victim of sexual abuse. She was arrested, handcuffed and taken to Wirral police station in 2010 after becoming drunk and abusive outside a kebab shop. In the police station, she was forcibly 'stripped for her own protection' by three female police officers, without her mother being informed. The police officers maintained that this was not a 'strip search' so the relevant part of PACE Code C did not apply; the appeal court judges dismissed the appeal but disagreed that PACE Code C safeguards should not apply in these cases (see *Davies v Merseyside Police & Anor [2015]*).

The High Court of Justice in 2015 found that in 2007, Basil Khan—then 16 years old—had endured wrongful arrest, assault and racial abuse from police officers (see *Mohidin & Anor v Commissioner of the Police of the Metropolis & Ors [2015]*). On the basis of false allegations from a police officer, Khan was then strip-searched at the police station. This again was found to breach PACE 1984 and its codes. Khan was awarded £11,900 in damages by the Metropolitan Police (BBC News 2015b).

Intimate Searches

The Police and Criminal Evidence Act 1984 s.55 provides police powers to conduct intimate searches. An intimate search is the physical examination of a person's body orifices other than the mouth. This is a particularly intrusive search which is usually only carried out with the consent of the person being searched, unless the situation is life threatening, for example, if the person is armed or has ingested drugs. If the person refuses to be searched 'without good cause', a police officer or member of police staff must warn that the refusal 'may harm their case if it comes to trial' (Home Office 2017a: Annex A, 2B).

Intimate searches can only be performed by a 'registered medical practitioner or registered nurse, unless an officer of at least inspector rank considers this is not practicable and the search is to take place under paragraph 2(a) (i) [ibid. Annex A], in which case a police officer may carry out the search' (Home Office 2017a: Annex A, 3). These searches are usually undertaken at a hospital, surgery or medical premises but in some cases, can be conducted at a police station (ibid.: Annex A 4).

National statistics for the year ending 31 March 2015 show that 75 intimate searches were carried out by 21 police forces in England and Wales (Home Office 2015b). Eighty-seven per cent of the searches were made in an attempt to find Class A drugs, which were found in 14% of cases. The remaining searches were conducted to find harmful articles, which resulted in one harmful article being found. Of all the searches, 74 were performed by a suitably qualified person and one was carried out by police officers (Home Office 2015b).

How individual police officers implement searches may give people a different experience of searches; office attitude and techniques of handling may be acceptable within Codes of Practice but still offer a varying experience. The same might be said of how different forces implement searches, and questions have been raised about the number of intimate searches being carried out. In 2009, Dyfed-Powys police, for example, were responsible for one-fifth of all intimate searches conducted in England and Wales (24 instances out of 123), despite only polling 488,000 people (less than 1% of the population (Owen 2009)).

Extensions of the Search Process

A number of processes have been added to the basics of a police search including the use of 'sniffer dogs', the use of metal-detecting archways and hand-held body scanners.

Drug Detection Dogs or 'Sniffer Dogs'

The use of drug detection dogs or 'sniffer dogs' by the police to search out drugs is an area of law enforcement that has proceeded without parliamentary discussion or new laws. In more technical language, the process has been referred to as 'olfactory surveillance' or the 'monitoring of odour'. The dogs can be conceived as an extension of the police search and go through houses, cars, pubs, luggage at airports and other useful police points of contact and either bark on finding something or alternatively sit quietly by the offending smell that they have picked up (so-called passive alert dogs). The location identified by the dog then simply becomes a field of police search for confirmation. There has been little research on the effectiveness of 'sniffer dogs' and it has more been 'common sense' that has allowed these developments (Marks 2007).

In a 2004 review of drug detection, sniffer dogs in New South Wales (NSW), Australia, the NSW Ombudsman found that 73% of people identified by the dogs were not carrying drugs; most drugs detected were small amounts of cannabis, and dogs were failing to detect drug dealers (NSW Ombudsman 2006). New South Wales Council for Civil Liberties (NSWCCL) issued a response stating that: (a) the dogs are getting it wrong in three out of five searches and (b) if speed cameras were getting it wrong in three out of five cases, there would be public outrage and we would stop using them. Given these poor results, the police should immediately stop using sniffer dogs, (c) the few people who are found to have drugs in their possession are overwhelmingly drug users, not dealers, and are cautioned by police under the cannabis-cautioning programme and (d) the police are constantly complaining about a shortage of resources. When they do, the public should be asking why they are wasting millions of dollars on useless sniffer dogs, instead of using the money to investigate serious crime (NSWCCL 2006).

There is a lack of evidence on the effectiveness of sniffer dogs, but current evidence does suggest that their use is counterproductive and an unnecessary intrusion on the privacy of people searched. Nonetheless in 2016, the US state of Utah won a bid to use a sniffer dog trained 'to detect chemical compounds on thumb drives, SIM cards, phones and iPads'. Known as 'porn dogs', it is believed they can assist law enforcement in the detection of devices which may contain child pornography (Best 2016; Micklethwaite 2016).

Police Metal Detectors

The IPCC bulletin in 2011, *Learning the Lessons*, highlighted that wand-style metal detectors were ineffective in detecting smaller metal items, in police custody searches. Consequently, a wand search should not be used by police officers as an alternative to a thorough strip search (IPCC 2011a). In contradiction to this finding, the police Ombudsman for Northern Ireland advocated that metal detectors should be used to search police custody cells, following an incident where a detainee self-harmed using a concealed razor blade (Police Ombudsman's Office 2012).

Metal detectors are usually static arrangements in the form of an arch. In November 2004, the Metropolitan Police introduced the knife crime initiative 'Operation Blunt'. The operation was targeted in London boroughs where knife crime had been assessed as a problem and was involved the creation of crime profiles for the areas, education and awareness programmes in schools, knife amnesties and the use of search arches in public places to detect people carrying metal objects (Metropolitan Police Authority 2005). The Metropolitan Police Authority (MPA) (2005) reported that recorded knife crime had dropped from 5.9% of all violent crime offences in 2003/2004 to 4.8% in 2004/2005. In 2006, the Metropolitan Police Service (MPS) reported that Operation Blunt had reduced knife-enabled offences by 'very approximately 1.7% of annual levels' (MPS 2006).

Operation Blunt 2 was launched on 19 May 2008 and spanned a wider area, including all aspects of youth violence and greater community engagement on police tactics (MPA 2008). The MPA reported in 2009 that overall recorded knife crime had fallen 13.3% in 2008/2009, but this could not be attributed directly to Operation Blunt 2. An evaluation of Operation Blunt 2 found that 'there was no discernible crime-reducing effects from a large surge in stop and search activity at the borough level during the operation'. (McCandless et al. 2016). This supports previous research findings on the weak impact of stop and search on crime reduction (see, e.g., Rosenfeld and Fornango 2014; Weisburd et al. 2016).

Despite the limited evidence base and calls for more research (BBC News 2008a), an increase in police use of metal detectors ensued in Scotland (STV 2009) and across England and Wales (see, e.g., Blackledge 2013; Knapper 2016); these initiatives included a new metal detector glove issued to police officers for use during searches (*Daily Mail* 2010). As noted by Karn (2013), the police do not routinely use research evidence to inform their practice in tackling crime.

Metal Detectors in Airports

Metal detectors have long been a part of the traveller experience in airports in the interests of security and particularly the prevention of terrorist attacks (see Butcher 2011 for an overview of aviation security). The airport security, 'experience of being touched, scanned and having your suitcase rummaged through' (Moskvitch 2015), is a familiar intrusion to personal privacy and integrity.

Following a failed attempt by Umar Farouk Abdulmutallab, to blow up Northwest Airlines Flight 253 from Amsterdam to Detroit in December 2009 using explosives sewn into his clothing, the government conducted an immediate review of aviation security measures, announcing: (a) an increase in the use of explosive trace detection, (b) plans for greater random searching of passengers and (c) the introduction of security scanners also known as body scanners or Advanced Imaging Technology (AIT) (Department for Transport 2010).

The attempted attack 'reminded policy makers of the limits of metal detectors, commonly used at airports' (FRA 2010: 1). This led to speeding up the 'further development and eventual deployment of body scanners' (ibid.: 1). Body image scanners were subsequently trialled at Heathrow and Manchester Airports in 2010; the £80,000 Rapiscan machines show a clear body outline and have been described by critics as the equivalent of 'virtual strip searching' (Travis 2010a)

A public consultation followed—notably *after* the introduction of the body scanners—with a final Code of Practice announced in November 2011 (see Department for Transport 2016a). An interim Code of Practice was introduced in the UK, which 'ensured that the operation of security scanners would be mindful of privacy, health and safety, data protection and equality issues' (Department for Transport 2016b).

Initially there was no alternative screening method offered to passengers, and a 'no scan, no fly' policy was implemented. The Code of Practice also stated that individuals could not be selected for scanning based on personal characteristics, and they can request that the person viewing the image be of the same gender (Department for Transport 2010). In practice, there appeared to be potential for disproportionate use based on personal characteristics. For example, two reported cases of Muslim women refusing to undergo the body scan, citing religious and medical reasons, were subsequently barred from their flight (Travis 2010a).

An inspection of Gatwick Airport revealed that women were being disproportionately singled out for *strip searches* and 'people of African/ Afro-Caribbean origin subjected to the highest proportion of searches'

(Vine 2011: 5). In 2015, the International Air Transport Association (IATA) reported that the majority of passengers welcomed the use of full body scanners (IATA 2015) which supported previous research (see Mitchener-Nissen et al. 2011). More recent studies have suggested differences in the predictive power concerning the attitude towards body scanners. For example, women demonstrate more worries and people who are better informed about body scanners are more concerned with possible discrimination through their use (Laib and Wolkenstein 2016a).

The use of full body scanners has received criticism from civil liberties groups for breaching privacy rights (see Crystal 2016a). The scanners used were 'millimetre wave' machines that use non-ionising radio waves to produce a three-dimensional image and Backscatter scanners that use X-rays (European Commission 2012). They produce a naked image, which caused concern at the intrusive nature of the scanners. The Equality and Human Rights Commission warned that airport body scanners are breaching rights to privacy (Crystal 2016b).

The government advocates that the image is permanently deleted after it has been assessed by the airport security officer of the individual being scanned (Gov.uk 2015b); however, experts have admitted that the images are being stored and still exist somewhere inside the machines (Mironmenko 2011), raising questions about how the data is being stored and protected. In addition, there were public health concerns raised with regard to the use of Backscatter body scanners (Brenner 2011) and possible discrimination against overweight passengers (Laib and Wolkenstein 2016b).

After a three-year trial in the UK, Backscatter body scanners were withdrawn and replaced with 'privacy-friendly' scanners (BBC News 2012a). The new scanners run software known as Automated Target Recognition (ATR), displaying a stylised (cartoon) figure of the individual, with graphical indicators showing any regions which the software considers suspect (Mowery et al. 2014). In November 2013, the government announced that the deployment of security scanners was to be extended to another 11 airports. In addition, passengers opting out of being screened by a body scanner would be allowed 'at least an enhanced hand search in private' (Department for Transport 2016a).

The Police and the Mental Health Act 1983

Privacy and autonomy are important factors to consider when searching or detaining a person suffering from a mental disorder. Katsakou and Priebe (2007) have demonstrated that when people are given the chance to participate in decisions, they find it easier to accept compulsory treatment. An 'Approved Mental Health Professional' (AMHP) and a doctor may compulsorily admit someone to a hospital from their home using the Mental Health Act 1983 ss. 2, 3 or 4. This is usually when they have been given access to the home; the presence of the police is not necessary but may be requested if a degree of force looks likely to be needed. An AMHP is usually a social worker or a nurse.

The Mental Health Act 1983 ss. 135 and 136 set out the particular circumstances covering how and when 'a person believed to be suffering from mental disorder' can be removed 'to a place of safety' and 'be detained there for a period not exceeding 72 hours' when they are (a) in a private dwelling which they refuse to allow admission to (s.135) and (b) in a public area (s.136). Neither section 135 or 136 constitutes an arrest by the police but force may be used to take the person concerned to a place of safety. Once in the 'place of safety', the person must be examined by a registered medical practitioner and be interviewed by an AMHP with a view to making any necessary arrangements for his or her continuing treatment or care.

Criticisms of s.136 have been longstanding (see, e.g., Department of Health and Home Office 2014) and not least concerning the definition of a 'place of safety'. The 1983 Act offers no definition but an accompanying Code of Practice does define 'a place to which the public have access' as places to which members of the public have open access, access if a payment is made or access at certain times of the day (Department of Health 2015: para.6.18). It does not include private premises, such as the person's own place of residence or private homes belonging to others, in which case a section 135 warrant is needed. Section 135 should be used if the person is in private premises.

The debate on what constitutes a public place can be found in relevant case law. For example, the grounds of a bail hostel may not be a public place (see *Harriot v DPP* [2005]). A front garden of a private house is not usually a public place (see *R v Edwards* [1978]; *R v Roberts* [2003]) neither is a private driveway shared by neighbouring private properties (*R v Bogdal* [2008]) whereas the upper landing or communal balcony of a block of flats can be a public place (see *Knox v Anderton* [1982]; *Carter v Metropolitan Police Commissioner* [1975]). Likewise, a car park is a public place (*David Lewis v Director of Public Prosecutions* [2004]; *May v Director of Public Prosecutions* [2005]).

Research has revealed that police officers have been known to encourage a person outside from their home in order to use section 136 powers:

> Section 136 is often used inappropriately as a person is often persuaded to leave a private property – in my experience a person is often invited outside to have a cigarette or similar and at this point [detained under] a Section 136 (Paramedic). (Department of Health and Home Office 2014: 26)

The use of s.136 does not require the presence of the AMHP or the doctor and can therefore be carried out by the police alone and to that extent may be viewed as less bureaucratic and useful in an emergency. On the other hand, that 'bureaucracy' is the person's civil liberty safeguard.

In the case of *Sessay, R v South London & Maudsley NHS Foundation Trust & Anor [2011]*, the court found that the claimant had been unlawfully detained by Maudsley Hospital and that her rights under Article 5 of the ECHR were infringed. Police officers entered the claimant's home in August 2010 following concerns about her mental health. They removed her from her (private) property and brought her to the hospital (a place of safety) using their powers under the Mental Capacity Act 2005. This Act has no legal authority for police to remove a person from their home and forcibly take them to the hospital. The hospital told the woman that she was being detained under the Mental Health Act s.136. She was subsequently detained under the Mental Health Act 1983 s.2.

A service user responding to the Department of Health and Home Office online survey highlighted the importance of personal privacy:

> You should not physically, psychologically or emotionally violate the privacy and dignity of a mentally ill person. The home has a special place in British law. To take that away from someone takes away our/their humanity/ human rights. (Department of Health and Home Office 2014: 27)

Regarding 'places of safety', the 2014 Department of Health/Home Office Report found that 'most service users who were detained in police cells found the experience "criminalising", distressing, and often dehumanising', along with 'strong support for police cells never to be used as a place of safety for people aged under 18' (Department of Health and Home Office 2014: 10). A Home Affairs Committee Report in February 2015 recommended the removal of police stations from the s.135 (6) definition of 'places of safety' (House of Commons 2015b: Recommendation 3). This recommendation was included in the planned Policing and Crime Bill, '[e]nsuring that those experiencing a mental health crisis receive the help they need' (*Hansard House of Commons Debates 13 June 2015 col.1595*).

The Policing and Crime Bill set out several points for action, which were enacted in the Policing and Crime Act 2017, including reducing the maximum time period for which a person can be detained under section 135 or 136 from 72 hours to 24 hours (with the possibility of an extension to 36 hours in certain specified circumstances) (Policing and Crime Act 2017 s.82).

Case

Martin Middleton, aged 23, was taken to a Leeds police station on 23 August 2004 by officers who had visited him in his home and noted his serious preparations for committing suicide. The officers believed they had removed Mr Middleton under section 136. When they arrived at the police station, no attempt was made to obtain a medical assessment as required for a detainee under s.136. The custody sergeant refused to detain Mr Middleton, as the removal had taken place from his private residence. The police officers therefore took him to a friend's home. Mr Middleton had spent only 15 minutes in the police station.

Mr Middleton was found dead at his home in Church Lane, Crossgates, Leeds, at midday on 24 August 2004. An inquest concluded on 1 December 2009 with a verdict of accidental death with a narrative. The coroner ruled the detention under section 136 as unlawful.

A report by the IPCC in 2011 concluded:

'The practice of relying on police forces to deal with mentally ill people in police stations is outdated and inappropriate. The practice must stop and the welfare and treatment of the individual must be the priority' (IPCC 2011b).

The resulting Policing and Crime Act 2017 s.83 introduced a new section 136C to the 1983 Mental Health Act which would permit the police to search someone removed under s.135 or s.136 if the constable has reasonable grounds for believing that the person (a) may present a danger to himself or herself or to others and (b) is concealing on his or her person an item that could be used to cause physical injury to himself or herself or to others. Any such item found may be confiscated by the police.

While the Policing and Crime Act 2017 has made some positive steps, it appears to have missed an opportunity to treat mental health through more appropriate means, such as qualified medical professionals and enhancing crisis care services rather than police intervention as a first point of call. The police have a core duty to protect life, as outlined in ECHR Article 2, but the Mental Health Act 1983 remains—unnecessarily so—one of the few pieces of legislation that allows people to be deprived of their liberty when they have not committed, or are not suspected of having committed, a crime. The Policing and Crime Act 2017 does improve the response to those in mental health crisis—including stopping those under 18 from being detained in a police station and restricting such detention for adults (Policing and Crime Act 2017 ss.80–83).

Powers of Entry, Search and Seizure

The police may enter and search a private household if they have the consent of the householder. If that consent is withheld, they have powers that may be invoked to give them a right of entry regardless of the householder's wishes. These powers come from either a warrant being issued by a magistrate (Justice of Peace [JP]) or common law being invoked to protect life and limb.

The rights of the occupier to refuse police entry were established in the eighteenth-century case of *Entinck v Carrington (1765)*. Searches were often made of publishers or booksellers selling material considered seditious or blasphemous, and the searches were made on the authority of the Secretary of State. *Entinck v Carrington* was one of the first to challenge this form of direct authorisation.

Piecemeal statutory powers were later granted to enable searches for stolen property and other material unlawfully detained (see, e.g., The Metropolitan Police Courts Act 1839 s.25).

With a Warrant

Powers of entry, search and seizure are contained in the PACE part 2. The police need judicial authorisation from a JP to obtain a warrant allowing them to force entry if necessary. The JP issuing the warrant must be satisfied that there are reasonable grounds for believing that:

(a) an indictable offence has been committed;
(b) there is material on premises which is likely to be of substantial value to the investigation of the offence;
(c) the material is likely to be relevant evidence; and
(d) it does not consist of or include items subject to legal privilege, excluded material or special procedure material (Police and Criminal Evidence Act 1984 s.8(1)).

'Relevant evidence', in relation to an offence, means anything that would be admissible in evidence at a trial for the offence.

The JP must be further satisfied that:

(a) it is not practicable to communicate with any person entitled to grant entry to the premises,
(b) it is practicable to communicate with a person entitled to grant entry to the premises but it is not practicable to communicate with any person entitled to grant access to the evidence,
(c) that entry to the premises will not be granted unless a warrant is produced, or
(d) that the purpose of a search may be frustrated or seriously prejudiced unless a constable arriving at the premises can secure immediate entry to them (Police and Criminal Evidence Act 1984 s.8 (3)).

A constable may seize and retain anything for which a search has been authorised by a JP (PACE 1984 s.8 (2)). The PACE Code of Practice B guides the police in the exercise of these powers of entry, and the code outlines the principles which should underpin the exercise of a warrant including:

> The right to privacy and respect for personal property are key principles of the Human Rights Act 1998. Powers of entry, search and seizure should be fully and clearly justified before use because they may significantly interfere with the occupier's privacy. (Home Office 2013b: para.1.3)

The PACE Code of Practice B further states that '[s]earches must be made at a reasonable hour unless this might frustrate the purpose of the search' (Home Office 2013b: para.6.2). The officer in charge of the search must try to communicate with the occupier to explain the purpose of the search and to obtain entry, unless the occupier is absent, the property unoccupied or *reasonable grounds* exist which 'would frustrate the object of the search or endanger officers or other people'. Searches made early in the day and often referred to as 'dawn raids' are carried out for the purpose of finding the occupier before they head out for their daily duties or gain a psychological advantage over the occupier (i.e., catch them unaware and reduce the chance of alerting others or of hiding incriminating evidence) (Campbell 2012).

The image of teams of police using mechanised battering rams to break down doors has become a mainstay of televised police documentaries and news bulletins. The raid on 91-year-old Lord Bramhall in 2015 as a part of Operation Midland involved 20 officers and forensic experts. Some officers reportedly wore a flak jacket as the body armour. Nothing was found and no charges ever laid (Barrett 2015). In 2011, five police officers from Merseyside police were sacked, after posing for an inappropriate photograph during a raid (Blake 2011).

The relationship between the police and the media came under scrutiny during a raid on the home of singer Sir Cliff Richard. In a high-profile intrusion of personal privacy, a Home Affairs Committee Report described the events as very unusual, stating that:

A BBC reporter and camera crew were present at the premises, having arrived before the police, and the BBC broadcast footage of officers entering and leaving the building, filmed by the camera crew on the ground and from a helicopter. During the course of this coverage, the BBC suggested that the police had given them advance notice of the search in order to maximise coverage of the case, in the hope that further witnesses might come forward. (House of Commons 2014: 3)

Special Procedures

PACE introduced the concept of 'special procedures' leading to access. This covered material that could *not* be taken by the police when executing a warrant of entry, search and seizure issued by a JP.

The Act describes this 'special procedure' material as:

(a) items subject to legal privilege; or
(b) 'excluded material'; or
(c) special procedure material consisting of documents or records other than documents (Police and Criminal Evidence Act 1984 ss. 9–14).

'Items subject to legal privilege' means any written transactions between lawyers and their clients (see Chap. 7), 'excluded material' means 'personal records' (such as those kept by healthcare professionals, social workers or counsellors) and 'special procedure material' covers journalistic material and material acquired by an employee or company.

If the police decide that they still need this 'special procedure' material, they are allowed to take their application for search and seizure to a higher level where a High Court judge will make the decision. The judge has to be satisfied that a serious offence has been committed and that the material the police are looking for will be substantive and relevant evidence. The judge must also be satisfied that other methods of obtaining the material have been tried without success and that there is a clear public interest in obtaining the material. The judge would then make an order requiring the material to be produced (PACE 1984 s.9 Schedule 1).

Special Groups

Registered sex offenders have regular visits from the police to monitor their progress; the number of visits increases in frequency if the registrant is assessed as posing a particularly high risk of reoffending. Mostly such visits are consensual, and the police wear no uniforms and do not use marked police cars to draw attention to the address they are visiting. If the police are refused admission or have received no reply on at least two occasions, then compulsory powers may be used. The police can apply to a magistrate for a warrant to enter premises where a registered sex offender lives in order to search and carry out a risk assessment (Sexual Offences Act 2003 s.96B as amended by the Violent Crime Reduction Act 2006 s.58 (Home Office 2007a)).

One registered sex offender has attempted to challenge this power in the courts. The registrant was referred to as M, and part of the claim was that allowing the police into his home on a consensual basis was not truly consensual because failure to agree to let the officer in was backed up by the possible use of section 96B, thereby breaching Article 8; the courts disagreed saying that the provisions were covered by Article 8.2 (*M, R v Secretary of State for the Home Department [2014]*).

People suspected of using child pornography or images of child abuse may also be the subject of a forced entry to their home if the police have been successful in applying for a JP's warrant to enter and search the premises (Protection of Children Act 1978 s.4). The evidence presented to the JP must be full and clear (see *G v Commissioner of Police for the Metropolis [2011] EWHC 331 (Admin)*)

Without a Warrant

The use of common law by the police covers a police officer without a warrant entering premises using force if necessary. This form of entry was considered in the case of *Handcock v Baker (1800)* where private citizens had entered a house to prevent a possible murder in a case of domestic abuse. Today, PACE, 1984 s.17 outlines situations in which the police can enter premises without a warrant, provided the constable has reasonable grounds for believing that the person whom he is seeking is on the premises, which include:

- deal with a breach of the peace or prevent it
- enforce an arrest warrant
- arrest a person in connection with certain offences
- recapture someone who has escaped from custody
- save life or limb or prevent serious damage to property

The police can, however, make mistakes which result in serious breaches of personal privacy. For example, in 2009, police paid out £560,000 in compensation for raiding the wrong properties (Daily Mail 2009). In 2012, Merseyside police apologised for the distress caused to a family whose house they had raided, by mistake (Forrester 2013). A business-man in Manchester claimed compensation—which was rejected—from Greater Manchester Police (GMP) in 2014. GMP had smashed down the front door of the premises, acting on intelligence that the cellar of the building was being used as a cannabis factory, but no drugs were found (Scheerhout 2014).

In a crime prevention initiative in Coventry, the police walked unan-nounced into a number of houses where doors had been left unlocked to demonstrate to householders the ease with which crime is committed if they did not take precautions. In a later public display, the police tweeted photographs they had taken in these houses to bring their demonstration to a wider audience; the home owner's consent had not been obtained for what was seen as a clear breach of privacy (Lillington 2016).

At the Police Station: Detention, Treatment and Questioning

The law covering detention in a police station is PACE Code C which outlines police powers for detention, treatment and questioning of indi-viduals. In most cases when an individual is arrested they will be trans-ported to and detained in police custody. The police can hold the individual for 24 hours, which can be increased to 36 or 96 hours for more serious offences (Gov.uk 2016). For terrorist-related offences, an individual can be detained for 28 days under the Terrorism Act 2006—the longest detention without charge period in the Western world. If the detainee is under the age of 18 years, they should be transferred after charge to local authority accommodation, and the local authority has the power to detain them pending appearance at court (Home Office 2017a: para.1.5A (a) (ii)).

DNA, Fingerprints and Photographs

The police have the right to take photographs of people, along with fingerprints and a DNA sample. They do not require the individuals' permission to do this. Permission is required from the individual to take samples of blood or urine or to take dental impressions, unless the arrest is in connection with drink or drug driving (Gov.uk 2016). The NDNAD was introduced in 1995 and until 2001, DNA was only collected when a person was *charged* with an offence; this DNA was destroyed if the person was acquitted. In 2001, this was amended to allow DNA to be held indefinitely, and in 2003 the law was reformed to allow DNA to be taken at the point of arrest for a recordable offence *instead of* the point of charge. The UK holds over five million DNA profiles, making it the second largest per capita DNA database in the world (Home Office 2015c). The database has been criticised for being highly discriminatory with hundreds of thousands of innocent people having their DNA permanently retained (Liberty 2016a; see also Chap. 5).

The Protection of Freedoms Act 2012 reformed legislation on DNA and fingerprint retention (together referred to as biometric information) in response to the case of *S. and Marper v. The United Kingdom [2008]*, in the European Court of Human Rights. The court ruled that the blanket and indiscriminate nature of the powers of retention of the fingerprints, cellular samples and DNA profiles of innocent people posed a disproportionate interference with the right to private life, in violation of Article 8 of the ECHR. Subsequently, a DNA sample must be destroyed within six months of being taken, except where it is required for use as evidence in court (Criminal Procedure and Investigations Act 1996). The retention of DNA profiles and fingerprints varies according to the situation. For those individuals convicted of an offence, unless under 18 years of age, their DNA profile and fingerprints will be held indefinitely. For non-convictions, the retention period is up to five years (see Home Office 2013c; see also Chap. 5 for more on biometric information).

Buildings and Custody

The College of Policing (2015b) provides guidelines on the design, planning, building and maintenance of police custody suites. With regard to privacy, it is stated that when entering the custody suite, detainees under escort should enter through a custody vehicle dock wherever possible, providing security and privacy. If the detainee is required to wait to see custody staff, a holding area which provides a reasonable degree of privacy should be provided, allowing space for the arresting/escorting officers to remain with the detainee to ensure their safety. The booking-in area should also allow the detainee a reasonable degree of visual and auditory privacy during the booking-in and charging process, using privacy screens or a separate, discreet charging area if required. Cell doors should open outwards and be fitted with a privacy cover. Cell blocks should contain appropriate separation allowing visual privacy to detainees.

CCTV in the Police Station

The College of Policing provides guidance on the use of CCTV in custody areas, which can be used for both monitoring the welfare of detainees and preventing and detecting crime. The guidance outlines the many areas CCTV can be used to record activity, while highlighting that there are different levels of privacy intrusion on detainees. CCTV cannot cover the examination area of the healthcare professional's consulting room or the shower area/wash areas. Under exceptional circumstances, such as detainee safety, CCTV may be used in WCs. Where this is the case, cameras should be positioned so that the WC is not in range or the image pixelated, for privacy reasons. While it is acknowledged that 'cameras sited in cell interiors are more intrusive of a person's privacy than those sited in corridors' (College of Policing 2015c), PACE 1984 Code C states that 'any request to have video cameras switched off shall be refused' (Home Office 2017a: para.3.11)

Questioning and Inferences from Silence

Detainees may be questioned at the police station about the offence for which they have been arrested. PACE 1984 Code C provides the guidelines for the police interview process. At common law, a suspect is not obliged to answer any questions, when being interviewed about possible involvement in a criminal offence, as outlined in the police caution (Home Office 2017a Code C, paragraph 10.1). The original police caution was:

> You are not obliged to say anything unless you wish to do so but what you say may be given in evidence.

The Criminal Justice and Public Order Act 1994 s. 34 (2) (d) permits the court to 'draw such inferences from the failure [to mention facts when questioned by the police under caution, charged or officially informed that they may be prosecuted] as appear proper' against the accused in the circumstances contained within those sections. The caution was duly changed to:

> You do not have to say anything. But it may harm your defence if you do not mention when questioned something which you later rely on in court. Anything you do say may be given in evidence.

If the suspect fails to mention a fact (to the police) that they later rely on in court that could reasonably have been expected to mention at this time, adverse inferences can be drawn. These allow the court to draw a negative conclusion from the defendant's silence. For example, the jury or magistrate may infer that the defendant remained silent as he or she had no adequate explanation for their conduct and has fabricated the facts for the defence at trial (Lexis 2016), even though the suspect may remain silent to maintain their integrity and their right to silence (Home Office 2017a: para.10.1).

The notion of an individual being 'innocent until proven guilty' and the emphasis on the criminal justice system to prove guilt appear to be missing in this piece of legislation. It also potentially undermines legal representation at the police station (Robins 2013) as a suspect may have remained silent under the advice of their legal representation. In the case of *R v Hoare and Pierce* [2004], the Court of Appeal held that when such an explanation is put forward, a jury should consider whether it was reasonable for a defendant to rely on such advice. The reasonableness of relying on legal advice was developed in the case of *R v Beckles* [2005]. The court advocated that the jury should consider (a) how *genuine* the defendant relying on the legal advice was and (b) whether it was *reasonable* for the defendant to rely on this advice.

The introduction of polygraphs (lie detectors) into the UK after years of dismissing them as an example of 'American exceptionalism' gave expectations of a whole new way of interviewing suspects in police detention (Offender Management Act 2007 ss.28–30). In Hertfordshire, the police were enthusiastic about the idea:

> The testing is undertaken ahead of any charges being brought and involves specialist officers from the constabulary's paedophile unit working with an expert who conducts the test on first-time suspected offenders who have volunteered to co-operate with police. (BBC News 2011)

But a later statement from Association of Chief Police Officers (ACPOs) based largely on the unreliability of the polygraph urged caution:

> The use of the polygraph during investigations is discouraged because it is a controversial technique that may well leave the integrity of the interview and the investigation unnecessarily exposed to challenge. In these circumstances it could be argued that at best the use of the polygraph will not get the investigation any further forward and at worse it could discredit it leading to a situation in which victims of crime are needlessly denied justice. (ACPO 2014)

The Offender Management Act 2007 s.30 precluded the evidence of a polygraph being used in court, and the polygraph has only been used for supervising known offenders (see Chap. 10).

The Investigation Anonymity Order

Rhys Jones was 11 years old when he was shot and killed in Liverpool in August 2007. The police eventually found his killer who was brought to justice in the courts. Jones had been an innocent bystander caught in cross-fire between street gangs operating near where he lived. The police had experienced considerable difficulty collecting evidence and witness statements in the area because of the witnesses' fear of repercussions from the gangs. These difficulties led to the Investigation Anonymity Order (IAO).

The IAO was included into the Coroners and Justice Act 2009 (ss.74–85) and offered anonymity to witnesses of serious crimes to encourage people to come forward in given circumstances. The police applied to a magistrate for an order if the offence under investigation was a 'qualifying offence' of murder or manslaughter where the death was caused by being shot with a firearm or injured with a knife (Coroners and Justice Act 2009 s.74). Other conditions had also to be met including that:

- the person likely to have committed the offence was at least 11 but under 30 years old at the time the offence was committed;
- that the person likely to have committed the offence is a member of a group engaging in criminal activity and the majority of its members are at least 11 but under 30 years old; and
- the person in respect of whom the order would be made has reasonable grounds to fear intimidation or harm if they were identified as assisting the investigation (Coroners and Justice Act 2009 s.78 (1–7)).

Finally, the person specified in the order had to be able to provide information that would assist the criminal investigation as it relates to the qualifying offence and is more likely than not, as a consequence of the making of the order, to provide such information (Coroners and Justice Act 2009 s.74 (8)). It is an offence for anyone to disclose the name of a person subject to an IAO (for further details see ACPO 2010).

Disclosing a Suspect's Identity

Once a suspect is detained at a police station or allowed to leave on pre-charge police bail while inquiries continue, there remains the continuing dilemma of whether information about the suspect should remain private. Should the police respond to media questions from journalists or should the privacy of the suspect be respected? Should the police at least wait until a charge has been laid before disclosing the suspect's name? There is no law offering guidance in this area which has often led to inconsistent practice between different forces.

Disclosing a suspect's name can prejudice a later trial. This was infamously demonstrated by the West Yorkshire Police when they arrested Peter Sutcliffe (the 'Yorkshire Ripper') in 1981 after an intensive five-year search for him. The police were so relieved that they called a press conference to announce the arrest while Sutcliffe was still making statements in the police station. Their expressions of triumph and being 'absolutely delighted' were widely published earning the conference the name the 'laughing policeman's press conference'; because of the sub-judice constraints, 'both the police and the press came in for a great deal of criticism ... including statements in both the House of Commons and the House of Lords' (Home Office 2006a: para.428).

At the other extreme, problems have arisen when journalists have been given a name of someone who is later not charged. This happened in the case of Christopher Jefferies, suspected and investigated for a murder in Bristol in 2010 that someone else had committed. *The Sun* and the *Daily Mirror* newspapers were fined £18,000 and £50,000, respectively, for reporting that presented a 'risk of serious prejudice' to any potential future trial of the killer (Halliday 2011; see also BBC News 2013a and Halliday and Mason 2015).

The identity of alleged sex offenders including celebrities known to the public has caused other problems. The police have used the disclosure of a name in some of these cases as a technique to see if other complainants will be forthcoming to help build a case. The radio presenter Paul

Gambaccini had his name disclosed in this manner and described it as being used like 'flypaper':

> he said he was a victim of a 'fly paper' investigation, whereby a suspect's name is hung up in public to see if it attracts further complainants. (House of Commons 2015c: para.12)

Gambaccini was never charged with any offences.

The formal advice to the police on naming suspects under investigation has been regularly updated. Current guidance from the College of Policing states that names should not normally be disclosed (College of Policing 2013: paras. 3.5.1–3.5.2). This guidance is being updated at the time of writing (May 2017); an initial draft has been published for consultation still maintaining that disclosure should be exceptional (Greenslade 2016).

Summary

There are many ways in which the police have face-to-face contact with the public. Each contact can be seen as a potential intrusion into an individual's privacy. On the other hand, it may be necessary for the enforcement of law. Notwithstanding the complex job the police face in balancing law enforcement and citizens' rights to privacy, there are evidently occasions where the implementation of the various laws, codes and rules is leading to unnecessary and improper intrusion into personal and information privacy. The efficient oversight and supervision of these operational police–public encounters should uphold the ideas of privacy wherever possible.

4

Police (2): Techniques of Investigation

Introduction

Police techniques of investigation might take place without face-to-face contact with the public and often without the public even knowing about it. The first part of this chapter considers the law and practice of the police interception of communications in the form of letters and telephone calls and other means of 'listening in' to private conversations. The problems raised by new electronic forms of communication are also examined along with the new laws required to keep up with these developments. The second part outlines the police use of Covert Human Intelligence Sources (CHISs)—often referred to as undercover policing—who infiltrate various organisations and networks; it also covers the use of non-police informers already in those organisations and willing to share information with law enforcement officials. These techniques have clear implications for the invasion of privacy in the name of crime investigation.

© The Author(s) 2017
D. Marshall, T. Thomas, *Privacy and Criminal Justice*,
https://doi.org/10.1007/978-3-319-64912-2_4

The Interception of Public Communications

Letters

In the early seventeenth century, the growth of literacy enabled people to write letters to each other. Rudimentary private letter collection and delivery systems emerged to be eventually overtaken by a public national system with the passing of the 1660 Post Office Act. This 'Royal Mail' constituted a new world of private information but it was a world that the government retained a right to intervene in and a right to intercept and open private letters in the name of national security. An ordinance of 1657 went so far as to say that a post office would be 'the best means to discover and prevent any dangerous and wicked designs against the Commonwealth' (Birkett Report 1957: para.15).

Porter even describes the post office as the first real intelligence agency in British history:

> Here then, was a genuine espionage agency, with a structure and personnel of its own, recognised by statute, independent (in one sense) of governments, but there for any minister to use when he wanted: a precursor, in a way, of today's GCHQ. (Porter 1989: 17)

The origin of the authority of the government to intercept communications in the name of national security has been difficult to identify but is now usually taken as the parliamentary proclamation of 25 May 1663, which forbade the opening of any letters or packets in the public post by anybody, except by the immediate warrant of the Principal Secretary of State (Birkett Report 1957: para.9). The later 1740 Post Office Act repeated the requirement that the opening of letters should only take place under warrant.

Difficulties arose in 1844 when it was revealed that the Home Secretary Sir James Graham was authorising the opening of the letters of Giuseppe Mazzini, an exiled political activist living in London but working for the unification of Italy; as many as 70 or 80 of his letters were suspected of having been read and their contents passed to governments of other countries such as Austria. The implication was that this was not about

UK national security at all (Vincent 2016: 104–5). The practice was condemned by parliamentarians as un-British and unconstitutional, and two Secret Committees were set up to inquire into the state of the law in respect of the detaining and opening of letters. The existence of the law was confirmed but the origin of the power given to the Home Secretary remained obscure; neither common law nor statutory law appeared to provide the source of the power (see *Hansard House of Commons 27 July 1844 Vol.76 cols. 211–59*).

In more recent times, the Interception of Communications Act 1985 put the opening of post on to a statutory footing requiring a warrant; any one opening a post without a warrant was committing an offence. Section 2 stated that:

> The Secretary of State shall not issue a warrant under this section unless he considers that the warrant is necessary
>
> (a) in the interests of national security;
> (b) for the purpose of preventing or detecting serious crime;
>   or
> (c) for the purpose of safeguarding the economic well-being of the United Kingdom (Interception of Communications Act 1985 s.2).

The pace of change in the telecommunications industry and postal market between 1985 and 2000 led to changes in the law, on the interception of communications, which rapidly became outdated. Since then, new legislation has contained the Home Secretary's powers to issue warrants and have letters opened (see, e.g., Regulation of Investigatory Powers Act 2000 ss.5-11), and the current powers are contained in the Investigatory Powers Act 2016, part 2, Chapter 1. The grounds for granting a warrant remain the same:

> *Grounds on which warrants may be issued by Secretary of State*
> (2)A targeted interception warrant or targeted examination warrant is necessary on grounds falling within this section if it is necessary:
>
> (a) in the interests of national security,
> (b) for the purpose of preventing or detecting serious crime, or

(c) in the interests of the economic well-being of the United Kingdom so far as those interests are also relevant to the interests of national security. (Investigatory Powers Act 2016 s.20)

Telephones

The invention of the telephone in late Victorian times provided a new challenge to the police. Although it was not until the 1930s that telephones became widespread in use, the police responded with new forms of interception of telephone communications often referred to as telephone tapping. These interceptions took place without warrant until 1937, at which point the Home Secretary and the Postmaster-General reviewed the policy and decided that interception of telephones should only take place in future on the authority of a warrant signed by the Home Secretary (Home Office 1999b: para.2.1).

In September 1951, in response to the increasing demands for warrants, the Home Office issued guidelines to the Metropolitan Police and Customs and Excise stating the conditions which must be satisfied before a warrant for interception of telephone communications could be authorised. These conditions were:

(a) The offence must be really serious;
(b) Normal methods of investigation must have been tried and failed or must, by the nature of things, be unlikely to succeed if tried; or
(c) There must be good reason to think that an interception would result in a conviction (cited in Birkett Report 1957: para.64).

The Home Office explained in a letter to chief constables that 'serious crime' offences were defined as offences for which a man or woman with no previous record could reasonably be expected to be sentenced to three years' imprisonment or offences of lesser gravity in which a large number of people were involved. A separate letter to Customs defined 'serious crime' as 'involving a substantial and continuing fraud which would seriously damage the revenue or the economy of the country if it went unchecked' (ibid.: paras. 65–66).

Patrick Marrinan was a practising barrister in the 1950s who appeared to have 'dodgy' associates among the criminal fraternity. The police intercepted and recorded some of his phone calls and passed the resulting tapes to his professional organisation, the Bar Council. Marrinan was struck off for unprofessional conduct. Arguments immediately arose as to whether this was a proper use of phone tapping and whether this passing of information to a professional body was an appropriate use of the arrangements; it was not helping solve any serious crimes or leading to any conviction (Vincent 1998: 186–8).

In response to the Marrinan case, a Committee of Privy Councillors was appointed to inquire into the interception of communications. The resulting Birkett Report reaffirmed the grounds for telephone interceptions that it is in the national interest for matters of national security and that normal methods of investigation must have been tried and failed or must, by the nature of things, be unlikely to succeed if tried (Birkett Report 1957: paras.67–68).

An area of concern has been the alleged interception of telephone communications involving Members of Parliament (MPs). This first arose in the 1960s and in response to several parliamentary questions. Prime Minister Harold Wilson made a statement in the House of Commons saying that MPs' telephones would not be intercepted by police or security services (*Hansard House of Commons Debates 17 November 1966 col.639*). This statement thereafter became known as the 'Wilson Doctrine' and successive governments confirmed that the doctrine remained in place (e.g., *Hansard House of Commons Debates 30 October 1997 col.680w*). Eventually, the 'Wilson Doctrine' was put on a statutory footing by the IPA 2016 s.26 (see below).

The question of telephone interceptions went quiet again for a few years but appeared again in the early 1980s. Home Secretary Willie Whitelaw published a White Paper on the subject. The White Paper brought the thinking of the Birkett Report up to date. It confirmed that interceptions may be undertaken only with the authority of the Secretary of State by means of a warrant, and it again listed the conditions which must be satisfied for the police, Customs and Excise or the Security Service to apply for a warrant:

(a) that the public interest which will be served by obtaining the information which is hoped will result from the interception of communications is of sufficient importance to justify this step;

(b) that the interception applied for offers a reasonable prospect of providing the information sought;

(c) that other methods of obtaining it such as surveillance or the use of
informants have been tried and failed or from the nature of the case
are not feasible;

(d) that the interception stops as soon as it has ceased to provide information of the kind sought or it has become apparent that it is unlikely
to provide it;

(e) that all products of interception not directly relevant to the purpose
for which the warrant was granted are speedily destroyed; and

(f) that such material as is directly relevant to that purpose is given no
wider circulation than is essential for carrying it out (Home Office
1980: para.2.7; see also *Hansard House of Commons Debates, 1 April
1980 col 207*).

Taking the same line as the Birkett Report, nothing was said in the
White Paper about judicial oversight of these warrants. Home Secretary
Whitelaw explained that the government had decided not to introduce
legislation on interception but had decided that it would be useful if
there was an annual independent report carried out in accordance with
the established purposes and procedures (*Hansard House of Commons 1
April 1980, col. 205*). Lord Diplock was appointed to produce the first of
these continuous independent reports which appeared in March 1981
(Diplock Report 1981). Diplock considered the procedures were working satisfactorily and with minimum interference in the individual's
rights of privacy. His first report was also his last report that would be
available to the public with Whitelaw having decided that future reports
should not be published (*Hansard House of Commons Debates 5 March
1981 cols 404–5*).

During the miners' strike of 1984–1985, allegations were made that the
National Union of Miners (NUM) had had their telephones tapped. Since
1973, Arthur Scargill, the leader of the NUM, had been the subject of a
warrant—authorising the interception of all the correspondence of suspects—due to his contacts with the Communist Party of Great Britain
(CPGB). Likewise, the NUM's Vice President Mick McGahey had been
the subject of interception since 1970 on the grounds of his communist

links. A former MI5 officer stated that Scargill 'would occasionally shout abuse into the phone of the people who were tapping him', and information on McGahey was gained from listening to his wife 'chatting about his movements, which he himself was careful to conceal' (Andrew 2009: 677).

Andrew argues that Milne's (2004: 341–3) claims that all NUM branches had had their phones tapped was fanciful, given that phone tapping during that time authorised by the Home Secretary was limited to leading communist and Trotskyist militants and those judged to have close links with them. Bonino and Kaoullas (2015: 826) highlight that the simultaneous surveillance of the NUM leadership in itself 'serves as a prime example of the coordinated action of the law enforcement's wing of the State in nationwide repression of political dissent'.

The debate on the interception of private communications was reignited during the criminal trial of James Malone in 1984 for allegedly handling stolen property. During Malone's trial, it became clear that the police had gathered evidence against him by intercepting his telephone conversations on the authority of the Secretary of State's warrant. When the interception was challenged in court it was revealed that no English law had been breached. Malone took his case to the European Court of Human Rights in Strasbourg who held that his right to respect for private life under Article 8 of the Convention on Human Rights had been infringed. The court acknowledged that detailed procedures existed governing the interception of communications but concluded that the law did not indicate with reasonable clarity the scope and manner of exercise of the discretion conferred on the public authorities (*Malone v UK (1984) 7 EHRR 14*). An earlier European case had ruled that the interception of a telephone call did fall within the definition of both 'private life' and 'correspondence' in Article 8(1) (*Klass v Germany (1978) 2 EHRR 214*).

The Malone case meant that the government was required to look again at the interception of communications and did so in the publication of another White Paper; this time the government stated that it would be introducing legislation (Home Office 1985). The White Paper described the proposals for statutory frameworks covering authorisation of interception, use and storage of intercept material, independent oversight of the warrant process by a Commissioner and a complaints procedure to be carried out by an independent Tribunal (Home Office 1985).

The Interception of Communications Act 1985

The new law was the Interception of Communications Act 1985 which put the interception of public communications onto a statutory footing. The Act set out the criteria by which an interception warrant could be issued. The Secretary of State could not issue a warrant under this section unless he or she considered that the warrant was necessary in the interests of national security; for the purpose of preventing or detecting serious crime; or for the purpose of safeguarding the economic well-being of the UK (Interception of Communications Act 1985 s.2 (2)). The Act also created the new office of the ICC who would review the Secretary of State's exercise of his or her power to make warrants. A new Interception of Communications Tribunal would hear complaints concerning interceptions; there was still to be no judicial oversight to the initial making of warrants.

The Interception of Communications Act 1985 (s.9) did not allow the use of intercept material to be used as evidence in court. In other words, the material could only be used by the police or security services to guide their investigations. The value of being able to use intercept material as evidence in courts has been the subject of much debate over the years (see, e.g., Privy Council 2008). One unspoken argument against using intercept evidence in court—or the need to obtain judicial oversight for warrants—was that the security services disliked their low-visibility activities being placed in the public forum of the court. A number of legal challenges were made that the 1985 Act still breached Article 8 of the ECHR but all of them were successfully resisted (see, e.g., *Campbell Christie v United Kingdom: decision 27 June 1994; Matthews v United Kingdom: decision 16 October 1996 Application No. 28576/95 Commission decision*).

The Interception of Non-public Communications

The Interception of Communications Act 1985 had been specific in covering 'the interception of communications sent by post or by means of *public* telecommunication systems' (Interception of Communications Act 1985 Introductory Text emphasis added). What the Act did not cover was interceptions made *privately* within an organisation of communications that had not been sent by post or by public telecommunications; this included the interception of internal telephone calls. The Halford case revealed the gap in provision.

Alison Halford was a senior officer in the Merseyside police who believed her promotion to even higher office was being denied because she was a woman. She had failed to win promotion nine times between 1987 and 1990 and finally made a formal complaint to the Equal Opportunities Commission in June 1990. At this point, she became suspicious that her internal work phone was being tapped by her own senior officers, who were anxious to head off her complaint (Halford and Barnes 1993). Halford left the force in 1992 without getting her promotion and later in 1997 laid a complaint before the European Court of Human Rights. In Strasbourg, it was revealed that her office and telephone had been tapped by her former colleagues but the 1985 Interception of Communications Act did not cover such internal phone calls. The ECHR found a breach of Article 8 (*Halford v. United Kingdom [1997] ECHR 32 (25 June 1997)*; Wynn Davies 1997).

The Halford case formed a central part of later discussions (Home Office 1999b) for the formulation and implementation of the RIPA in 2000. This Act regulated the interception of communications on all private networks, including mobiles and voicemail (see below for further discussion of RIPA).

Property Interference

An allied area of concern to post and phone call interceptions was that of placing listening devices on properties to try to gain evidence of crimes, a practice sometimes referred to as 'bugging'. In 1992, the police placed a listening device on the property of a man under investigation for dealing in heroin; at this time, the only guidance for the police on planting such devices came from a Home Office (1984) circular. A Mr Khan who visited the house was recorded saying that he had been involved in the importation of drugs. At Khan's trial the judge admitted evidence from the tape recording, and Khan was sentenced to three years' imprisonment. The House of Lords rejected an appeal stating that even if they were to take into account a possible breach of Article 8 of the Convention (which they were not obliged to do prior to the Human Rights Act 1998), this did not necessitate exclusion of the evidence gained as a result (*R v Khan [1996] 3 WLR 162 at 175*; Spencer 1997).

The government responded with the Police Act 1997 part 3 introducing authorisations for the planting of such devices and replacing the 1984 guidance. Until the passing of the Police Act 1997, the police's use of electronic surveillance devices ('bugs') on private property—rather than telephone tapping—was subject to Home Office guidelines (Home Office 1984) but not to any statutory regulation. The grounds for 'bugging' held that:

This subsection applies where the authorising officer believes:

(a) that it is necessary for the action specified to be taken on the ground that it is likely to be of substantial value in the prevention or detection of serious crime, and
(b) that what the action seeks to achieve cannot reasonably be achieved by other means (Police Act 1997 s.93 (2))

The police were allowed to authorise such surveillance for themselves if it was straightforward 'normal' surveillance, but a Surveillance Commissioner (created by the Act) had to further approve the authorisation if it was considered particularly 'sensitive' surveillance, covering a person's home, a bedroom in a hotel and office premises or if there was any likelihood of the investigation seeing legally privileged papers, confidential personal information or journalistic material (s.97). The Police Act 1997 introduced a Code of Practice (s.101) and the new Office of Surveillance Commissioner had a general oversight (see Police Act 1997 part 3).

The Rise of the Internet, Mobile Phones and Social Media

Towards the end of the 1990s, the telecommunications systems in use began to proliferate. New companies were allowed to deliver services and the nature of the services became more varied including mobile phones, e-mail and other internet-based forms of communication. These new systems and their market-based ownership presented problems for those who wished to intercept communications. A Home Office White Paper summarised the difficulties:

- The number of telecommunications companies offering fixed line services has grown from 2 to around 150.
- Mobile telephones have developed from being virtually unheard of to the mass ownership which is seen today.
- The emergence of totally new services such as international simple resale, which offers cut price telephone calls abroad—there are currently over 200 of these.
- The satellite telephone market, while still in its infancy, will evolve rapidly in the next few years.
- Communications via the internet have grown dramatically in the last few years, and this part of the market continues to grow.
- The postal sector has also developed rapidly, with a huge growth in the number of companies offering parcel and document delivery services (Home Office 1999b).

A new law was called for that would expand the 1985 Act to deal with all interception of communications in the UK, regardless of the means of communication, how it is licenced or at which point on the route of communication it is intercepted. This would expand the Interception of Communications Act 1985 in three specific areas: non-public networks, wireless telegraphy and interception of mail. The result was the RIPA.

The Regulation of Investigatory Powers Act 2000

The Regulation of Investigatory Powers Bill received the Royal Assent on the 26 July 2000 to govern the use of covert surveillance powers to 'ensure that the relevant investigatory powers are used in accordance with human rights' (Home Office 2000: para.3). The Act would cover:

- the interception of communications
- the acquisition of communications data (e.g., billing data)

- intrusive surveillance (on residential premises/in private vehicles)
- covert surveillance in the course of specific operations
- the use of CHISs (agents, informants, undercover officers)
- access to encrypted data (ibid.: para3)

For each of these powers, the Act intended to ensure that the law clearly covered:

- the purposes for which they may be used
- which authorities can use the powers
- who should authorise each use of the power
- the use that can be made of the material gained
- independent judicial oversight
- a means of redress for the individual (ibid.: para4)

RIPA divided surveillance into two main forms—directed and intrusive surveillance. Directed surveillance was considered to be non-intrusive or occurring outside of a private home or vehicle, including the monitoring of a person's movements and conversations. Intrusive surveillance was in relation to a private residence or vehicle (Home Office 2014c: paras.2.2 and 2.11).

Warrants for post or telephone interceptions still came from the Secretary of State unless urgent, and the grounds for granting a warrant remained similar to previous legislation:

(a) in the interests of national security
(b) for the purpose of preventing or detecting serious crime
(c) for the purpose of safeguarding the economic well-being of the UK
(d) for the purpose, in circumstances appearing to the Secretary of State to be equivalent to those in which he would issue a warrant by virtue of paragraph (b), of giving effect to the provisions of any international mutual assistance agreement (RIPA 2000 s. 5(3))

A Code of Practice elaborated on the Secretary of State's duty is:

The Secretary of State must also believe that the interception is proportionate to what is sought to be achieved by that conduct. Any assessment of proportionality involves balancing the seriousness of the intrusion into the privacy or property of the subject of the operation (or any other person who may be affected) against the need for the activity in investigative, operational or capability terms. (Home Office 2016a)

Five Codes of Practice were published to accompany the Act covering the interception of communications, equipment interference, the acquisition, disclosure and retention of communications data, covert surveillance and CHISs (see below) and the investigation of protected electronic information (i.e., only accessible by password or de-encryption). All of these codes are available at Home Office 2016a.

The Act also introduced the Investigatory Powers Tribunal (IPT) (RIPA 2000 s.65) which investigated and determined complaints which alleged that public authorities or law enforcement agencies had unlawfully used covert techniques and infringed a person's right to privacy as well as claims against the security and intelligence agencies for conduct which breached a wider range of human rights.

One of the unforeseen outcomes of RIPA was the number of non-police and security agencies who decided that they wanted access to the Act. While law enforcement agencies that included the police and the security services were to be the primary users in tackling terrorism and serious crime, a whole series of local authorities, and agencies from the NHS to the Department of Work and Pensions, were included in the Act as potential users (Regulation of Investigatory Powers Act 2000 Schedule 1).

Case Study

Local authorities have used RIPA to investigate minor offences; for example, Derby City Council, Bolton, Gateshead and Hartlepool used surveillance to investigate dog fouling (BBC News 2008b). Poole Council used RIPA to mount surveillance on parents claiming to live within a given school catchment area to see if they were breaking local authority rules (BBW 2010). Cambridgeshire County Council sent undercover officers to monitor whether eight children delivering papers in the village of Melbourn were doing their rounds without the correct paperwork. Rashmi Solanki, who ran the local shop, received a six-month conditional discharge at Cambridge Magistrates' Court for employing delivery boys without a valid permit (Bingham 2008).

> Sir Simon Milton, the then chairman of the Local Government Association, insisted that the powers were necessary to deal with legitimate concerns from local people about 'fly tippers, rogue traders and those defrauding the council tax or housing benefit system' (Hope 2008).

RIPA has been criticised for lack of clarity about the authority it provides and despite amendments, for being out of date in a social-media age (BBW 2014). QC David Anderson in his report *A Question of Trust* was a critic of the obscurity of the legislation, stating that:

> RIPA, obscure since its inception, has been patched up so many times as to make it incomprehensible to all but a tiny band of initiates … [t]his state of affairs is undemocratic, unnecessary and – in the long run – intolerable. (Anderson 2015a: para.35)

RIPA was eventually replaced by the IPA 2016 (see below).

The Retention of Communications Data

Apart from powers to intercept communications, the police and security services have long been keen to obtain and retain digital communication data from private service providers. This would be information such as the dates of communications and who was contacting who; it would not allow access to the content of those communications. Under the Anti-Terrorism, Crime and Security Act 2001, telecommunications operators were asked to retain this information on a voluntary basis. A Code of Practice setting out the voluntary agreement was created through the Retention of Communications Data (Code of Practice) Order 2003 SI no. 3175.

In 2006, an EU initiative took this idea of retention further and issued its own Directive on the matter requiring all member states to store citizens' telecommunications data for a minimum of 6 months and a maximum of 24 months (EC Data Retention Directive 2006/24/EC). The UK's response was the Data Retention (EC Directive) Regulations 2009 SI no. 859 which required Britain's Communication Service Providers to keep such data for 18 months; the 2003 voluntary Code of Practice was also made mandatory.

The new Coalition government of May 2010 announced its intention to continue this path towards retention of communications data. It wanted to:

> introduce a programme to preserve the ability of the security, intelligence and law enforcement agencies to obtain communication data and to intercept communications within the appropriate legal framework. This programme is required to keep up with changing technology and to maintain capabilities that are vital to the work these agencies do to protect the public. (HMG 2010a: para.4.A.5)

A new primary law was considered necessary to replace the existing 2009 Data Retention (EC Directive) Regulations, and the Draft Communications Data Bill was duly published in June 2012. The Bill was widely criticised for being too intrusive on privacy. A Joint House of Lords and House of Commons Committee, for example, reported:

> Our overall conclusion is that there is a case for legislation which will provide the law enforcement authorities with some further access to communications data, but that the current draft Bill is too sweeping, and goes further than it need or should. We believe that, with the benefit of fuller consultation with CSPs [Communications Service Providers] than has so far taken place, the Government will be able to devise a more proportionate measure than the present draft Bill, which would achieve most of what they really need, would encroach less upon privacy, would be more acceptable to the CSPs, and would cost the taxpayer less. (House of Lords/House of Commons 2012: para.281)

The Bill was ultimately withdrawn.

A further blow for data retention came in April 2014 when the European Court of Justice (ECJ) declared the 2006 EC Data Retention Directive invalid:

> It entails a wide-ranging and particularly serious interference with the fundamental rights to respect for private life and to the protection of personal

data, without that interference being limited to what is strictly necessary. (Court of Justice of the European Union 2014)

The decision of the ECJ (*Digital Rights Ireland (C-293/12) and Seitlinger and Others (C-594/12) ECJ (Grand Chamber) 8 April 2014*) rendered any regulations under the Act such as the UK's 2009 Data Retention (EC Directive) Regulations as ultra vires.

In response to the ECJ ruling, emergency legislation was rushed through parliament in less than one week and introduced in July 2014. The government stated that the Data Retention and Investigatory Powers Act (DRIPA) ensured 'that critical capabilities to fight crime and protect the public [we]re maintained', clarifying 'existing law without extending current powers' (Home Office 2014d). Critics were not convinced and called for an urgent review of all UK surveillance laws (BBW 2014). DRIPA was amended through the Counter Terrorism and Security Act 2015, providing the Home Secretary with powers to require communications companies to retain 'relevant internet data', but in July 2015, MPs David Davis and Tom Watson had argued in court that the law allowed the police and security services to spy on citizens without sufficient privacy safeguards. The High Court agreed with them and ruled that DRIPA was 'inconsistent with European Law' and hence unlawful (see *Davis and Watson vs Secretary of State for the Home Department [2015] EWHC 2092 (Admin)*).

In November 2015, the Draft Investigatory Powers Bill was published. This Bill purported to place the existing arrangements on to a new statutory footing. Campaign groups raised concerns at the speed with which the Bill was to be passed through parliament and apparent lack of due diligence of recommendations made (DSOU 2016).

The Snowden Files

Following revelations made by former US National Security Agency (NSA) contractor Edward Snowden in 2013, we now know much more about global surveillance and one of the largest intrusions of privacy in history. The leaked documents to the *Guardian* revealed mass collection of citizen's data by the NSA in the USA and the GCHQ in the UK. In addition, telephone and internet companies were sharing information with the security agencies (Lyon 2015).

Through a programme called *Prism* the NSA collected material including search history, the content of e-mails, file transfers and live chats from a number of internet companies including, Google, Facebook, Microsoft, Apple, Yahoo and Skype (Hopkins and Watt 2013). The documents further revealed that the UK-based GCHQ had access to *Prism* since at least June 2010, generating 197 intelligence reports from it in 2012 (Hopkins 2013).

The Guardian further reported that through another operation named *Tempora*, GCHQ had the ability to collect metadata—the 'who, when, where and how' of communication—from communication channels across the world (MacAskill et al. 2013).

In 2015, Privacy International filed a legal challenge in the IPT centred on whether the acquisition, use, retention, disclosure, storage and deletion of bulk personal datasets are in accordance with the law and necessary and proportionate. The legal challenge was amended following disclosures regarding the use of section 94 of the Telecommunications Act 1984 to require telecommunications companies to provide bulk access to communications data outside the protections of the RIPA regime (Privacy International 2015; Corera 2015). The IPT ruled that, over a period of 17 years (1998–2015), some data collection by GCHQ, MI5 and MI6 did not comply with Article 8, the *Right to a Private and Family Life*, of the ECHR (*Privacy International v. (1) Secretary of State for Foreign and Commonwealth Affairs and others* 2016).

As the Campaign group Liberty put it:

GCHQ acted unlawfully in accessing millions of people's private communications collected in bulk by the USA's National Security Agency, the Investigatory Powers Tribunal has ruled today.

The Tribunal found that the intelligence-sharing relationship was unlawful prior to December 2014 because rules governing the UK's access to the NSA's mass electronic surveillance programmes PRISM and Upstream were secret.

Today's landmark ruling is the first time the Tribunal – which considers complaints brought against GCHQ, MI5 and MI6 – has found against the intelligence agencies in its 15-year history. (Liberty 2015a)

Following the Snowden leaks, MP Caroline Lucas brought a case to the IPT (a successor to the Interception of Communications Tribunal) on the way in which GCHQ had been collecting metadata—the 'who, when, where and how' of communication. Lucas argued that the Wilson Doctrine, which protects MP's communications, was being breached. The Tribunal ruled that the Wilson Doctrine was not enforceable in law (*Lucas MP and Ors v. Security Service and Ors 2015*).

The Investigatory Powers Act 2016

The IPA received Royal Assent on Tuesday, 29 November 2016. The Act aimed to consolidate and update the existing law on the interception of communications and thereby replace the RIPA 2000. It also legalised the bulk collection of communications data held by Communication Service Providers in the form of phone records, Internet Connection Records (ICRs) and personal messages.

What exactly the government had done was immediately contested. The Home Secretary Amber Rudd announced it as:

world-leading legislation that provides unprecedented transparency and substantial privacy protection. (Home Office 2016b)

while a spokesperson for the campaign group Liberty said:

It's a sad day for our democracy as this Bill – with its eye-wateringly intrusive powers and flimsy safeguards – becomes law. (Liberty 2016b)

Even before the Investigatory Powers Bill was published and in anticipation that something needed to be changed following the 2013 Snowden revelations, a number of reports had appeared on the subject of surveillance.

Privacy and Security: A Modern and Transparent Legal Framework came from the parliamentary Intelligence and Security Committee (ISC) in March 2015 and expressed concern at the 'opaque' and 'unnecessarily complicated' myriad of legislation governing the activities of the agencies.

It was in favour of a new legal framework governing the intelligence and security agencies.

The report outlined the so-called triple test used by the agencies to justify intrusions on privacy. The triple test drew on Article 8 from the ECHR Rights and required agencies proposing action to ask themselves:

(a) Was the action in accordance with the law?
(b) Was it necessary in a democratic society?
(c) Was it proportionate and no more intrusive than is justified for the purpose of the investigation? (House of Commons 2015a: para.23)

While the 'triple test' looked good on paper, the Committee had received submissions from those who thought implementation of the test in practice might not be so neat and tidy (ibid.: para.25).

QC David Anderson, the government's own Independent Reviewer of Terrorist Legislation, published *A Question of Trust: Report of the Investigatory Powers Review* in June 2015. Anderson was concerned by the polarisation of the debate and the lack of understanding on the two sides:

> The silent majority sits between those poles, in a state of some confusion. The technology is hard to grasp, and the law fragmented and opaque. Intelligence is said to have been harvested and shared in ways that neither Parliament nor public predicted, and that some have found disturbing and even unlawful. Yet this was brought to light not by the commissions, committees and courts of London, but by the unlawful activities of Edward Snowden. Informed discussion is hampered by the fact that both the benefits of the controversial techniques and the damage attributed to their disclosure are deemed too secret to be specified. Politics enters the picture, and for informed debate in the media are substituted the opposing caricatures of 'unprecedented threats to our security' and 'snoopers' charter. (Anderson 2015b: para.13.2)

In anticipation of new laws, the then Deputy Prime Minister Nick Clegg in 2014 commissioned an independent report on all aspects of surveillance. The resulting comprehensive and independent report by the Royal United Services Institute (RUSI), *A Democratic Licence to Operate:*

Report of the Independent Surveillance Review (July 2015), outlined, among other things, ten tests that showed if privacy had been intruded upon. The first three constituted the 'triple test':

1. Rule of law: All intrusion into privacy must be in accordance with law through processes that can be meaningfully assessed against clear and open legislation and only for purposes laid down by law.
2. Necessity: All intrusion must be justified as necessary in relation to explicit tasks and missions assigned to government agencies in accordance with their duly democratic processes, and there should be no other practicable means of achieving the objective.
3. Proportionality: Intrusion must be judged as proportionate to the advantages gained, not just in cost or resource terms but also through a judgement that the degree of intrusion is matched by the seriousness of the harm to be prevented. (RUSI 2015: para.5.35)

Others of the ten tests included a need for 'restraint', 'effective oversight' and a degree of 'transparency'.

Other privacy and rights groups, including Privacy International (2015) and BBW (2016a), had voiced their concern about the proposed Bill which they described as a 'draconian bill'. Several NGOs including the Open Rights Group, Liberty, Privacy International, BBW and Index on Censorship joined forces to run high-profile campaigns against the Bill, such as the 'Don't Spy on Us' campaign (see DSOU 2017)

The Draft Investigatory Powers Bill was published in November 2015. As a Draft Bill, a Joint Parliamentary Committee was formed to provide pre-legislative scrutiny. The Committee reported on 11 February 2016 declaring an overall support for the Bill and, in particular, on the desirability of having a new Bill that did not stop them from saying that numerous points were needing of further discussion as the Bill passed through parliament even to the extent that the Bill was 'flawed' (House of Lords/House of Commons 2016); the Home Secretary was also accused of rushing the Bill through (McTague 2016).

The House of Commons Science and Technology Committee published yet another report in February 2016 entitled *Investigatory Powers Bill: technology issues*. This report steered clear of wider ethical issues and, as its title stated, focussed on the technology issues. The report still placed a sense of 'balance' at the heart of the new law—balance between 'protecting the law-abiding majority from the criminals and terrorists against protecting the very democratic freedoms these terrorists are seeking to undermine' (House of Commons 2016a: para.9).

These reports were responded to by the government in a Command Paper. The government was certain that the Bill was still on track to become law and the concept of privacy was clearly stated within it:

> The Investigatory Powers Bill will protect both privacy and security. Part 1 of the Bill provides an overview of the privacy safeguards contained throughout the Bill. The revised Bill and the accompanying Codes of Practice make clear the strong privacy safeguards that apply to all of the powers in the Bill. (Home Office 2016c: para.9)

Almost at the same time as the Bill received its Royal Assent, the IPT ruled that British security agencies had secretly and unlawfully been collecting massive volumes of confidential personal data, including financial information, on citizens for more than a decade; Article 8 had been breached. The IPT said:

> the security services [MI5, MI6 and GCHQ] operated an illegal regime to collect vast amounts of communications data, tracking individual phone and web use and other confidential personal information, without adequate safeguards or supervision for 17 years (*Privacy International v. (1) Secretary of State for Foreign and Commonwealth Affairs (2) Secretary of State for the Home Department, (3) Government Communications Headquarters, (4) Security Service, (5) Secret Intelligence Service – Investigatory Powers Tribunal case no. IPT/15/110/CHIPT 2016*; see also Travis 2016).

The fear was that the IPA 2016 was doing little more than legalising what had been going on illegally for 17 years.

One thing the Act did do was put the 'Wilson Doctrine', that MPs should not have their communications intercepted, onto a statutory footing for the first time; the Act now requires the relevant Secretary of State to consult with the prime minister before agreeing for a warrant to intercept an MP's communications (Investigatory Powers Act 2016 s.26).

Covert Policing: Covert Human Intelligence Sources

Covert policing refers to police investigation of a subject who does not know if they are under surveillance and that the investigation may infringe upon their private life (Sharpe 2002). The introduction of police detectives in CIDs in 1878 represented a shift of emphasis in policing from crime prevention to crime detection. Unlike other police officers, detectives did not have to wear a uniform, making them effectively 'invisible'. They investigated the most serious crimes, knew all the local villains and were well connected (James 2013). They were viewed as symptomatic of an intrusive system of spies and surveillance similar to those operating in France, which caused some public resentment.

Unlike traditional, overt forms of policing in England and Wales, which are regulated (since 1985) by the PACE (see Chap. 3) until RIPA 2000 in the UK, the gathering of information via secretive means was enforced by informal, non-statutory mechanisms—such as Home Office Guidelines. The case of James Malone in 1984 led to the introduction of the Interception of Communications Act 1985 and subsequent measures such as the DPAs 1984 and 1998, the Police Act 1997 and the Intelligence Services Act 1994 (Clark 2007). It is important that statutory, due process rights applied to overt police investigation are also applied to covert police investigations. Failure to enforce these rights allows police to act without due ethical consideration, weakening an individual's human right to privacy. This may also contribute to a decrease in trust and respect for the law (Sharpe 2002).

RIPA defines someone as an undercover police agent or CHIS as someone who establishes or maintains a personal relationship for the covert purpose of obtaining information or to provide access to any information to another person (Regulation of Investigatory Powers Act 2000 s.26 (8)). HMIC recognises three types of undercover officers:

- an advanced undercover officer;
- a foundation undercover officer; and
- an undercover online officer (HMIC 2012: para.21)

and estimates a total of 1229 police officers who are or could be deployed as undercover officers (HMIC 2014: para.4.7).

For present purposes, we should note that the RIPA Code of Practice for CHISs sets out the requirements of the police to:

- consider whether use of an undercover officer is necessary or if the intelligence can be secured through other, low-risk means
- consider whether the deployment of an undercover officer is proportionate (the seriousness justifies intrusion into people's lives)
- conduct an assessment of the safety of police officers (Home Office 2014e: paras.3.2–3.5 and 6.14)

The Special Demonstration Squad

Following the 1968 London demonstrations against the Vietnam War and in particular the outbreaks of violence outside the US embassy in Grosvenor Square on 18 March 1968, the Metropolitan Police Special Branch formed a new Special Operations Squad (SOS). The first detailed 'Statement of Purpose' for the SOS was dated 26 November 1968:

> The primary object is to provide information in relation to public order problems, the secondary by-product is that our knowledge of extremist organisations and individuals active in them is considerably enhanced (cited in Ellison and Morgan 2015: 13)

The squad operated as SOS between 1968 and 1972/1973, when it was renamed the 'Special Demonstration Squad' ('SDS'). The SDS deployed undercover officers for long periods to gather 'high-grade intelligence' on protesters during 'deep infiltration operations' in London with the aim of preventing serious crimes associated with protest.

The Home Office required the MPS to cover the operation of the SOS and the SDS with the strictest of secrecy, in order not to compromise the government or its sensitive operations. Significant dedicated funding was provided by the Home Office to the MPS until 1989 when the MPS took over and exercised all financial as well as managerial control (Ellison and Morgan 2015).

Undercover officers would meet, usually with a sergeant, at least weekly, to provide a handwritten or typed report of anything they thought might be of interest to those collating intelligence. Sometimes they would also telephone in a report if it was urgent. This raw intelligence would then be reviewed back at the SDS office, alongside other intelligence from other officers. It was then 'sanitised' to remove all references which might identify that it had come from an undercover officer, before it was disseminated out to 'specialist desks' within the Special Branch. They, in turn, would pass it on to the units that had to plan for and deal with public disorder, typically describing the intelligence as 'from a secret and reliable source' (Ellison and Morgan 2015).

The SDS planted more than 100 undercover officers (usually just 10 at a time) in more than 460 political groups, until it was wound up in 2008. The undercover officers adopted intricate fake personas and pretended to be campaigners for spells of usually five years. The SDS officers were deployed to gather information about protests organised by campaigns including those of grieving families seeking the truth about police misconduct, environmentalists and anti-racist groups. A Tradecraft Manual was written at the time to assist undercover police officers; in 2015 it was made public through a Freedom of Information Act request but the heavy redaction it has been subject to makes it of little use to the researcher (MPS 2015a).

Undercover officers were effectively:

- supplying information about the intentions of militant political extremists in relation to public order events
- identifying those who engage in preliminary planning or who take part in such demonstrations
- identifying suspects involved in breaches of the law before, during and after demonstrations
- gathering and recording information about the formation and development of target organisations for long-term intelligence purposes
- providing intelligence on the criminal activities of individuals or groups involved in support of terrorism and animal rights extremism (Ellison and Morgan 2015)

In 1997, the squad was again renamed as the 'Special Duties Section' ('SDS'); eventually, it was closed down in 2008.

In 2009, the Metropolitan Police made an internal retrospective review of the work the SDS had completed. The review was critical and found that the SDS had operated without tight controls, ignored ethical issues and gathered information that had little use in fighting crime and that:

> a number of ethical/moral dilemmas arose from the activity of SDS operatives and the management of them … [the review adds]. … In some instances apparent 'ethical/moral dilemmas' were simply not addressed as they formed part of the 'accepted consequences' of such operational deployments. (cited in Evans and Lewis 2015)

and

> Clearly the SDS preferred the less bureaucratic approach and directed their operational activity without intrusive senior supervision and management at that time. … The SDS directed their own operations with significant tactical latitude with minimal organisational constraints. … Inappropriate targeting occasions and reporting upon peripheral subjects whom, on the face of it, were not worthy of mention is further evidence of this. … There appears to be no value to the policing of London derived by recording and retaining such information. It neither prevents nor assists in the detection of crime or helps secure the economic well-being of the UK or protect National Security. (Ellison and Morgan 2015: 15)

The National Public Order Intelligence Unit

The National Public Order Intelligence Unit (NPOIU) of the MPS worked in parallel with the SDS and operated from 1999 to 2011; its brief, however, was national compared to the London-based work of the SDS.

According to HMIC, a small number of staff and managers had worked for both the SDS and the NPOIU. The work that they undertook included training, providing guidance, recruiting staff and authorising undercover operations. In 2006, control of the NPOIU was transferred to the ACPO. In January 2011, in the wake of the emerging revelations concerning undercover officers, it was transferred back to the control of the MPS, where it remains as part of the National Domestic Extremism Unit (NDEU) (HMIC 2012: 30).

Recent Events

That might have been the end of the SDS and NPOIU story as far as the public were concerned if it had not been for certain details coming to light in the press about the work and activities of its undercover officers after 2010. Rob Evans and Paul Lewis working for *The Guardian* newspaper reported on the activities of a police officer called Mark Kennedy who had been using the undercover name 'Mark Stone'. Kennedy was alleged to have had countless sexual liaisons and an endless supply of cash, earning him the nickname 'Flash' (Evans and Lewis 2013a: 4). He had decided to go public about his infiltrating and reporting on environmental campaign groups and their activists.

Stories emerged of undercover officers forming sexual relationships with the people they were reporting on (i.e., suspects) and even becoming fathers; they were also said to be using the names of dead children for their new identities (Evans and Lewis 2011b, 2013b; Evans et al. 2011; Hirsch 2011). In Nottingham, a case against activists collapsed in court because the undercover officers would have had to be named (Evans and Lewis 2011b). Evans and Lewis collated their stories in the book *'Undercover – the True Story of Britain's Secret Police'* (Evans and Lewis 2013a). Another undercover police officer—Peter Francis—came forward to tell his story, when he appeared on the *Channel 4 Dispatches* programme on 24 June 2013 (Channel 4 News 2013).

In total, the media articles, the television programme and the book broadly reported on the following allegations:

- That SDS officers engaged in sexual relationships while deployed.
- That the SDS used deceased children's identities in the creation of their covert identity.
- That the SDS targeted 'Black Justice Campaigns'.

- That SDS officers appeared at court in their covert identities.
- That SDS officers were tasked to gain information that might be used to 'smear' the Stephen Lawrence family.
- That family liaison officers assigned to the Stephen Lawrence family reported intelligence to Special Branch.
- That SDS officers were tasked to gain information that might be used to 'smear' Duwayne Brooks.

The Home Secretary instituted a series of inquiries into what had been going on:

Operation Herne tasked the police to complete a detailed and timely investigation into the above claims and report on them; Operation Herne was led by Derbyshire Constabulary's Chief Constable, Mick Creedon, and three reports were made:

- Report 1: Covert Identities
- Report 2: Allegations of Peter Francis
- Report 3: SDS Reporting

Operation Herne revealed that a number of SDS officers had been arrested in their undercover identity, often along with other activists. The figure was later put at 26 SDS officers arrested on a total of 53 occasions. Nine of those occasions were when they were 'in role' and in the company of other co-defendants (Ellison and Morgan 2015: 35). The question was that if the undercover police were released without charge, what had happened to their non-police co-defendants (see Creedon 2013, 2014a, b)?

HMIC provided reports in 2012, 2013 and 2014 into the effectiveness of the arrangements in place in all police forces to carry out, manage and scrutinise undercover operations. The first two were of their own initiative and the third was requested by the Home Secretary and constituted the most detailed of the three (HMIC 2012, 2013b, 2014). The 2014 report found inconsistencies across police forces, making 49 recommendations for reform.

The **Ellison Report 2014:** This inquiry looked into the role of undercover policing in the Stephen Lawrence case. It found that the evidence fell short of making it certain that corruption or collusion had infected the initial murder investigation (Ellison 2014).

The **Taylor Report 2015** was a review of the Home Office's knowledge of SDS activities. The report found that there was no evidence that the Home Office was aware of:

- the practice, by some officers, of using the identities of dead children
- the risk of SDS officers forming relationships with individuals within groups under false pretences
- any justice campaign groups being 'targeted' by the SDS
- any direct knowledge of any criminal activity and court appearances by SDS operatives that could lead to miscarriages of justice (Taylor 2015)

The **Ellison and Morgan Review 2015** was another independent report to the Attorney General on the possibilities of miscarriages of justice having taken place caused by undercover police activities. Its results were inconclusive and a bigger public inquiry was recommended:

> The relative lack of progress of this Review over the last year, the complexity which has been encountered in making progress over any reasonable timescale, and the limitations that may exist as to either the CCRC or the CPS referring cases back to an appellate court, all suggest that it may now be appropriate for the Public Inquiry to become engaged in these issues. (Ellison and Morgan 2015: 50)

All these revelations led to then Home Secretary Theresa May establishing a full public inquiry under the chair of Lord Justice Sir Christopher Pitchford to examine undercover policing in England and Wales (see UCPI 2016). The inquiry is considering the deployment of police officers as CHISs by the SDS, the NPOIU and by other police forces in England and Wales. It is also reviewing undercover policing practices, identifying lessons learnt and making recommendations about the way undercover policing is conducted (Home Office 2015d; for the full terms of reference see the Home Secretary's Written Statement at *Hansard House of Commons 17 July 2015 col.58WS*).

Meanwhile, seven women claiming compensation for their abusive treatment by undercover officers from the Metropolitan Police have settled out of court. The settlement was agreed after a process of mediation. Assistant Commissioner Martin Hewitt said:

> it has become apparent that some officers, acting undercover whilst seeking to infiltrate protest groups, entered into long-term intimate sexual relationships with women which were abusive, deceitful, manipulative and wrong. … I unreservedly apologise on behalf of the Metropolitan Police Service. I am aware that money alone cannot compensate the loss of time, their hurt or the feelings of abuse caused by these relationships … at the mediation process the women spoke of the way in which their privacy had been violated by these relationships. I entirely agree that it was a gross violation. (MPS 2015b)

Some reports suggested compensation amounted to an estimated £3 million (Morgan 2015).

Sir Christopher Pitchford announced in February 2017 that his ill-health meant that he would not be able to complete the inquiry but he would continue for as long as he could; a new chair was being sought. At the time of writing (May 2017), the Pitchford Inquiry remains ongoing with one estimate that it will not be completed until 2018 (see *Hansard House of Lords 27 October 2015 col.GC174*).

Informants: Covert Human Intelligence Sources

Informants who are not police officers are regarded as an effective source of information by law enforcement and are not confined to the most serious offences. Part Two of RIPA 2000 provides the statutory controls for the use of informants, which the Act labelled CHISs. The CHIS is a witness afforded special status and protection on the grounds of public policy (Clark 2007).

In 2014, the Home Office published a Code of Practice, which provides guidance and rules on authorisation procedures to be followed for the grant, review, renewal and cancellation of authorisations for the use of CHISs. The code highlights that:

> particular care should be taken in cases where the subject of the intrusion might reasonably expect a high degree of privacy, or where confidential information is involved. Confidential information consists of matters subject to legal privilege, confidential personal information, confidential constituent information or confidential journalistic material. Home Office (2014e: 24)

The use of informants presents many ethical problems (see Sharpe 2002; Clark 2007). Applied correctly, and supported by appropriate training, it is a proportionate, lawful and ethical tactic which provides an effective means of obtaining evidence and intelligence (College of Policing 2016a). Recent criticism has centred on the cost of paying informants—reported to have been £25 million between 2008 and 2013—and breaches of data protection, with the (electronic) information of informants being lost (Robinson 2013).

Summary

The techniques of investigation used by the police have had to keep pace with the complex and changing nature of communication. Technological advances, such as the internet, have meant that crime investigation has evolved significantly since the days of needing to be physically present to 'eavesdrop' on a suspected offender. As the Snowden files revealed, in the twenty-first century, 'eavesdropping' can be conducted remotely and from one country to another. The introduction of the IPA 2016, allowing bulk data collection by the government, raises significant questions for the future of crime investigation and the safeguarding of individuals' privacy. As the following chapter explores, the storage of this information is of critical importance when considering privacy issues.

5

Police (3): Data Collection and Retention

Introduction

The police collection and storage of personal information on people inevitably leads to accusations of our privacy being invaded. Some people may be happy with the adage 'if you're innocent what have you got to fear?' But others may ask the questions, why do the police need this information? How did they obtain it? Who are they sharing it with? How accurate is it? How long will they keep it for and will it be kept safe? Contemporary use of computers and digital forms of managing millions of items of personal information with the means of instant retrieval only enhances the 'Big Brother' metaphor of the police officer looking at his screen as agents of the all-encompassing state encroaching upon our privacy.

The police, for their part, can state exactly why they need all this information. They need it for:

(a) protecting life and property;
(b) preserving order;
(c) preventing the commission of offences;
(d) bringing offenders to justice; and

© The Author(s) 2017
D. Marshall, T. Thomas, *Privacy and Criminal Justice*,
https://doi.org/10.1007/978-3-319-64912-2_5

(e) any duty or responsibility of the police arising from common or statute law (Home Office 2005a: para.2.2.2).

These are the stated police purposes as required by the DPA 1998 and the chief officer of police is the person responsible for the information's use or misuse. The police are also beholden to the ECHR as brought into domestic law by the Human Rights Act 1998 and including the Convention's Article 8 and the right to privacy.

Police Data Collection: Personal Information

Police-held personal information is often divided into what can be called 'soft' and 'hard' information. The first category of 'hard information' is taken to be information that is verifiable and includes criminal conviction records and sentences that could be verified by the court that made them, photographs, fingerprints and other biometric forms of identification such as DNA samples based on scientific knowledge; 'hard information' can usually be presented in court by the police as evidence or antecedents of past behaviour.

The second category of 'soft information' is information that is not so clearly verifiable and consists of crime reports, allegations, background information, family connections, suspicions and possibilities. It is often the aim of the police to turn this 'soft information'—also referred to as 'police intelligence'—into 'hard information' that could be used by them to present as evidence in court.

In general terms, there are two main databases used by the police to store information. These are the PNC holding 'hard information' and the PND holding 'soft information'. These two computers have a number of applications and other police databases do exist alongside them.

Police National Computer

The PNC is the primary national police computer system in the UK and is used for facilitating investigations and sharing information between police forces. The system holds extensive information on people, vehicles, crimes and property. It is accessible over a secure network within seconds and from thousands of terminals across the country at any one time.

The UK police were told of the centralised initiative being developed to give all forces access to a single computer network in 1969 (Home Office 1969), and the PNC was launched in 1974 from its headquarters in Hendon, north London. It incrementally built up a number of applications for the storage of information (see below) and has periodically caused ripples of concern about police records becoming more extensive and more quickly retrieved. An upgraded PNC2 was introduced in 1990 (Grundy 1990; Watts 1991).

The PNC has grown from a basic record-keeping service into an online intelligence and investigatory tool consisting of various databases assisting in investigations and other areas of the criminal justice system and law enforcement.

PNC Databases

The main PNC databases are as follows:

Names File This contains information about people (referred to as nominals) who have been convicted, cautioned or recently arrested. The PNC also holds information on all recent previous arrests, convictions and what sentence was delivered as well as all previous addresses, co-defendants, marks/scars and descriptions and will include links to fingerprints and DNA.

Vehicle File It is a file with details of the registered keeper of a motor vehicle, as well as other information from the Driver and Vehicle Licensing Agency (DVLA) as to the vehicle status such as whether the tax has expired. The police can add their own reports as to whether a vehicle is, for example, stolen, missing or believed to be involved in a crime. The vehicle file is in turn linked to the Motor Insurance Database maintained by the Motor Insurers Bureau (MIB). Vehicle Online Descriptive Search (VODS) is a software that allows users to search the vehicles' file in the search for potential suspect vehicles; the search can be based on criteria such as registration, colour and postcode, sometimes using only partial descriptions or limited pieces of information.

Drivers File This contains information on the several million people who hold a driving licence, including details on those who are disqualified and information relating to test passes and endorsement licence entitlements. The DVLA is responsible for maintaining this database.

Property File Different types of stolen and found property can be placed onto the PNC system including firearms, trailers, plant and equipment, engines, animals and marine craft.

Criminal Records

In Chap. 2, we briefly outlined the Victorians concern to keep better records on former prisoners returning to the community on discharge. These concerns led to the 1869 creation of a national criminal record collection and the 1913 establishment of a central CRO in London. By 1924, the number of criminal records held by the CRO totalled 770,000 (Commissioner of Police for the Metropolis 1925: 14); today, there are over ten million nominal criminal records held on the PNC (at December 2016) although this does include not only those with convictions but also those with impending prosecutions, cautions, cases that require no further action and any other criminal justice activity on their record, for example, arrested but not charged (House of Commons 2016b: para.80).

The national criminal records collection in the 1970s and 1980s was still maintained on cards and paper with the PNC offering only a computerised Names Index acting as a means of directing officers to the full cardboard file. The accuracy of the Names Index and the criminal record files at this time was being called into question. Evidence to a Select Committee reported that the collection was 'in a terrifying condition of inaccuracy' (House of Commons 1990: para.1). The Home Office took a closer look and confirmed the picture:

> By the standards of what is technologically feasible today, the present [criminal] record system is in a very unsatisfactory state. The handling, searching, up-dating and disseminating of manual ... records is a slow, labour intensive and cumbersome business. (Home Office 1991: para.19)

The answer was seen to lie in computerisation of the full criminal record information (i.e., not just the Names Index). This information was duly added to the PNC records in 1995 with the application known as Police Home Office Extended Names Index (PHOENIX) (Home Office 1995b). A 'back record conversion' exercise continued for a number of years afterwards to ensure the full changeover to computerisation.

The PNC also opened up its criminal record databases to other non-police agencies. These included the National Ports Office, Her Majesty's Revenue and Customs, the Port of Dover police, the Office of Fair Trading and the Criminal Record Bureau. In 2011, the government's independent advisor on Criminality Information Management recommended that HMIC's audit role be extended to cover all these extra PNC users (Mason 2011: 34–36; see also HMIC 2016b).

Software has been developed called Query Using Extended Search Facilities (QUEST) launched in 1998 to help officers trawl through PNC records at a much faster pace. Searches can be made on the basis of physical descriptions and on limited pieces of information:

> Quest unlocks the full potential of the Phoenix application and realises its role as an investigative tool. Provided the information entered into Phoenix is up to date and complete Quest will find who you are looking for. (PITO n.d.:9; see also Orr-Munro 2001)

Police National Database

The PND is a complementary computer system to the PNC that links all police forces together to share 'police intelligence' or soft information. It started operation in 2011. Local forces have long had Force Intelligence Bureaus (FIBs) to record police intelligence on the residents of their local communities but until recently the collation of force intelligence was largely a paper and card exercise (Campbell 1979). At one time, the officers who did this work were known simply as 'collators':

> The collator will update files from every possible information source within a police station – officer's daily reports, crime investigations, cases before the courts, information from police files elsewhere, hearsay from any kind

of source, stop checks and vehicle checks and so on. All of these are entered on a person's record and are available to police officers on demand, and to all others either directly or via their own local collators. (Campbell 1980: 118–9)

Sometimes, the indexing system was unusual if not crude:

In one collator's office … there was a file marked 'cows, queers and flashers'. (ibid.: 129)

The Thames Valley police had developed a computerised system of holding intelligence as far back as the 1970s (Campbell and Connor 1986: 207–11), but it was only after the turn of the century in 2000 that computers got heavily engaged in holding 'soft' information culminating in the PND.

The big move in this direction followed the conviction and sentencing of Ian Huntley for the murder of two children in the village of Soham in Cambridgeshire during the summer of 2002. In the aftermath of Huntleys, trial questions were asked about 'soft information' that the police had held on him and why this information had not been made available to the Cambridgeshire local authority when they had screened him for work as a school caretaker. Huntley had not met his victims through this work but the amount of information the police held on him demonstrated a pattern of behaviour that meant he should not have been given the job (Morris 2003). Sir Michael Bichard was asked to conduct an enquiry into what had gone wrong.

Bichard's Inquiry found that Huntley had been reported to the police on some nine occasions for sexual improprieties sometimes including girls under the age of consent; none of these reports had led to a prosecution. These reports had been collated by the Humberside police when Huntley had lived at his previous address. The Humberside police had held these paper reports separately, not recognised the growing pattern of behaviour and had not passed this information to Cambridgeshire police when they had requested it as part of his screening. The Bichard Report now recommended a nation-wide computerised system of holding police intelligence to improve the ease of sharing this 'soft information' around the country; such a system 'should be introduced as a matter of urgency' (Bichard Inquiry 2004: para.4.31).

Developing such a system was going to take time and money. The Home Office allocated some £367 million for developmental work describing the new database as 'a new technology based system designed to connect information held locally and nationally by police systems, as well as the Police National Computer' (Home Office 2006b: 1). The result was the PND launched in 2010 and operationally starting in June 2011 (Hall 2011).

Guidance on the handling of police intelligence was provided in the National Intelligence Model (NIM), produced by the National Centre for Policing Excellence on behalf of the ACPOs. A Code of Practice relating to the operation of the model was issued in January 2005 by the Home Secretary under sections 39 and 39A, Police Act 1996, sections 28 and 73, Police Act 1997 and sections 28A and 73A, Police Act 1997 (National Centre for Policing Excellence 2005).

A *Code of Practice on the Operation and Use of the Police National Database* was published in 2010. The code emphasised that the PND had to be compliant with the DPA 1998, the Human Rights Act 1998 and the common law duty of confidence (NPIA 2010a: para.3.1) and that its information was designated confidential in accordance with the Government Protective Marking Scheme (GPMS). Staff using it had to be duly trained and vetted.

At the time of writing (May 2017), plans are afoot to join up the PND and the PNC in the police and Home Office initiative called 'Law Enforcement Data System' (LEDS); the ANPR database will also be joined to this initiative (see Chap. 6 for more on the ANPR arrangements). The Surveillance Camera Commissioner (SCC) explains that he will be closely watching this development:

> The plan is to create a services channel whereby access can be provided to the data and intelligence. … Proportionality will be a design feature of the system with permission-based access, with a full audit trail and a description of purpose of access. There is much work to do in terms of exact detail. My office will maintain contact to provide advice against some key issues such as visibility and transparency of system. (SCC 2016: 22–23)

Biometric Data

Biometric data was originally referred to in Chap. 3 and is returned to here. It is taken to mean fingerprints and DNA samples.

Fingerprints

The use of fingerprints as a form of identification was first used in colonial India by the British authorities who had difficulty identifying the native population (Sengoopta 2003). The idea was brought back to the UK and adopted by Scotland Yard as a means of identifying known offenders; a national collection of fingerprints was started in 1902 with the opening of the Metropolitan Police's Fingerprint Office which was later merged into the CRO in 1913 (Beavan 2001).

Fingerprints at this time were taken on a wet-ink basis with fingers, thumbs and palms suitably inked in black and then rolled and pressed on to a paper record. This system held a certain ritual 'rite of passage' to it as the officer would hold down the hand to ensure a good impress and at the end the person concerned had to wash their hands clean. It was a system that lasted well into the 2000s.

PACE s.61 granted the police power to take fingerprints without consent if there were reasonable grounds for suspecting the involvement of that person in a criminal offence, and fingerprints would tend to prove or disprove his or her involvement. The Criminal Justice Act 2003 s.9 extended these powers to allow the taking of fingerprints without consent upon arrest for a recordable offence. Reasonable force can be used to take fingerprints after arrest, charge or conviction.

Today the process is done digitally with Livescan consoles having replaced the old ink system in 2005. The fingers, thumbs and palms are impressed on the clean consoles where the fingerprint is captured and stored on the IDENT1 database. IDENT1 provides the UK's central national service for holding, searching and comparing fingerprint information on those who come into contact with the police as detainees after being arrested. It was designed and developed by Northrop Grumman and replaced the earlier software National Fingerprint Identification System (NAFIS) in 2004.

On their website, Northrop Grumman describes the nature of IDENT 1:

IDENT1 provides an integrated fingerprint and palm print system and computing infrastructure to connect 57 police forces and agencies, with over 1200 workstations and 440 Livescan units, throughout England, Wales, and Scotland, utilizing a dedicated data communications network service. The system's image-based finger and palm print data is integrated with Phoenix, the criminal records database on the Police National Computer (PNC). (Northrop Grumman ND)

The police can access fingerprints on mobile systems carried in cars. 'Project Lantern' was a pilot scheme started in 2006 to make fingerprints available to mobile police units and enable confirmation of driver details when police are carrying out a vehicle check; these fingerprint checks are voluntary. Mobile systems have also been used by police operations at railway stations or during stops for searches for knives. The checks go back to the IDENT database. The Mobile Identification at Scene (MIDAS) project that followed the pilots reportedly allows police access to information on 7.5 million individuals (Bowcott 2008).

In order to create greater oversight of the collection and use of biometric materials in the wake of *S and Marper v UK 48 EHRR 1169 2008*, the government introduced more safeguarding laws (see Chap. 3) and created a new independent post of Commissioner for the Retention and Use of Biometric Material (the 'Biometrics Commissioner') (Protection of Freedoms Act 2012 s.20–21).

National DNA Database

The UK claims to have been the first jurisdiction to create an NDNAD to enable samples to be matched against those found at scenes of crime and elsewhere (Home Office 1995a). The original database grew exponentially and in 1999 the Home Office expanded it with an input of £34 million (Home Office 1999a) and with a further £109 million pounds a year later (Home Office 2000).

In 2008, two people challenged the police ability to retain DNA samples on them when they had been arrested but subsequently never charged. They thought it wrong that as innocent people, the police were allowed to keep these samples. Their case was taken through the UK courts—who upheld the police's right to do this—and ended up in the European Court of Human Rights in Strasbourg where it was held that this blanket and indiscriminate retention policy breached the right to privacy under Article 8 (*S and Marper v UK 48 EHRR 1169 2008*).

The Labour administration prepared plans to remedy this, but they were replaced by the Coalition government in May 2010 who made their own changes in the Protection of Freedoms Act 2012 Chapter 1. Under the new regime, DNA (and fingerprints) of individuals arrested or charged but not convicted of an offence has to be destroyed, unless one of the exceptions in the Act is triggered. For example, where someone has been arrested but not charged with a serious offence their DNA can be retained for up to five years. The 2012 Act also provides for the destruction of DNA samples and profiles already retained under the current regime.

In the year 2015–2016, nearly 300,000 people's DNA samples were added to the NDNAD:

As at 31st March 2016, NDNAD held 5,860,642 subject profile records and 519,678 crime scene profile records. In 2015/16, 292,311 new subject profile records were loaded to NDNAD, together with 36,250 new crime scene profile records …

In 2015/16, 205,977 subject profile records were deleted from NDNAD (including 53 under the 'Deletion of Records from National Police Systems guidance ('the Record Deletion Guidance'); see '2.4 Early Deletion'). Additionally, 4,547 crime scene profile records were deleted. (NPCC et al. 2017: para.1.2.1)

The Biometrics Commissioner has pointed out that:

despite deletions and the more restrictive retention regime that has been in place since October of 2013, some 12.5% of men and some 3% of women in the United Kingdom continue to have their DNA profiles and/or fingerprints retained on those national databases. (Commissioner for the Retention and Use of Biometric Material 2016: para.15)

National Special Branch Intelligence System

Police Special Branches have their own database known as the National Special Branch Intelligence System. Special Branches are those units from which the police are gathering, evaluating and disseminating information among police forces; this intelligence relates to threats to public order, including those arising from domestic extremism.

The police routinely collect information at public demonstrations using Evidence Gathering Teams (EGTs) and Forward Intelligence Teams (FITs) who undertake overt information and intelligence gathering, identify and engage with individuals/groups who may become involved in, or encourage, disorder or violence, or may increase levels of tension, and provide commanders with fast-time updates so that resources can be deployed efficiently and effectively. They are specifically advised to take Article 8 into account when carrying out their task to ensure that any potential interference with the right to privacy is necessary, proportionate and legal (College of Policing 2016b).

ViSOR

ViSOR is the database that supports Multi-Agency Public Protection Arrangements (MAPPA) work. The Police Service and the Probation Service were given a legal duty in 2000 to cooperate and work together as the 'responsible authorities' in MAPPA (Criminal Justice and Court Services Act 2000 ss. 67–68). MAPPA is not an agency in itself but a set of administrative arrangements to assist the participating agencies; each MAPPA has its own coordinator. This legal duty to cooperate was later extended to Her Majesty's Prison Service and together the now three 'responsible authorities' (police, prison and probation) worked closely with other agencies under a 'duty to cooperate' (see Criminal Justice Act 2003 s.325 (6) for the complete list).

This cooperative work was to be focussed on three categories of offenders:

(1) Offenders on the sex offender register
(2) Violent and other sexual offenders
(3) Other dangerous offenders

ViSOR facilitates the effective sharing of information and intelligence on violent and sexual offenders between the three MAPPA 'responsible authority' agencies, as well as the recording of joint risk assessments and risk management plans. ViSOR was initially an acronym for the Violent and Sexual Offender Register, but its role was expanded by the police to record information on some non-convicted subjects (known as potentially dangerous persons) and terrorist offenders. ViSOR is no longer an acronym but is the formal name of the database. ViSOR is to be used by MAPPA responsible authorities in discharging their statutory duties to assess and manage the risks presented by known sexual and violent offenders (see, e.g., Probation Instruction 2013).

The categories of people now with their information stored on ViSOR are:

MAPPA

- Registerable Sexual Offender
- Violent Offender
- Other Sexual Offender
- Other Dangerous Offender

Non-MAPPA (sub-categories)

- Registerable Violent Offender
- Registerable Terrorist Offender
- Potentially Dangerous Person

A Registerable Sexual Offender is one defined in the Sexual Offences Act 2003 ss.80–93 and Schedule 3, a Registerable Violent Offender is defined in the Criminal Justice and Immigration Act 2008 ss.107–12 and a Registerable Terrorist Offender is one listed in the Counter Terrorism Act 2008 ss.41–42. Violent Offenders and Other Sexual Offenders are decided upon by the police and other agencies guided only by the Criminal Justice Act 2003 s.325 (2) (b). The Potentially Dangerous Person is not defined in law but the Criminal Justice Act 2003 Chapter 5 and Schedule 15 again lists the sort of offences that should indicate such a person (for an overview see NPIA 2010b).

The police have been using ViSOR since 2005 but, since June 2008, ViSOR has been fully operational allowing, for the first time, key staff from the Police, Probation and Prison Services to work on the same system, thus improving the quality and timeliness of risk assessments and of interventions to prevent offending.

The agencies regard ViSOR information graded as CONFIDENTIAL, according to the GPMS. This places specific obligations on users of the system and their organisations, and users of the system are required to be vetted or security cleared or both, depending on which agency they work for and which role they occupy (NOMS 2012a: paras 8.1–8.25; Home Office et al. 2013).

HOLMES

Home Office Large Major Enquiry System (HOLMES) is a database used to support major inquiries and incidents. Its origins can be traced back to the late 1970s. The search by the West Yorkshire police for Peter Sutcliffe, known to the press as the Yorkshire Ripper (1975–1981), was beset with problems of too much information—some 9000 interviews were made and much of it was stored on card indexes and statement sheets making it hard to analyse and cross-refer. Afterwards, an enquiry was set up to see why it had taken so long to detect Sutcliffe. The Byford Report recommended a new computerised system for major incidents (Home Office 2006a).

In 1986, UK police forces started to employ the HOLMES as recommended by Byford in all major incidents including serial murders, multi-million-pound fraud cases and major disasters. In 2004, HOLMES 2 was introduced as an updated version; HOLMES 2 is now an investigation management system to assist law enforcement organisations in their management of the complex process of investigating serious crimes. It enables them to improve effectiveness and productivity in crime investigations, helping to solve crimes more quickly and improve detection rates.

Problem Areas in Data Collation and Retention

The remainder of this chapter looks at the accuracy and completeness of the data held by the police (data quality), the improper use of data held by the police and the arguments about how long data should be retained by them before becoming obsolete and in need of deletion. All of these features can impact on privacy: We start with data quality.

Data Quality

We noted above that it was the poor quality of criminal records held on the PNC that had triggered the move to computerisation in 1995. But within three years, a Home Office Report stated that the data quality remained poor (Russell 1998; see also HMIC 2000). The importance of this finding increased because of the pending start of the Criminal Records Bureau (CRB).

Since 1986, local police forces had been given the job of supplying local authorities and other employers with criminal record information to help them screen potential employees seeking work with children and other vulnerable people. The CRB was designed to take this work off the police and provide the same information from a national base in Liverpool (Home Office 1996; for more on this see Chap. 10). The CRB was due to start operations in March 2002. The Home Affairs Committee now returned to the subject of data quality in the national criminal record collection and again emphasised the importance of keeping the records accurate and up to date:

> The Home Office must ensure that improvements are made to the quality of data stored on the Police National Computer. The Criminal Records Bureau should closely monitor the number of complaints it receives that certificates are incorrect in the first year of operation. (House of Commons 2001: para.50; see also Thomas 2001)

Part of the problem was that records of criminal convictions and sentences were made by the courts and then passed to the police for input to the PNC; the courts had no direct way of inputting to the PNC. As a result, the police had limited 'ownership' of the records when they first arrived on their desk, and officers tended not to prioritise the updating of the PNC among all their other work. HMIC started to look at the issues:

HMIC subsequently produced three reports, the last of which, in December 2002, showed that, while there had been significant improvements in clearing the backlog of case results, few forces were consistently achieving the required performance criteria (HMIC 2002). In 2003, the HMIC PNC Compliance Audit Team was formed to carry out focussed PNC inspections of all forces in England and Wales and on invitation from HMIC (Scotland) to inspect the eight Scottish forces.

A new law in 2002 had given new powers to the Home Secretary to issue Codes of Practice to chief police officers in the interests of making the police more efficient and effective (Police Act 1996 s.39A as amended by the Police Reform Act 2002 s.2). Two such codes were now issued on the Management of Police Information (MOPI) (Home Office 2005a) and on the PNC itself (Home Office 2005b). The MOPI Code was supplemented by a volume of guidance (ACPO/Centrex 2006); the guidance was updated in 2010 and its latest version is now to be found on the College of Policing website (College of Policing 2016c).

All this attention has had some effect on data quality but problems still crop up and not least because of the large number of criminal record disclosures made to employers each year. Between 2003 and 2012, an estimated 20,000 people had complained of mistakes and been given records they did not have. Sometimes a record was attributed to the wrong person and sometimes PNC entries were wrong. Some people lost jobs they should have been entitled to, having waited months for errors to be corrected (Whitehead 2012). An ACPO spokesman said:

> While we regret there will be some errors made, as a result of a number of enquiries, including the Bichard Inquiry, and advances in technology, record keeping and data collection is far better and on the whole the accuracy is very good. (quoted in ibid.)

Case

The data quality of police, which held biometric information, has also been called into question. For the best part of the twentieth century, the fingerprint was taken as the gold-standard method of ensuring a person's identity. A case in Scotland revealed all was not as it seemed. Shirley McKie was a police woman until February 1997 when she was accused of leaving her fingerprint at a crime scene and then lying about it. McKie was part of a police team investigating a murder in Kilmarnock. At the trial of the accused she was asked as a Crown witness why her fingerprints were to be found at the crime scene. McKie said she had never actually been at the crime scene and therefore the fingerprints could not be hers.

At McKie's trial for perjury, Scottish police fingerprint experts maintained that the fingerprints belonged to McKie whilst two American experts testified that the fingerprints found were not hers. McKie was acquitted, left the police and in 2006 was awarded a compensation pay out of £750,000 from the Scottish Executive. An inquiry into what had gone wrong maintained that whilst individual prints may be unique, forensic analysis depends on the clarity of reproduction and, for example, the degree of contamination on the surface the print has been taken from (Campbell 2011; O'Neill 2011).

Improper Use

Police officers and civilian staff working for the police have been guilty of misusing the information they have collected. This improper use of information has direct implications for privacy. Much of this misuse has been for the personal use of police officers. The ICO has reported that 'the unlawful disclosure of information from police systems is an issue of particular concern as many professional standards units within the police are investigating corrupt practices by serving officers' (ICO 2006: para.4.6); the Metropolitan Police have admitted that hundreds of their officers have improperly accessed police databases (Lewis 2011).

The campaign group BBW reported no less than 2315 data breaches carried out by police officers and civilian staff between June 2011 and December 2015. These included:

- 869 (38%) instances of inappropriate/unauthorised access to information
- 877 (38%) instances of inappropriate disclosure of data to third parties

Specific incidents revealed officers misusing their access to information for financial gain and even passing sensitive information to members of organised crime groups (Big Brother Watch 2016b).

A different example of more organised police disclosure of information improperly has come to light in investigations into the practice of 'blacklisting'. Blacklisting is the name given to the illegal screening of potential workers by private employers to ensure that no 'trouble makers' were ever employed. To employers in the construction and building, trade 'trouble makers' meant active trade unionists and those concerned about health and safety issues, both perfectly legal activities. Information on workers was gathered by secretive organisations who shared the information on a national level between different employers who subscribed to their illegal databases. The Economic League lasted from 1919 to 1993 (Hollingsworth and Norton Taylor 1988), and this was superseded by the Consulting Association from 1993 to 2009 (Smith and Chamberlain 2015).

The databases held by these two organisations comprised information gathered from other employers, observations at union meetings and cuttings from union and other radical newspapers. Suspicions that the police were also contributing information emerged after 2009 when the ICO started investigating (Boffey 2012). A House of Commons Select Committee took evidence that suggested police information had been finding its way on to the databases (House of Commons 2013 Ev105), and later the IPCC made further investigations and declared that it is 'likely that all [police] special branches were involved in providing information' to the Consulting Association that had kept certain individuals out of work, sometimes for years:

> The [IPCCs] admission has been welcomed by campaigners for the 3,200 workers whose names were on the blacklist that was run for construction companies as 'absolute evidence' of a conspiracy between the state and industry that lasted for decades. (Boffey 2013)

Police officers are subject to a number of different laws and procedures should they improperly disclose police-held information. These include the common law of 'misconduct in public office', the Official Secrets Act

1989, the DPA 1998, the Criminal Justice and Courts Act 2015 and other wider regulations such as the Police (Conduct) Regulations 2012 No. 2632. Officers are also bound by the College of Policing's Code of Ethics and may be subjected to investigation by the IPCC established by the Police Reform Act 2002.

Official Secrets Act 1989

Security and intelligence officers as well as police officers and prison officers are all bound by the Official Secrets Act 1989 which introduces the idea of 'damaging' disclosures of information. It is for the attorney general to decide whether a disclosure is deemed damaging and to bring a prosecution; the relevant parts of the Act indicating 'damage' are sections 1(3), 2(1), 3(1), 4(2), 5(3)(a) and 6(2).

Data Protection Act 1998

Police officers and other public officials are all expected to comply with the DPA 1998 and its incorporated eight principles that include Principle 7 that appropriate measures shall be taken against unauthorised or unlawful processing of personal data and against accidental loss or destruction of, or damage to, personal data (Data Protection Act 1998 Schedule 1 part 1 and part 2).

Codes and Guidance

In general terms, all police officers are expected to comply with the College of Policing's Code of Ethics where Standard of Professional Behaviour number 7 on confidentiality states 'I will treat information with respect, and access or disclose it only in the proper course of my duties' (College of Policing 2014a: 11). The more specific *Code of Practice on the* MOPI issued in 2005 under the Police Act 1996 (as amended) requires all police forces to establish and maintain an information management strategy and advises that:

Chief officers' should ensure that arrangements within their forces for managing police information include procedures and technical measures to prevent unauthorised or accidental access to, amendment of, or loss of police information. Such procedures should comply with guidance issued under this Code. (Home Office 2005a: para.3.4.1)

The code required forces to have in place current written information strategies but again, almost ten years on, the inspectorate 'were disappointed to find that this was not always the case' (HMIC 2015: 12). The report concluded that 'greater rigour in the implementation of management information policies is required so that all forces are brought up to the standards of the best' (ibid.: 61).

This MOPI Code states that it is 'supported by more detailed and extensive guidance' (ibid.: para.1.1.7). The latest version of this guidance is now provided by the College of Policing (2014a).

Misconduct in Public Office

Misconduct in public office as common law offence is not well defined but the offence over the years has come to mean a public officer such as a police officer or prison officer who wilfully neglects his or her duty and/or wilfully misconducts him or herself in their role. Their behaviour has to be to such a degree as to amount to an abuse of the public's trust in the office holder without reasonable excuse or justification. Mark Turner was a West Midlands police officer imprisoned in 2009 after passing on information to criminals. He pleaded guilty to two charges of misconduct in public office. The misconduct charges related to restricted intelligence that Turner had accessed between April 2004 and October 2007, while he worked for West Midlands police (Lewis 2011).

The Home Office produces regular guidance to the police on the subject which makes specific reference to matters of confidentiality:

Police officers treat information with respect and access or disclose it only in the proper course of police duties. (Home Office 2015e: para.1.21)

An earlier version of the same guidance had been more expansive:

> The police service shares information with other agencies and the public as part of its legitimate policing business. Police officers never access or disclose any information that is not in the proper course of police duties and do not access information for personal reasons. Police officers who are unsure if they should access or disclose information always consult with their manager or department that deals with data protection or freedom of information before accessing or disclosing it.
>
> Police officers do not provide information to third parties who are not entitled to it. This includes for example, requests from family or friends, approaches by private investigators and unauthorised disclosure to the media. (Home Office 2012a: paras.1.51–1.52)

Misconduct in public office became the subject of a Law Commission consultation exercise in late 2016 in order to clarify its meaning and consider whether it should become a statutory offence (Law Commission 2016). The consultation exercise also wanted to look at possible overlaps with the Criminal Justice and Courts Act 2015.

Criminal Justice and Courts Act 2015

The Criminal Justice and Courts Act introduced the new offence of police corruption:

> Corrupt or other improper exercise of police powers and privileges
> (1) A police constable listed in subsection (3) commits an offence if he or she:
>
> (a) exercises the powers and privileges of a constable improperly
> (b) knows or ought to know that the exercise is improper. (Criminal Justice and Courts Act 2015 s.26)

This Act clearly makes it an offence for a police officer to exercise their powers and privileges 'improperly', and this would include improper disclosure of police-held information.

Retention and Deletion

One thing that has bothered critics is the length of time the police should keep personal information, especially when that information is on material that is trivial or clearly outdated. In particular, these critics included those people who had old and minor criminal records that years later were stopping them from getting jobs if those jobs required pre-employment screening. What use was this information to the police and why could it not be deleted?

The recent history of policies and laws on data retention is a complex and confused one. The first DPA in 1984 had reproduced the Council of Europe's eight data protection principles (CoE 1981) in its Schedule 1. Principle 6 stated that:

> Personal data held for any purpose or purposes shall not be kept for longer than is necessary for that purpose or those purposes. (Data Protection Act 1984 Schedule One)

ACPO in turn used these principles as the basis for its first published guidance on how long police records should be kept and this became the ACPO starting point for the police. As the Act gave no legal interpretation of Principle 6, ACPO decided that:

> it is not possible to lay down absolute rules about how long particular items of personal data, which form part of a collection, should be retained. (ACPO 1987: para.2.6.2)

It would all depend on the particular circumstances, what purpose it served and how useful it was likely to be in future. In practice, this meant keeping it under review which at best would be on an annual basis. At the end of the day the length of retention would be a police decision.

ACPO did recommend that offences could be deleted after 20 years if an offender had not been prosecuted again; meanwhile, such deletion was not to take place where a six-month or more sentence had been imposed for offences of indecency or for offences of homicide. Cautions could be deleted for adults and juveniles after three years provided there had been no additions to the record and for juveniles they could also be deleted when they reach 17 years of age (ibid.:13).

A second version of this guidance increased the number of exceptions for deletion after 20 years to include convictions for violence, drug possession or dealing and offences where the victim was a child or vulnerable adult. Cautions now had to stay on record for five years with no further additions to the record in the meantime (ACPO 1995: 21–22).

Having stated in both these codes that 'it is not possible to lay down absolute rules about how long particular items of personal data ... should be retained', ACPO now produced guidance entitled *General Rules for Criminal Record Weeding on Police Systems*. Aimed specifically at criminal records rather than any other information, the period of retention was said to be dependent on the sentence disposal type. Ten years after a conviction the offences could be deleted unless they had led to a six month (or more) custodial sentence or were sentences related to sexual or terrorist offences. To make the point, this document included a list of nearly 500 offences that would lead to records being retained for life (ACPO 2000)

This discernible trend towards keeping information for longer periods before deletion was continued in another version of the ACPO Code of Practice for Data Protection published in 2002 (ACPO 2002). By this time the relevant Principle 6 had become Principle 5 as reproduced in the new DPA 1998:

> Personal data processed for any purpose or purposes shall not be kept for longer than is necessary for that purpose or those purposes. (Data Protection Act 1998 Schedule One)

ACPO still maintained that that it was not possible, in all instances, to lay down absolute rules about data retention (ACPO 2002: para.8.2) but still advised 'such rules should be established where possible' (ibid.). The new rules that it came up with now were that records could be deleted after ten years unless certain offences had been committed. The list of excepted records was as in the last edition of the Code of Practice for data protection but with the addition of sexual offences and terrorist offences. In the case of all these offences the records would now be deleted on the death of the subject or when the subject reached 100 years of age (ibid.: 21). Police cautions for adults would be deleted after five years unless for an offence against a vulnerable person; reprimands and final warnings (as juvenile cautions were now called) would last for five years, if no further record had been added (ibid.: 22).

Members of the public still felt frustrated when they lost jobs because of old or minor offences still being on their records. The ICO was asked to intervene and in 2007 ordered the police to delete all the old and minor convictions kept on file (ICO 2007). The police appealed against this decision to the Information Tribunal but on 21 July 2007, the Tribunal upheld the Commissioner's decision and also ordered the police to start deleting the relevant records.

Still not happy with losing some of their records, the police took their case to the courts. The case became known as the 'Five Constables case' having been brought by the Humberside, GMP, Northumbria, Staffordshire and West Midland's police. This time the courts over ruled the ICO and the Information Tribunal and allowed the police to maintain all the records they thought were necessary (*CC of Humberside Police and Ors v The Information Commissioner and Anor [2009] EWCA Civ 1079*).

In 2013, a number of people took further legal action to challenge the police, the Home Office and the Ministry of Justices' right to retain old and minor criminal records on them. A 21-year-old man referred to as T had received warnings from the police for stealing two bicycles when he was 11, which later stopped him from getting a place on a sports study course. A woman referred to as JB similarly lost a job caring for vulnerable people because she had been cautioned for stealing a packet of false nails some eight years earlier. The Court of Appeal agreed with them and declared the criminal record collection to be in breach of Article 8 of the ECHR (*R on the Application of T, JB and AW v Chief Constable of Greater Manchester, Secretary of State for the Home Department and Secretary of State for Justice [2013] EWCA Civ 25*). A spokesman for Liberty said:

> This sensible judgement requires the Government to introduce a more nuanced system for disclosing this type of sensitive personal data to employers ... we hope that long overdue reforms – properly balancing the aim of public protection with privacy rights – will now be forthcoming. (Liberty 2013)

A new 'filtering' mechanism to take out the old and minor records was introduced on 29 May 2013. It meant the applicant for employment could safely leave out the old minor offences in any self-declaration; serious offences would remain disclosable. Applicants were directed to the details of the system (Gov.uk 2013) or the relevant new laws in the Rehabilitation of Offenders Act 1974 (Exceptions) Order 1975 (Amendment) (England and Wales) Order 2013 SI 2013 No. 1198 and the Police Act 1997 (Criminal Record Certificates: Relevant Matters) (Amendment) (England and Wales) Order SI 2013 No. 1200. The new arrangements did not mean the conviction or cautions would be 'removed' or 'wiped' from the PNC, just that they would not be disclosed and therefore did not have to be declared.

For reasons best known to themselves and despite having already introduced the new 'filtering' system, the government still decided to challenge the Court of Appeal decision in the Supreme Court. The Supreme Court eventually agreed with the lower court and decided that the old arrangements were incompatible with Article 8 (*R (R on the application of T and Another) v Secretary of State for the Home Department and Another [2014] UKSC 35*).

In many ways, the new 'filtering' mechanism replicated the old 'step-down system' that had only lasted from 2006 to 2009. For present purposes, it is worth noting that under the new arrangements, adult convictions would only be removed from a DBS certificate if:

- 11 years have elapsed since the date of conviction
- it is the person's only offence
- it did not result in a custodial sentence

Some people with more than one old and minor offence took exception to the wording '[if] it is the person's only offence' and mounted yet another challenge in the High Court to the disclosure arrangements. Once again, the government lost because of its unwillingness to consider more than one old or minor conviction and once again the new arrangements were said to be incompatible with Article 8 (*R (on the application of P and A) v Secretary of State for Justice, Secretary of State for Home Department and Chief Constable of Thames Valley Police [2016] EWHC 89*

(Admin)). The Home Office took it higher but the Court of Appeal agreed with the High Court that the current system was 'unlawful' (*P and Others v. Secretary of State for the Home Department, and the Secretary of State for Justice [2017] EWCA Civ 321*).

Case

Another legal challenge to police retention of information has been made by John Catt. This did not relate to pre-employment screening but to the inclusion of Mr Catt's personal details on a police database despite him never having committed any crimes. His inclusion was on the National Special Branch Intelligence System because of his regular appearance at demonstrations and political protests. All these attendances were perfectly legal and he was never arrested by the police for violence or other criminal activity.

The arguments again went to the Supreme Court who ruled that the retention by police of information about the 91-year-old activist's presence at political protests was (1) in accordance with the law and (2) of proportionate interference with his right to a private life under Article 8(1) of the ECHR.

Only Lord Toulson on the Supreme Court sounded a note of dissent in favour of Mr Catt describing the records as unnecessary and disproportionate:

One might question why it really matters, if there is no risk of the police making inappropriate disclosure of the information to others. It matters because in modern society, the state has very extensive powers of keeping records on its citizens. If a citizen's activities are lawful, they should be free from the state keeping a record of them unless, and then only for as long as, such a record really needs to be kept in the public interest (*R (Catt) and R (T) v Commissioner of Police of the Metropolis [2015] UKSC 9* at para. 69).

At the time of writing (May 2017), Mr Catt is taking his case to the European Court of Human Rights claiming violation of Article 8.

Summary

The police collect and retain personal information on various databases including the PNC and the PND; new databases have periodically started. Personal biometric information, including fingerprints and DNA samples, is also collated and retained in digital form. A number of problem areas have been identified in the management of this personal information, and here we have noted the question of improper use by officers having access to the databases, matters of data quality and ensuring that records are fully correct, and debates about how long some of this personal information should be maintained to be of use to the police. The future development and expansion of digital technology looks likely to be able to provide the police with more opportunities to retain items of personal information.

6

Photographs, CCTVs and Other Cameras

Introduction

The UK is often said to be one of the most watched countries in the world with its extensive CCTV cameras gazing on public places as well as indoors in retail outlets, football grounds, libraries and in fact just about every kind of work premise (Norris and Armstrong 1999). More recently, as the technology improves and gets smaller, cameras have appeared on buses and trains as well as police officers' uniforms to capture the personal interactions of officers with members of the public. ANPR uses cameras able to link in real time with police computers to identify Vehicles of Interest (VOI). Police helicopters have reportedly been equipped with infrared cameras that can read car licence plates from 610 metres (Lewis 2008). Further developments in CCTV have led to better quality photographs and to experiments with such software as 'facial recognition technology'.

Whether or not the CCTV that watches us in the streets is an invasion of privacy has been debated. If you are in a public space, have you forfeited any rights to privacy? Or can your movements and, for example, who you might be meeting not be an activity you might want to keep private? Does a UK citizen have a right to lose themselves in the crowd of

© The Author(s) 2017
D. Marshall, T. Thomas, *Privacy and Criminal Justice*,
https://doi.org/10.1007/978-3-319-64912-2_6

the city rather than be singled out by cameras using 'facial recognition technology'?

People arrested and taken into police custody are liable to have their pictures taken. In this chapter, we start by considering the process by which that photography takes place and the problematic absence of a regulatory regime to govern the police retention of these photographs.

Police Photographs

Police Custody Photographs

Today, the law on police powers to photograph people in their custody is in the PACE, but the law on the digital and legal storage of custody pictures taken by the police is somewhat of a grey area.

People who have been arrested may have a custody photograph taken. In law and following the PACE Codes of Practice, photographs are included with the taking of fingerprints and other samples such as DNA or blood samples. The photographs can be taken with or without consent and reasonable force may be used if necessary; items of clothing or other substances may be removed and again reasonable force may be used. Children can only be photographed if a parent or guardian is present and a person cannot be arrested for the sole purpose of a photograph being taken (Police and Criminal Evidence Act 1984 ss.54A and 64A; Home Office 2017b: paras.5.12–5.24).

The photographs are used for such purposes as checking to see if a match is already held in existing photographs, to establish a time of arrest or verify an identity (Home Office 2017b: para.5B). The police are allowed to retain the photographs:

> PACE, section 64A, see paragraph 5.12, provides powers to take photographs of suspects and allows these photographs to be used or disclosed only for purposes related to the prevention or detection of crime, the investigation of offences or the conduct of prosecutions by, or on behalf of, police or other law enforcement and prosecuting authorities inside and outside the United Kingdom or the enforcement of a sentence. After being

so used or disclosed, they may be retained but can only be used or disclosed for the same purposes. (ibid.: para.3.30)

Regulating Police Custody Photographs

Although the PACE and its accompanying Codes of Practice set the overall framework for taking custody photographs, the regulation and retention and compilation of these photographs in database form is more of a grey area.

Two people who had been arrested challenged the police right to retain their custody photographs when neither had been charged or prosecuted. The High Court ruled in their favour and stated that such retention was a breach of their Article 8 rights:

In my judgment, therefore, the retention of the claimants' photographs in application of the existing policy amounts to an unjustified interference with their right to respect for their private life and is in breach of Article 8. (*R (RMC and FJ) v Metropolitan Police Service [2012] EWHC 1681* at para.55)

As part of this ruling the High Court stated that the police's 'existing policy concerning the retention of custody photographs … was "unlawful"'. The police were given 'a reasonable further period' of time within which to revise the existing policy; the Courts clarified that a 'reasonable further period' was to be 'measured in months, not years' (*R (RMC and FJ) v Metropolitan Police Service [2012] EWHC 1681* at para58).

Two years later it emerged that nothing had been done to revise the policy. The Biometrics Commissioner had been created by the Protection of Freedoms Act 2012 to provide oversight to the police use of biometric information such as DNA and fingerprinting; the Act had said nothing about police photographs but the Commissioner took it upon himself to start asking questions. The Biometrics Commissioner was informed in April 2014 that 12 million custody photographs had been uploaded to the PND and that an automated facial recognition searching system had been implemented without any formal form of governance (Office of the Biometrics Commissioner 2014: paras 336–44). The campaign group

Liberty asked its own questions: 'when will the police stop showing such contempt for our privacy?' The Home Office response was that 'this is a complex issue' and they 'are currently reviewing the framework through which the police use custody images, and expect to be able to report in the spring' (Home Office 2015f).

The Biometrics Commissioner decided to then bring the lack of regulation of police custody photographs to the attention of the House of Commons Science and Technology Select Committee. This time, the ACPO advised the Committee that they were 'undertaking concerted work to ensure that the regime under which images are taken, retained and used meets the same thresholds as they set for other biometric data' (House of Commons 2015d: para2.3), and the Home Office again made reassuring statements that 'work is underway to ensure the retention of photographs by the police, including those taken of detainees under Section 64A of PACE, is proportionate in the light of developing case law' (ibid.: Home Office evidence para.4.1).

The Select Committee was not that reassured:

> We are concerned that it has taken over two and half years for the Government to respond to the High Court ruling that the existing policy concerning the retention of custody photographs was 'unlawful'. Furthermore, we were dismayed to learn that, in the known absence of an appropriate governance framework, the police have persisted in uploading custody photographs to the Police National Database, to which, subsequently, facial recognition software has been applied. (ibid.: para.99)

The Committee recommended that the Biometrics Commissioner has the brief extended to cover photographs (ibid.: para.23).

The police, for their part, seemed to have spotted the gap in the law and taken advantage of it. Leicestershire police were reported to be well advanced in their use of facial recognition technology using NEC software. Senior Leicestershire officers downplayed suggestions that this was invasive of privacy:

> Concerns over privacy were rejected by senior officers who said a match did not constitute evidence ... the system would not impact on civil liberties and could be a huge boost to the delivery of justice. (BBC News 2014a)

Speaking to the BBC, one chief constable said forces had to stay up to date with new technology:

> Everybody is very keen that the police enter the cyber world. … I hear much criticism of policing that we're not up to speed and it does come as a surprise to me that we're now being admonished for being ahead of the game. (quoted in BBC News 2015c)

Case

NEC advertises one example of their software online:
Designed for operational security users, NeoFace Watch integrates with existing video surveillance systems, enhancing security by extracting faces in real time from surveillance or even web cameras and instantaneously matching them against a watchlist of individuals. Multiple alert options are available within NeoFace Watch (available at https://www.necam.com/Biometrics/doc.cfm?t=FaceRecognition accessed 31 October 2016).

Some four years after the legal position had first been made clear by the High Court, the Biometrics Commissioner could see no progress at all. In his second Annual Report, he stated:

> the upshot of the Home Office review has yet to be published and it is my impression that, in the absence of any clear 'steer' from the Home Office:

- police forces in England and Wales have continued to upload custody images to the PND regardless of whether the individuals in question have or have not been convicted of, or even charged with, an offence
- all the custody photographs on the PND have continued to be searched against by forces using facial recognition software
- few, if any, steps have been taken to remove from that database the custody photographs which, in the light of the judgement in *R (RMC and FJ) v MPS*, seems likely that the police should no longer be retaining (Commissioner for the Retention and Use of Biometric Material 2016: para.343)

The campaign group Big Brother Watch described the situation as a 'disgrace':

That police forces are still uploading custody photos; of often innocent people, to the Police National Computer with no oversight or regulation is a disgrace. Concerns were raised 18 months ago but still we await Government guidance on oversight and regulation. (BBW 2016b)

At the time of writing (May 2017), and over five years since the High Court made its comments, no revised policy on police custody photographs has ever been produced, and in the absence of an appropriate governance framework, the police have persisted in uploading police custody photographs to the PND. This would appear to be a direct invasion of privacy by the police and an ignoring of requirements laid down by the courts to correct this invasion. No doubt if pressed they would argue the need to counter terrorism activities and other serious crimes but at the moment no one appears to be pressing them. Whether this retention of police custody photographs does contribute to the prevention of terrorism and the detection of terrorists remains an unknown that should be researched.

Police Photographs of Crowds

Police officers taking photographs have become a familiar part of a police response at large crowds where there might be public disorder. This enables retrospective examination and possible arrests if they have not taken place at the time. One man has challenged the police right to take such photographs and raised the question of whether police action is compatible with the right to private life protected by ECHR Article 8. The Court of Appeal considered these issues in *Wood v Commissioner of Police of the Metropolis* [2009] *EWCA Civ 414*.

The court held that Article 8 was engaged if the circumstances of the case were sufficient. The bare act of taking a photograph in a public place was not of itself capable of engaging Article 8 but the taking of the pictures had to be considered in context and especially if the images were going to be retained for any length of time. Once it had become clear that the person in the photograph had not committed any offence, it was for the police to justify as proportionate the interference with his Article 8 rights. It was the retention without good and proportionate cause that violated the right to privacy; keeping the photographs just because they might come in useful was insufficient ground.

The College of Policing has published a summary of the principles relating to review, retention and storage of overt images. These include the need to regularly review retention to ensure that the images remain necessary for a policing purpose with any records that have no evidential or intelligence value being disposed of securely. Any images retained should not be excessive and must be proportionate to the risk the person poses to the community. Film footage taken to record the character of a public order event without targeted individuals may be retained in accordance with relevant statutory limitation periods for civil actions. Where the footage shows significant criminal activity, the retention period is 50 years. Records should otherwise be disposed of when there is no longer a policing purpose for retaining them (College of Policing 2016d).

The College of Policing's summary provides some reassurance but still raises difficulties with the vagueness of language that often surrounds questions of privacy. What, for example, does 'regularly reviewed' mean or 'remain necessary' and 'not be excessive'? All such words demonstrate the elasticity of the concept of 'privacy' and the difficulties of pinning it down at any one time.

Closed Circuit Television

The 1930s saw the first known uses of the new technology of the film camera becoming available to the police. A primitive form of CCTV was used in Chesterfield in 1935 where the police used the techniques of targeted secret filming to gather evidence of illegal street betting; this pilot exercise was discontinued as being 'too expensive' (Williams et al. 2009).

The mid-1970s saw the development of CCTV as a renewed means of policing public areas. Improved technology in the form of cheaper and better equipment made filming in the 1970s more accessible to more authorities compared to the early 1930s experiments in Chesterfield. Some of this filming started in football grounds to try and contain the hooliganism that accompanied professional football at the time. Today CCTV is a widespread phenomenon with the conventional wisdom being that a person will be filmed 300 times during a walk through most UK city centres (BBC News 2006). CCTV is now subject to a form of governance under the DPA 1998 and the Protection of Freedoms Act 2012 and the auspices of the ICO and the SCC.

> ## Case
>
> As consumers we are monitored by the routine use of cameras in retail out-lets; whether in the supermarket, department store or corner shop. When we leave the store our image, in all probability, will be captured by high street, town centre and shopping mall camera systems. On our journey home, traffic cameras will monitor our compliance with speed and red light restrictions and, if we travel by rail, cameras at stations and along platforms will ensure a record of our presence. In other roles, whether it be as workers on the factory floor or at the office, as students, from kindergarten to university, as hospital patients, football fans or even customers at a local restaurant, cameras are probably watching over us. Put simply, in urban Britain … in almost every area to which the public have access we are under surveillance from CCTV (Norris and Armstrong 1999: 1).
>
> While precise figures are hard to come by, it is estimated that Britain is monitored by over four million CCTV cameras, making us one of the most watched nations in the world. CCTV is also spreading. It is no longer restricted to private property, shops and city centres but is increasingly being rolled out in school classrooms, bars and pubs and even swimming pool changing rooms (Liberty n.d. – CCTV and ANPR).
>
> https://www.liberty-human-rights.org.uk/human-rights/privacy/cctv-and-anpr

Sophisticated systems of cameras provided by the police and local authorities can be used to watch over a town or city centre. We have become used to images of banks of screens with operator 'watchers' in their control rooms homing in on suspicious activities. We have also become used to the resulting photographs being passed to the local newspapers for their readers to try and identify the people caught; police websites carry similar photographs (see, e.g., West Yorkshire Police 2017a).

A defining moment in the growth of CCTV has been identified as February 1993 when cameras picked up images of a two-year-old Jamie Bulger being abducted in the Bootle Strand shopping centre in Liverpool. The recordings served to help formulate peoples' images of the crime, and as Anthony Young suggests in his book 'Imagining Crime' as we look at them, we experience feelings of 'helplessness and horror as we watch the boys slowly disappear from view with the voyeuristic knowledge that death is to follow' (Young 1996).

Research has shown that CCTV does make a limited impact on levels of crime generally:

> The results suggest that CCTV caused a small (16%) but significant decrease in crime in experimental areas compared with comparable control areas. However, this overall result was largely driven by the effectiveness of CCTV schemes in car parks, which caused a 51% decrease in crime. Schemes in most other settings had small and nonsignificant effects on crime: a 7% decrease in city and town centres and in public housing. Public transport schemes had greater effects (a 23% decrease overall), but these were still non-significant. Schemes evaluated in the U.K. were more effective than schemes evaluated in other countries, but this effectiveness was largely driven by the studies in the car parks. (Welsh and Farrington 2007: 8)

In Middlesbrough, they went a step further and introduced technology that allowed the camera operators to talk to people in the streets. A disembodied voice would tell you to stop doing whatever was causing concern or simply pick up the litter you had just dropped. Other local authorities like the London Borough of Camden followed this model. The Home Office was approving of the initiative, and £500,000 development money was set aside for local authorities to bid for with some 20 authorities receiving grants from this funding (Clout 2007). Home Secretary John Reid said 'talking CCTV is another tool in creating safer communities. We know from Middlesbrough's example that this works' (Home Office 2007b). Local authorities do not appear to have kept up the use of 'talking CCTV'; Camden council turned theirs off following technical problems (Warman 2012). According to Middlesbrough Council website, the 'Talking Cameras' are still being used (Middlesbrough Council 2017).

Regulating CCTV

The CCTV networks that watch our movements in public space have grown up without any real political discussion and little regulation. CCTV is seen as just the extra 'eyes' of the police and as such a matter of simple 'common sense'. People being watched will not commit crime.

The cameras offer 'crime prevention' and if a crime still takes place they offer an additional 'investigative tool' to catch the wrongdoer. In practice, it is not so simple because crime may be 'displaced' to other areas where there are no cameras or their positioning in the first place is so poor that they never see anything untoward happening. The apocryphal story is told of the cameras catching people leaving car parks and passing their 'pay and display' tickets to newcomers. A communal act of kindness is made criminal by the cameras who know these tickets are 'non-transferable'.

A legal intervention was made when a man in the streets of Brentwood in Essex in 1995 was caught on CCTV self-inflicting injuries. The local authority camera controllers later released pictures from the tape to various local news outlets who decided to broadcast and publish them. The man in question, Geoffrey Peck, challenged their right to do this in the High Court; the court rejected his claim and refused to allow him to appeal to a higher court. Peck went higher to the European Court of Human Rights who ruled against the local authority for failing to get the man's permission and for failing to obscure his identity and against the UK for giving him no redress in UK law. The ECHR decided there had been a clear breach of Article 8, the right to privacy, and declared a 'disproportionate and unjustified interference with the applicant's private life'. The case was particularly significant in establishing that the publication of pictures taken in a public space may infringe a person's Article 8 right to privacy (*Peck v UK (2003) 36 EHRR 41*; Liberty 2003).

No doubt aware of the pending Peck case, the ICO issued a Code of Practice under the DPA 1998 covering the use of CCTV in 2000. The Code was developed to explain the legal requirements operators of surveillance cameras were required to meet under the Act and promote best practice. The Code also addressed the inconsistent standards adopted across different sectors at that time and the growing public concern caused by the increasing use of CCTV and other types of surveillance cameras.

The original code was updated in 2008, to account for new legal, practical and technological developments. CCTV moved away from simply being a camera on top of a pole in the town centre where the images were recorded on to video tapes to much more sophisticated operations using digital technology; the most recent code appeared in 2015 (ICO 2015).

The Protection of Freedoms Act 2012 s.30 required a surveillance camera Code of Practice to be issued by the Home Secretary, and s.34 of the same Act created the statutory post of the Surveillance Camera Commissioner (SCC) (SCC 2017). The Commissioners' role is tied closely to the code where his or her functions are described as:

(a) encouraging compliance with this code
(b) reviewing the operation of this code
(c) providing advice about this code (including changes to it or breaches of it) (Protection of Freedoms Act 2012 s.34 (2))

The code elaborates the role to be one where 'the commissioner must work closely with other regulators including the Information Commissioner and the Chief Surveillance Commissioner' (Home Office 2013d para. 5.2). The code expects system operators to adopt 12 guiding principles which include specifying the purpose of the cameras, publishing a contact point for access to information and complaints about the cameras and clear policy documents outlining responsibility and accountability for all surveillance camera system activities including images and information collected, held and used. The second principle states that:

> The use of a surveillance camera system must take into account its effect on individuals and their privacy, with regular reviews to ensure its use remains justified. (Home Office 2013d: para.2.6 details all 12 of these principles)

The Code elaborates on the second principle to add that CCTV arrangements should not normally include facilities to record conversations:

> Any proposed deployment that includes audio recording in a public place is likely to require a strong justification of necessity to establish its proportionality. There is a strong presumption that a surveillance camera system must not be used to record conversations as this is highly intrusive and unlikely to be justified. (ibid.: para.3.2.2)

The ICO code makes the same point (ICO 2015: 34–36). This has proved problematic in some situations where such audio recording does take place. In Southampton, the local taxis have used CCTV and audio equipment recording the activities and conversations of their passengers. A notice in the taxi informs the passengers. The Information Commissioner issued a notice telling Southampton City Council to stop the audio recording. Southampton in turn appealed against the notice but the First-Tier Tribunal dismissed the Appeal (*Appeal No: EA/2012/0171 Southampton City Council v. The Information Commissioner* 19 February 2013). Oxford and Doncaster have also used video and audio equipment in their taxis (BBW 2012).

The SCC produces an annual report on developments in CCTV to the Home Secretary which comments on such subjects as:

- launch of a third-party certification scheme
- completion of the review into the impact and operation of the code
- a draft national surveillance camera strategy for England and Wales
- working with all principal local authority chief executives to encourage completion of the self-assessment tool
- work with the National Police Chiefs' Council (NPCC) lead on ANPR to promote transparency of its use across all forces (SCC 2016: 6)

The 'third-party certification' scheme referred to had started in November 2015 to enable any organisation to outwardly demonstrate compliance with the Surveillance Camera Code; organisations can be awarded the Commissioner's certification.

Automatic Number Plate Recognition

ANPR cameras were developed by the then Home Office Police Scientific Development Branch (PSDB) throughout the 1980s. These are cameras that can 'read' vehicle number plates and by links to other databases know the licenced driver and such details as insurance arrangements. ANPR cameras are not the same as the more straightforward speed cameras because alerts can be put on police systems in real time to show if this is a VOI.

Terrorism activities were the trigger to the growth of ANPR cameras. After the 1996 IRA bombing of Canary Wharf, a so-called ring of steel was built around the London financial districts that included the first major deployment of ANPR cameras. These ANPR cameras could watch the traffic and cross-reference suspect numbers on the PNC.

The Department of the Environment, Transport and the Regions started a consultation in 1999 on improving and standardising vehicle registration number plates. The stated reasons for this were various but included:

- the introduction of a mandatory requirement for the use of registration plates conforming to the most recent British Standard specification BS AU 145d;
- the introduction of a mandatory standard character font for registration marks on vehicles;
- the prohibition of fonts which is not substantially the same as the mandatory font and of layouts which make a registration mark relatively difficult to read or which disguise one character as another or part of another; and
- the prohibition of number plates fitted or treated in such a manner as to obscure or disguise the mark or make it difficult or impossible to photograph (DETR 1999).

The Vehicle Excise and Registration Act 1994 was amended with a new s.27A (inserted by the Vehicles (Crime) Act 2001 s.34) and regulations were brought in to make the number plates more readable (The Road Vehicles (Display of Registration Marks) Regulations 2001 no. 561).

In 2002, a number of police forces made more effective use of their ANPR systems by linking the cameras to dedicated intercept officers. The intention was that targeted enforcement would 'detect, deter and disrupt' criminality, and initial evaluation showed good results (Home Office 2004). Bradford in West Yorkshire became a lauded testing ground for ANPR cameras and not least when they had helped arrest the murderers of a local police woman:

The 24-hour digital anti-crime network, funded by West Yorkshire Police and Bradford Council, combines CCTV and Automatic Number Plate Recognition (ANPR) and is one of the most sophisticated in the country. The £300,000 state-of-the-art system brings 80 hi-tech fixed cameras on line and expands on the existing 'ring of steel'. The system helped solve several major crimes in Bradford, including the capture of the murderers of PC Sharon Beshenivsky in Bradford in 2005. (Wright 2009)

Not all was well with the ANPR arrangements. In the north east, three police forces—Cleveland, Durham and North Yorkshire—were unable to respond to a series of alerts that might have saved a murder had they been acted upon (IPCC 2010). On the other hand, the police use of ANPR technology and enforcement using the Motor Insurance Database held by the MIB is described as 'very effective'. According to the chief executive of the MIB, 'the number of uninsured vehicles on UK roads has halved over the last decade from around 2 million vehicles to 1 million within a vehicle parc of 36 million' (MIB 2016).

Project Champion was a joint operation by West Midlands Police and Birmingham City Council which showed the difficulties of working without any regulation. The lack of regulation allowed the installation of hundreds of cameras—CCTV and ANPR—in two predominantly Muslim residential areas of Birmingham. The anti-terror funding and purpose of the project were kept secret from the residents until national newspapers got hold of the story:

About 150 automatic number plate recognition (ANPR) cameras have been installed in Washwood Heath and Sparkbrook in recent months. Birmingham's two predominantly Muslim suburbs will be covered by three times more ANPR cameras than are used to monitor the entire city centre. They include about 40 cameras classed as 'covert', meaning they have been concealed from public view. (Lewis 2010a)

This degree of surveillance inevitably raised tensions in the community. All the cameras associated with the scheme were eventually dismantled after the campaign group Liberty threatened to bring judicial review proceedings on behalf of a group of affected residents, arguing that it breached principles of personal privacy and equal treatment protected by the Human Right Rights Act (Liberty 2010a; Lewis 2010b).

The West Midlands Police asked the chief constable of Thames Valley Police to take an independent and retrospective look at what they had been doing. Her report was critical:

> While such a security ring exists in the City of London, this proposal was to create something similar in a semi-residential, predominantly Asian area. This thinking should have been challenged from the start and questions should have been asked about its proportionality, legitimacy, authority and necessity; and about the ethical values that underpinned the proposal.
>
> Moreover the use of CCTV and ANPR is subject to the Regulation of Investigatory Powers Act in respect of covert cameras and Codes of Practice in respect of overt cameras. … Yet I found little evidence of thought being given to compliance with the legal or regulatory framework. (Thames Valley Police 2010: 48)

The use of CCTV and ANPR cameras on highways and even motorways is clearly very different to the proposed use in Birmingham where there was a planned move into residential areas that was kept secret from the residents. Only the intervention of journalists and observant residents stopped this from being a major intrusion on privacy.

Regulating ANPR

Rather like CCTV, before it, the development of ANPR in a legal vacuum showed all the elements of 'mission creep'. Starting out as a device to tackle the most serious crimes like terrorism as part of a city centre 'ring of steel', it was easily able to move over to more contentious residential areas and other crimes like stolen cars and insurance offences. The very title of the ACPO strategy document 2005–2008 for ANPR *Driving down Crime: denying criminals the use of the road* demonstrated the move away from just terrorism (ACPO 2004). The establishment of a National ANPR Data Centre (NADC) for storing ANPR 'reads' meant that rather than just finding a wanted car on the road for immediate interception, data mining could take place at a later date to see who was moving on a road at any one time. The NADC started work in 2007 (Mathieson 2007; see also parliamentary answer from the Minister of State for Security, Counter-Terrorism, Crime and Policing *Hansard House of Commons 6 July 2009: Column 574–5W*).

The regulation of ANPR was on the agenda of the new Coalition government that came in to power May 2010:

> The options being looked at by the Home Office for regulating the system, known as automatic number plate recognition (ANPR), include establishing a lawful right for the police to collect and retain such details as well as defining who can gain access to the database and placing a legal limit on the period information can be stored for. (Travis 2010b)

The police, for their part, have not been as transparent as they might have been (Mathieson 2011). An ACPO working group in 2013 admitted that there was variation between forces but that details of any national ANPR infrastructure were best kept secret:

> The details of the national infrastructure of police ANPR systems are not published and the police service is opposed to publishing that information in order to safeguard the systems and the benefits that can be obtained from them. It is acknowledged that at present consistent national standards for the development of ANPR infrastructure are not in place. (ACPO 2013)

The Home Office did publish guidance for how an ANPR system can be set up and maintained in order to achieve the maximum performance and how this performance could be measured (Home Office 2014f).

An attempt was made in 2015 to use the Freedom of Information Act to obtain details of the governance arrangements for ANPR from the NPCC. It was carried out by William Perrin, a member of the government's transparency panel:

> In reply he was told: 'There is no record which details the structure and governance of the ANPR.' Perrin said he was disturbed by that response. The FOI request also revealed that the police proposed to increase the retention of number plate data from two years to up to seven years. (Weaver 2015)

According to Perrin:

> The police may well be acting unlawfully in storing data past their agreed two-year period, the proposals to extend to seven years are implausible against this background. If new guidelines are being drawn up it is wrong in principle to do this in secrecy. (quoted in Weaver 2015)

Tony Porter, the SCC, expressed his concerns about the growth of the NADC containing billions of number plate 'reads' and the lack of transparency from the police about how this database was being used. He expressed these concerns directly to national meeting of the police ANPR user group (SCC 2015), and in his annual report for 2015–2016, Porter said:

> In last year's report I highlighted ANPR cameras role in policing and explained how I had engaged with their senior police leaders and its National User Group; encouraged the police to publicise the efficiency and effectiveness of these systems and listened to views expressed by civil liberties groups as to the legality of the camera network. I also pressed the police to enumerate the exact numbers of ANPR cameras operating in England and Wales. (SCC 2016: 22)

Porter had posed a number of questions to the police:

- Are you happy that you, the police, have done everything in your power to establish a governance structure that reflects the current public mood?
- Where do I go to understand the layers of responsibility?
- Are you, the police, happy that your consultation and engagement with the public is thorough, robust, informed and informative?
- Given the size of the ANPR operation are you, the police, happy that it should continue to operate outside of any legislative framework? (ibid.)

One immediate response was the publication in December 2015 of a press release from the NPCC on how the ANPR data is used and how long it would be kept. DCC Paul Kennedy, the NPCC lead on ANPR, explained, in rather convoluted fashion, that there was no proposal to extend the retention period of ANPR data but that it was being considered:

> There are no proposals at present for extending the ANPR data retention period. However, the ANPR User Group is exploring the legal and operational implications of extending the data retention period. This work will involve an independent and impartial academic exercise. If, as a result of that exercise, further consideration is judged to be appropriate, it will be subject to a privacy impact assessment and consultation. There is no proposal at present for a public consultation, as there is no existing proposal to extend the current data retention period. (NPCC 2015)

Another response in April 2016 was publication of a five-page Fact Sheet on ANPR by the NPCC. From this we learnt that 'approximately 9000 [ANPR] cameras submit between 25 and nearly 40 million "reads" daily to the NADC [National ANPR Data Centre]. Data is retained for two years on the NADC. Approximately 20 billion "read" records are held'. The NADC allows investigators to search for matching data on a national basis (once their forces have connected their Back Office Facility (BOF) to the NADC). The NADC records the location of the read using GPS coordinates sent via the BOF from the camera, irrespective of whether it is fixed, covert, overt, mobile or portable (NPCC 2016b; see also College of Policing 2016e).

In his third annual report, the SCC outlined his concerns about ANPR developments and its integration with the PNC and PND (see Chap. 5):

> I remain of the opinion that we have a burgeoning surveillance capability on the cusp of being integrated into a new platform called 'LEDS'. We have a system that grows exponentially in its functionality – from tracking vehicles believed to be involved in Irish related terrorism in the 1980's and 1990's to tracking MOT, insurance and vehicle theft. Its use as an intelligence tool is self-evident in that there are now approximately 8,500 cameras in use capable of capturing 35 million and 40 million 'reads' a day and storing upwards of 30 billion 'reads' a year … so, whilst governance and transparency remain key issues, we are still left with a system that is not subject to any parliamentary oversight yet is one of the largest intelligence

gathering tools in the world. A legislative framework would provide democratic oversight and strengthen the voice of the citizen. (SCC 2016: 23)

There is no statutory authority for the creation of the national ANPR database, and no report on its operation has even been laid before parliament.

Police Body-Worn Video

In the UK, police BWV cameras were first used in 2005 by Devon and Cornwall Constabulary (Home Office 2007c). These 'head cameras' were found to increase detection of offences and reduce complaints against police officers (Home Office 2007d; James and Southern 2007). Police forces around the UK have since been conducting pilots of BWV, the largest by the London MPS in 2014 which saw the distribution of 500 BWVs to police officers in 10 London boroughs (College of Policing 2014a).

A number of evaluations have been conducted as part of the trials and all have confirmed the Devon and Cornwall evaluation that police officer BWV reduces the number of allegations and complaints against officers and increases the proportion of detections resulting in a criminal justice charge, although there is some variation (see, e.g., Grossmith et al. 2015; Owens et al. 2014; Katz et al. 2014; Ellis et al. 2015), reducing police use of force (Ariel et al. 2014) and benefits to police officer professional development (Phelps et al. 2016).[1] By the end of 2016, the majority of UK police officers will be equipped with BWV cameras (Peachey 2016).

Case Study

West Yorkshire Police's technological transformation is taking another step forward. The Force has agreed a contract that sees officers and staff across the county wearing the latest state of the art body worn video cameras during their duties. Following a recent pilot of the devices in the Bradford District, a phased roll out will now begin. West Yorkshire Police and Crime Commissioner, Mark Burns-Williamson, has invested £2 million pounds from a 'Transformation Fund' to support the project (West Yorkshire Police (2016) Body Worn Cameras Increase Safety 'Focus' (press release) Monday 8 August).

Privacy concerns have been raised about the use of police BWV (see, e.g., Siddique 2013; BBW 2015; Bud 2016). The mobility of BWV cameras raises a unique privacy issue. They collect and preserve information (images and audio) but, unlike CCTVs, these body cameras can collect information from within private homes. This may be distressing for private citizens *and* police officers (Telegraph 2013).

A 2016 review of the Home Office *Surveillance Camera Code of Practice* (see Home Office 2016c) highlighted the increasing use of BWV cameras by public *and* private organisations, such as supermarket chains (SCC 2016). This increases the volume of data which is being collected and concerns are raised with regard to how the footage will be used, how it will be stored and for how long, who will have access to the data and the potential for it to be tampered with. Furthermore, what happens if footage goes missing or is unusable (Greenfield 2014)? Each police force is responsible for conducting a Privacy Impact Assessment (PIA) (see, e.g., the MPS 2015c). The ICOs provide general guidelines on conducting such assessments (ICO 2014).

There is the issue of consent from those being filmed, as acquiring consent from citizens to be filmed is challenging (Bud 2016). For example, consent for the use of CCTV is usually given by a person reading signage associated with the camera—which is, in many cases, obscured (Lippert 2009). In the UK, police officers are not required to obtain consent of the person(s) being filmed. The College of Policing (2014c) provides guidance on police officer use of BWV. Police officers retain discretion whether or not to film a specific incident, which should be relevant to the incident and necessary in order to gather evidence. Non-evidential material will be retained for a maximum of 31 days and the recorded material remains as police information and cannot be disclosed to third parties unless prescribed by law and can be accessed by the recorded individual in accordance with the Freedom of Information Act 2000 or via a subject access request in accordance with the DPA 1998. Crucially, the police officer retains discretion to switch the BWV off and the guidelines state that:

[t]here should always be a tendency to record (within the confines of legislation) unless circumstances dictate otherwise. An officer who fails to

record an incident will be required to justify their actions as vigorously as any officer who chooses to record a similar encounter. (College of Policing 2014c: 27)

Part 2 of the Protection of Freedoms Act (2012) section 33(5) specifies that relevant authorities must have regard for the *Surveillance Camera Code of Practice* which states that officers should consider if the necessary objectives can be met by less intrusive means. In addition:

Any proposed deployment that includes audio recording in a public place is likely to require a strong justification of necessity to establish its proportionality. There is a strong presumption that a surveillance camera system must not be used to record conversations as this is highly intrusive and unlikely to be justified. (Home Office 2013d: para: 3.2.2)

This places the BWV user (i.e., the police officer) in a precarious position of making sense of the legislation and police guidelines, while balancing evidence/intelligence gathering and intruding upon the personal privacy of the individual(s) being recorded. Indeed, the SCC (2016) highlighted the need for greater clarity regarding standards and what compliance with these standards should look like. The balance between technologies for law enforcement, police transparency and intrusion on public and information privacy continues to be debated (Lippert and Newell 2016; Peachey 2016).

In the meantime, the use of BWV is spreading to other non-police practitioners ranging from hospital staff (Weaver 2017a), local authority staff (BBW 2017) and private-sector staff working with asylum seekers (Weaver 2017b); suggestions have also been made that all school teachers should be wearing BWV (Walker 2017).

Unmanned Aerial Vehicles

Unmanned Aerial Vehicles (UAVs), or drones as they are popularly known as, have begun to interest the police as a new form of surveillance with cameras attached.

Assistant Chief Constable Barry who acts as lead for the NPCC on drones has said:

> We have consulted extensively with the Information Commissioners Office (ICO) and the Office of Surveillance Commissioners (OSC), both of whom are satisfied with the approach we have taken over privacy and data protection. The OSC recently saw the Gatwick drone being operated and was impressed with our operational protocols. (Surrey Police 2016)

The Inspire 1 drone, from the Hong Kong-based company DJI, is one design the police have favoured. Michael Perry, PR manager at DJI, says:

> The Inspire 1 has a 4K camera on board for really high-resolution images. It has a retractable leg design so that while it's in the air, the camera can rotate 360 degrees, allowing you to have a lot more control of the image while you're in flight. You also have a two operator set up. One person operates the platform. Another person can operate the gimbal. You can also operate everything by a single operator but sometimes you want a little more control over the image while it's flying. (quoted in Krol 2015)

The surveillance data is fed back to control rooms via monitoring equipment such as high-definition cameras, radar devices and infrared sensors.

Kent police has said their drone scheme was intended for use over the English Channel to monitor shipping and detect immigrants crossing from France. However, the documents suggest the maritime focus was, at least in part, a public relations strategy designed to minimise civil liberty concerns. A minute from one of the earliest meetings, in July 2007, states that, 'there is potential for these [maritime] uses to be projected as a "good news" story to the public rather than more "big brother"' (Lewis 2010c).

Facial Recognition Technology

The matching of new photographs or images from CCTV to existing databanks of photographs of known people is lengthy and labour intensive. The Metropolitan Police has now designated special officers known to be good at recognising people. This is the 'super-recogniser' programme, developed to identify officers with exceptional face-recognition talents:

> The Super-recogniser Unit is based on the third floor of a grey stone police building in Lambeth in south London. It is the only unit of its kind in the world. It was set up in May 2015, and moved from Scotland Yard in July … the team consists of six officers – five men and one woman. (Manzoor 2016)

Advances have been made in the technology of facial recognition by the cameras themselves. Anyone applying for a new passport or renewing a passport that has expired will know that they must get a new up-to-date photograph of themselves and that they should remember not to smile in that photograph but should present a neutral expression and keep their mouths closed. Other requirements of the photograph include that it must:

- be a close up of your full head and upper shoulders
- contain no other objects or people
- be in clear contrast to the background

In your photo, you must:

- be facing forward and looking straight at the camera
- have a neutral expression and your mouth closed
- have your eyes open, visible and free from reflection or glare from glasses
- not have hair in front of your eyes (Gov.UK 2017a)

These requirements are to facilitate the facial recognition currently being technologically developed.

The Mosquito

Although not strictly a form of camera or filming arrangement, it is appropriate to mention here the use of the so-called Mosquito in public areas. The *Mosquito* is an electronic device for emitting a high-frequency sound that only young people can hear and is designed to make them move from where they would otherwise publicly congregate and act in an anti-social, noisy fashion, littering, smoking and drinking, playing music and generally preventing other people from enjoying their home or business. The device was introduced around 2005 and by 2008 there were said to be over 3000 in use in the UK (Office of the Children's Commissioner 2008). The *Mosquito* makes a pulsing sound that is just out of the range of an adults' hearing, which is why it only bothers people under the age of about 25. The sound is not loud or painful, just highly annoying to young people after a short period of time.

The *Mosquito* has been criticised for being discriminatory against children by assuming they will all behave badly and yet does not affect adult law breakers at all. Both Liberty (quoted in Ward 2007) and the Parliamentary Assembly of the Council of Europe believe it contravenes Article 8 of the ECHR:

> The Assembly considers that the use of 'Mosquito'-type devices constitutes a disproportionate interference with Article 8 of the European Convention on Human Rights, which protects the right to respect for one's private life, including the right to respect for physical integrity. (Council of Europe 2010)

The Home Office has declared the *Mosquito* to be a private matter best dealt with locally and 'in relation to the Council of Europe report and the issue of guidance, our stance is that we do not see this as an issue on which we should intervene' (*Hansard House of Commons Debates 28 June 2010 col. 432W*). The use of the Mosquito remains, therefore, a localised and mostly private affair with individuals buying the necessary equipment from private companies (see also Little 2015).

Summary

The police and other agencies take photographs and film of people and various activities; these images are retained for varying lengths of time. Cameras cover public areas and also the roads and highways. New technologies have enabled better images to be taken and smaller cameras to be used which can be worn on the clothing of police officers or mounted on flying drones. There is evidence that these developments have made a modest impact on crime levels and that when worn by police officers video cameras make an overall improvement to police–public interactions. Concerns do remain, however, that databanks of photographs and images have been collated with the minimal of regulatory oversight, and this is an area that does require attention.

Notes

1. See the Body Worn Video Steering Group (BWVSG) (http://www.bwvsg.com/resources/studiesreports/) and the National Institute of Justice (NIJ) (http://www.nij.gov/topics/law-enforcement/technology/pages/body-worn-cameras.aspx) for a collection of resources and links to BWV evaluation and research.

7

The 'Open' Court

Introduction

People in the criminal court, whether as defendants or witnesses, must expect that the most private details of their lives may become public. In order to discover the truth, and that justice is achieved, trial proceedings work from the basis that all private information will become public; in general terms trial proceedings do not recognise information as being constrained by such concepts as privacy or information privacy. In a sexual offence case, details of the most intimate kind will be made public, and to assist with deciding on the correct sentence, a person's previous criminal convictions will be revealed to the court.

Criminal courts start from the premise that they should be open to the press and public so that justice can be seen to be done. This has long been a principle of British common law and is now a fundamental principle enshrined in the ECHR, Article 6, the 'Right to a Fair Trial':

> In the determination of his civil rights and obligations or of any criminal charge against him, everyone is entitled to a fair *and public hearing* within a reasonable time by an independent and impartial tribunal established by law. (ECHR Article 6 (1) emphasis added)

© The Author(s) 2017
D. Marshall, T. Thomas, *Privacy and Criminal Justice*,
https://doi.org/10.1007/978-3-319-64912-2_7

In practice, this means that a prosecution witness must be identifiable not only to the defendant but also to the open court. It supports the ability of the defendant to present his case and to test the prosecution case by cross-examination of prosecution witnesses.

The right to a fair and public trial is, however, qualified and from this starting point, various circumstances rule that the public may be excluded and the press restricted from reporting certain matters. A full reading of Article 6 gives us these qualifications and indicates the exceptions that may be made:

> Judgment shall be pronounced publicly but the press and public may be excluded from all or part of the trial in the interests of morals, public order or national security in a democratic society, where the interests of juveniles or the protection of the private life of the parties so require, or to the extent strictly necessary in the opinion of the court in special circumstances where publicity would prejudice the interests of justice. (ibid.)

One area that is always regarded as private is the working relationship between the defendant and his or her solicitor or barrister which is regarded as both confidential and privileged.

'Confidential and Privileged'

Anyone being advised or represented in criminal proceedings by a professional lawyer—solicitor or barrister—has a right to confidentiality and legal privilege being accorded with all their communications. That right extends to relevant documentation which is also accorded confidentiality and legal privilege. The Bar Standards Board states concisely that:

> The duty of confidentiality is central to the administration of justice. Clients who put their confidence in their legal advisers must be able to do so in the knowledge that the information they give, or which is given on their behalf, will stay confidential. In normal circumstances, this information will be privileged and not disclosed to a court. (BSB 2015: para. gC42)

The conduct of the solicitor in these arrangements is regulated by the Solicitors Regulation Authority (SRA 2016: esp. Chap. 4) and the barrister by the Bar Standards Board (BSB 2015).

The Police and Criminal Evidence Act 1984 gives a legal definition of 'items subject to legal privilege' when it looks at material that is excluded from a police search:

Meaning of 'items subject to legal privilege':

(1) Subject to sub-section (2) below, in this Act, 'items subject to legal privilege' means:

(a) communications between a professional legal adviser and his client or any person representing his client made in connection with the giving of legal advice to the client

(b) communications between a professional legal adviser and his client or any person representing his client or between such an adviser or his client or any such representative and any other person made in connection with or in contemplation of legal proceedings and for the purposes of such proceedings; and

(c) items enclosed with or referred to in such communications and made—

(i) in connection with the giving of legal advice or

(ii) in connection with or in contemplation of legal proceedings and for the purposes of such proceedings when they are in the possession of a person who is entitled to possession of them. (Police and Criminal Evidence Act 1984 s10)

The police may not take any confidential privileged documents in any search of premises they make.

Items held with the intention of furthering a criminal purpose are not items subject to legal privilege, and any information that a lawyer becomes aware of that might involve money laundering or fraud must be passed on to the police at the National Crime Agency (NCA). The Proceeds of Crime Act 2002 sections 327–9, 330 and 332 require lawyers working for banks and other businesses to report knowledge or suspicion of money laundering to the NCA Financial Intelligence Unit. These reports are commonly known as Suspicious Activity Reports (SARs) (NCA 2015).

Pre-trial

Even before a trial starts the courts may make several decisions in what is referred to as the 'pre-trial' stage; these may have implications for a person's liberty or privacy.

Remands

If a trial is not ready to start the case will be adjourned until it is ready. In the meantime, the defendant may be remanded in custody (in prison or a young offender institution) or remanded on bail. A remand on bail is usually preferred as the less restrictive option for the defendant and as the less costly option for the Ministry of Justice.

Remands on bail are covered by the Bail Act 1976. A remand on bail may have various conditions attached including living at a particular address, not contacting certain people, giving your passport to the police so you cannot leave the UK or reporting to a police station at agreed times, for example, once a week. If a curfew condition is attached requiring someone to, say, be at home for a given time period, an electronic monitoring arrangement can also be imposed; the time period is usually a 12-hour period overnight.

The use of electronic monitoring involves the wearing of an ankle tag which sends a constant signal to a monitoring or receiver device set up in the person's home. In turn, the monitoring unit sends a signal to the suppliers of the electronic tag. If the person breaches the curfew and leaves the home, the signal is interrupted and the police duly notified:

> If the defendant is not located and arrested quickly the police will record on PNC that the defendant is wanted and a 'wanted file' including evidence of the breach will be held in the Warrants Office. The local intelligence unit will alert officers, and efforts to track down the defendant will be made. (Home Office 2006c: para. 55)

Bail curfews with electronic monitoring for adults started around 1989 and are not referred to in law as such but just as 'conditions' of bail (Mair and Nee 1990). Pre-trial electronic monitoring of young people (aged 12–18) is outlined in the Criminal Justice and Police Act 2001 ss131–2 which has amended the Bail Act 1976.

The impact of electronic monitoring on privacy is to some degree clear cut but no doubt different individuals will experience the restrictions to a greater or lesser degree. Its low visibility worn around the ankle helps to reduce any stigma attached to it being seen in the street. Presumably, the alternative of a remand in custody makes the wearing of the tag less onerous. Electronic monitoring is further used at the court sentencing stage to support a community sentence and at the end of a custodial sentence to enable early release from prison (see Chap. 8).

Adult Courts

The principle that all aspects of court proceedings should be conducted in public has been a fundamental tenet of the UK's criminal justice system for centuries. In a number of high-profile cases of serious crime or terrorism, this has sometimes led to difficulties in persuading witnesses to give evidence out of fear of the consequences should they be identified by the defendants or their associates; measures have been taken by the courts under common law and statutory powers to preserve the anonymity of witnesses. Children have also been helped to give evidence in what can be an intimidating forum.

Children's Evidence in the Adult Courts

The adult courts have always been cautious of the evidence that comes from children. In Victorian times, such evidence was referred to as coming from a 'child of tender years' reflecting the terminology of the Prevention of Cruelty to, and Protection of, Children Act 1889 s.8. The fear was that a child might be intimidated by the court or the defendant, not understand the significance of the oath or have sufficient intelligence to understand what was going on; at worst, they may simply not under-stand the duty of telling the truth. Evidence to corroborate children's statements would routinely be needed to prevent adults being convicted on the word of a child.

To try and improve the status of children's evidence, attempts have been made to use technology and allow the child to speak to the courts from a safe and private area. The Criminal Justice Act 1988, s.32 intro-duced live video links for children under 14 to give their evidence to the court. The same Act (s.34) also abolished the need for a judge to give a warning when a child's uncorroborated evidence had been heard; s.34 did not extend to sexual offences, but the later, Criminal Justice and Public Order Act 1994, ss. 32–33, did make that extension. The importance of the 'live' link was emphasised to allow for cross-examination.

The government held back from introducing any pre-recorded tapes of statements or cross-examinations being used as evidence in court, and the 'live' element was considered critical. This did not stop the arguments being made for pre-recorded testimony. The Children's Legal Centre was in favour ('CLC calls for legal reform to end trauma for child witnesses', *Childright*, October 1987) but the chair of the Criminal Bar Association was clear that the defence lawyer's right to cross-examine a witness must be preserved and challenged what he described as the 'dangerous climate of opinion that children virtually never lie about sexual abuse' ('Warning on child video evidence', *The Guardian*, 2 October 1989).

The Home Office convened an Advisory Group, chaired by Judge Thomas Pigot, which was asked to review the practical implications of allowing pre-recorded video statements. The resulting report was in favour of pre-recording statements and even in favour of pre-recording a cross-examination (Pigot Report 1989). On this basis, the Criminal Justice Act 1991 introduced the use of pre-recorded video interviews of children in court by amending the Criminal Justice Act 1988 with a new s.32A; the child was still expected to be available for cross-examination. The Act did not go so far as to contain provisions for pre-recorded cross-examinations.

The Home Office and the Department of Health jointly produced a *Memorandum of Good Practice* for police officers and social workers who would be conducting the pre-recorded video sessions (Home Office/

Department of Health 1992). In practice, the police, with their greater understanding of criminal evidence and the needs of the criminal courts, tended to take the lead over social workers when it came to videoing, and today the taking of recordings is a standard part of the investigation of sexual offences against children.

An Inter-Departmental Working Group report *Speaking up for Justice* (Home Office 1998) reexamined the position of children as witnesses but this time also recognised that adults could be equally intimated or vulnerable when it came to speaking in court. The Youth Justice and Criminal Evidence Act 1999 that followed brought in new provisions for both children and adults as intimidated and vulnerable witnesses as well as new guidance replacing the *Memorandum of Good Practice* on videoing children's evidence (Home Office 2002); this guidance has been reproduced in subsequent new editions (see MoJ et al 2011).

Intimidated and Vulnerable Witnesses

Adult witnesses may fear that if their identity is revealed to the defendant, his or her associates or the public generally, then they or their friends and family will be at risk of serious harm. It is the police who first alert the CPS that a witness is in fear and should inform the prosecutor who will apply for 'special measures' in the court.

The Youth Justice and Criminal Evidence Act 1999 introduced eight 'special measures' for what it termed the 'eligible witness' (ss16–17); in effect this meant the child witness and the vulnerable or intimidated adult witness and the 'special measures' were designed to provide more protection and privacy and in turn improve the quality of the witnesses' evidence. The 'special measures' were:

- screening to prevent the witness seeing the defendant (section 22);
- live CCTV links to speak to the witness in another room (s23);
- the witness giving evidence in private (s25);
- the removal of wigs and gowns by court personnel (s26);
- pre-recorded witness statements ('evidence in chief') (s27);
- pre-recorded cross-examination of the witness (s28);

- use of an 'intermediary' by a witness (s29); and
- use of an aid to communication by a witness (s30).

The use of an 'intermediary' (s29) was to assist a witness with, say, learning disabilities or other communication problems to present their evidence as clearly as possible to the court. A 'Witness Intermediary Scheme' was started and all intermediaries had to be accredited and registered; a 'match' was made between the witness and an appropriate intermediary. The 'special measures' were initially the subject of 'pilot schemes' but were all up and running by 2007 with just the exception of the pre-recorded cross-examination of witnesses (s28). The pilot schemes were evaluated regarding young witnesses (Plotnikoff and Woolfson 2009).

Although the use of pre-recorded cross-examinations of witnesses were now on the statute book (s28), the government still held back from implementing the relevant sections of the Act. The position was explained by the Under-Secretary of State at the Home Office:

> The Government are disappointed not to be implementing one of the eight special measures for vulnerable or intimidated witnesses that we provided for in good faith five years ago. But we believe it is better to take the advice of one of the leading experts in the field and many senior practitioners, and revisit this complex issue. (*Hansard House of Commons Ministerial Statement 21 July 2004 cols. 41WS – 42WS*)

Three years later the government returned to the subject of achieving best evidence in the criminal courts. The Coroners and Justice Act 2009 made further amendments to the Youth Justice and Criminal Evidence Act 1999 and the 'special measures' provisions and:

- raised the upper age limit of child witnesses automatically eligible for special measures from those under 17 to include those under 18
- provided child witnesses with more choice and flexibility about how they give their evidence;
- made specific provision for the presence of a supporter to the witness in the live link room

- relaxed the restrictions on a witness giving additional evidence in chief after the witness's video-recorded statement has been admitted as evidence in chief
- make special provision for the admissibility of video-recorded evidence in chief of adult complainants in sexual offence cases in the Crown Court (Coroners and Justice Act 2009 ss98–103; see also MoJ 2011)

The search to make life easier for vulnerable and intimidated witnesses in criminal courts continued (MoJ 2012a) with the government still trying to resolve the question of pre-recorded cross-examinations:

> We are working to resolve the complex issues associated with implementation of pre-trial video-recorded cross examination (section 28 of the Youth Justice and Criminal Evidence Act 1999) with a view to establishing whether the provision can be made to work in practice. (MoJ 2012b: para.91–94)

Pilot measures for recorded pre-trial cross-examinations of children and other vulnerable witnesses eventually started in Leeds, Liverpool and Kingston on Thames in April 2014 (MoJ 2014b), 15 years after the Pigot report had first recommended it (see also MoJ 2016a). The Ministry of Justice eventually announced that the pre-recorded cross-examinations of children would be extended to all adults as complainants in rape cases; 'the rollout of pre-recorded evidence offers further protection, as questions can be edited out of the recording if barristers flout these rules' (MoJ 2017).

Sexual Offences: The Complainant's Previous Sexual History

A recurring area of concern regarding privacy in the adult courts concerns sexual offences and the ability of defending barristers to bring a woman's sexual history into the case as part of the defence of the male concerned. The truth was that the court should only be dealing with the facts of the case in front of them rather than any non-relevant sexual history. The purpose of bringing it in was often to use the previous history to smear the woman's reputation in order to show the defendants behaviour in a better light and effectively put the woman on trial or make the jury believe she was someone not to be believed. It has been surmised that this public cross-examination of a woman's previous sexual history has been one of the reasons women have been reluctant to report sexual offences in the past (Home Office 1998: para.9.57).

The law has long ruled that:

> Except with the leave of the judge, no evidence and no question in cross examination shall be adduced or asked at the trial, by or on behalf of any defendant at the trial about any sexual experience of a complainant with a person other than that defendant. (Sexual Offences (Amendment) Act 1976 s.2 (1))

The judge was expected to only give such leave 'if he is satisfied that it would be unfair to that defendant to refuse to allow the evidence to be adduced or the question to be asked' (Sexual Offences (Amendment) Act 1976 s.2 (2)). It was this wording of the law and the idea of it being 'unfair' that left open the opportunity to bring in a woman's sexual history. The feeling was that defence barristers were using s2 (2) as often as they could to discredit the complainant's character, and judges were reluctant to block anything that might make the trial 'unfair'. It led critics to suggest that 'the existing law was not achieving its purpose' and the law should be amended (Home Office 1998: para.9.64 and Recommendation 63).

The Youth Justice and Criminal Evidence Act 1999 attempted to tighten up the law in favour of the complainant. A similar wording to the 1976 Act was used to say that except with the leave of the court, no evidence may be adduced, and no question may be asked in cross-examination, by or on behalf of any accused at the trial, about any sexual behaviour of the complainant (Youth Justice and Criminal Evidence Act 1999 s41 s1). This time leave of the court could only be given if the evidence was not about consent and the sexual history to be disclosed was about behaviour close to the time of the alleged offence demonstrating similar behaviour to that in the case being heard; if the prosecution had brought up evidence of the complainant's sexual history that allowed the court to give leave if the evidence was to directly rebut that from the prosecution (Youth Justice and Criminal Evidence Act 1999 s41 ss3 and 5). It was not long before section 41 was tested in the courts as to whether or not it denied a defendant a fair trial. The case of *R v A (No2) [2001] UKHL 25* ruled that it did not deny the man a fair trial, and section 41 has remained until this day as the attempt to keep personal sexual histories private during rape trials.

Case

Sexual history was a matter that arose in the case of Ched Evans in 2016. Evans was a professional footballer who had served a prison sentence for a rape conviction but who continued to try and prove his innocence. Evans' conviction was later quashed by a court of appeal but a retrial was called for; at the retrial Evans was found not guilty. The retrial, however, had heard evidence of the complainant's sexual history which the court had allowed and according to some critics, 'the young female complainant was subjected to the kind of grilling about her sexual behaviour that was a throwback to 30 years ago' (Laville 2016). Forty women Labour MPs signed a letter to the Attorney General calling for a tighter law (Mason 2016) and during a debate on the Policing and Crime Bill, the government announced a review of s41 would take place (*Hansard House of Lords Debates 16 November 2016 cols 1471–5*).

A study of rape cases in Newcastle Crown Court revealed that sexual history was still produced in court in 11 out of 30 cases observed by a panel made up of lay members of the public. Three out of the 11 had received no leave of the court and the histories were just brought in without warning. In 6 of the 11 cases, no link was made to the case being heard, and 'it seems that previous sexual conduct was used to discredit each complainant, in precisely the way that Section 41 was intended to prevent' (Durham et al. 2017: 39).

Witness Anonymity Orders

Some witnesses may require even more protection of their identity than 'special measures' and particularly so when serious organised crime is being examined by the court. Witness Anonymity Orders were introduced in 2008 to protect such witnesses following the *Davis* case.

Iain Davis was charged with the murders of Ashley Kenton and Wayne Mowatt in Hackney, East London, on the morning of 1 January 2002. Davis claimed to have left the scene of the crime before the shooting and said he had an alibi defence. Three prosecution witnesses identified Davis as the gunman. To protect their identity, the judge ordered that:

• they would be allowed to give evidence under pseudonyms
• any details which might identify them were to be withheld from Davis and his legal advisers, and they could not be asked any questions which might lead to their identification
• they would be allowed to give evidence from behind screens and their voices disguised electronically

Despite appeals against this anonymity from Davis' counsel, these arrangements were allowed to remain in place. Further Appeals were made and eventually the House of Lords was asked to decide:

Is it permissible for a defendant to be convicted where a conviction is based solely or to a decisive extent upon the testimony of one or more anonymous witnesses?

On 18 June 2008, the Law Lords unanimously held that Davis had not received a fair trial, since his counsel had been unable to adequately challenge the prosecution evidence or test the reliability of the anonymous witnesses; any effective cross-examination had been hindered. The common law had developed incrementally in such a way that while no single step towards trials with anonymous witnesses had been obviously wrong, their cumulative effect had now gone too far (*R v Davis [2008] UKHL 36).*

The Davis case led to an emergency Bill to clarify and replace the common law on witness anonymity. The Criminal Evidence (Witness Anonymity) Bill was introduced on 4 July 2008 and had become law by 21 July 2008. In future, the new rules allowed trial judges to grant Witness Anonymity Orders provided that they met three conditions:

(a) that they were necessary to protect personal safety, prevent serious damage to property or 'to prevent real harm to the public interest';

(b) that in all the circumstances the measures will be consistent with the defendant receiving a fair trial; and

(c) that the interests of justice require the witness to testify and that the witness will not testify if an Order is not made. (Criminal Evidence (Witness Anonymity) Act 2008 s4)

Because of the emergency nature of the bill, the Criminal Evidence (Witness Anonymity) Act 2008 contained a 'sunset clause' which stated that the Act would expire on 31 December 2009 and the Act was duly replaced by the Coroners and Justice Act 2009 ss86–97 which came into force on 1 January 2010.

Witnesses Anonymity Orders should be differentiated from Investigation Anonymity Orders (IAO) (see Chap. 3). The two are independent of each other and one does not automatically lead to another. If an investigation proceeds to trial then a Witness Anonymity Order must be applied for to protect the witness during and after the trial. Guidance on Witness Anonymity Orders is provided by the CPS (CPS 2009).

Witness Protection: The UK Protected Persons Service

There have been times in the past when witnesses in trials have felt so intimidated that they have refused to testify in court. Cases have often collapsed because witnesses have refused to come to court with their evidence. Sometimes these witnesses have been offered safety in police-run Witness Protection Schemes to help persuade them to come to court. This has been a particular problem when the threat and the intimidation have come from serious organised crime.

Following a double murder in Lincolnshire by organised criminals seeking revenge (Britten 2004), the Home Office led plans to improve the ad hoc arrangements then made by local police to protect witnesses. A new national scheme was proposed (Home Office 2004: para.6.4) and implemented through the Serious Organised Crime and Police Act 2005 ss.82–94 and Schedule 5. This became the UK Protected Persons Service and was launched in October 2013 (NPCC 2013). A minor amendment to the 2005 Act was made by the Anti-social Behaviour, Crime and Policing Act 2014 s178 to open this new service up to anyone who was considered a 'person at risk'.

NCA was the central standardising part of the new service which was then delivered on a regional basis by police officers:

> The UK Police Service has dealt with thousands of cases in the last 20 years or so. Protected Persons quietly get on with their new lives in the knowledge that they are supported by the authorities, and safe in their new locations. (NCA 2017 web site)

The UK Protected Persons Service works only with those at serious and high risk, and the experience of being moved to a new location in the country without ties to your home community is described as quite traumatic.

Secret Justice?

Criminal trials have also been heard, at least partly, in private when considerations of 'national security' have been taken into account. The Home Secretary had signed 'Public Interest Immunity' (PPI) certificates for the trial of Wang Yam charged with murder in 2009 because of his connections to the secret services. As a result, the whole of Wang Yam's defence was held in private. He was found guilty of the murder and sentenced to life imprisonment (Campbell and Norton Taylor 2014). It was later revealed that Wang Yam had links to the intelligence services:

> Before the PIIs were granted it was reported that MI6 had requested secrecy, that Yam was a 'low-level informant' for the intelligence services and that 'part of his defence rested on his activities in that role'. (Campbell and Norton Taylor 2015)

Later Wang Yam argued that he had not been given a 'fair and public' hearing and tried to take his case to the ECHR. The UK Supreme Court has examined Wang Yam's case and confirmed that the government can decree that a criminal court take place in private where 'national security' is an issue (*R (on the application of Wang Yam) (Appellant) v Central Criminal Court and another, (Respondents) [2015] UKSC 76*). In the meantime, the Criminal Cases Review Commission (CCRC) has referred his case back to the Court of Appeal (CCRC 2016).

Others have been tried in these conditions of 'closed court'. Two 28-year-old men on charges related to terrorism were also allowed a partially secret trial. The men were referred to only as AB and CD. Reports in *The Guardian* suggested it was part of a move towards secret justice in the UK:

> The case of AB and CD has been widely described as 'Britain's first secret trial'. It would be more accurately described as the latest of a number of creeping moves towards secret justice. (Campbell et al. 2014)

In this case, representations were made by journalists and the names of the two men were revealed as Erol Incedal and Mounir Rarmoul-Bouhadjar who were accused of having a bomb-making manual. The trial was eventually heard in three parts—an open session, a closed session and an intermediate session; the last allowed journalists in but they could not report any of the proceedings. Despite further applications, that was as far as the journalists could go. The Court of Appeal stated its opinion:

> We are quite satisfied from the nature of the evidence for reasons which we can only provide in a closed annex to this judgment that a departure from the principles of open justice was strictly necessary if justice was to be done. It was in consequence necessary that the evidence and other information heard when the journalists were present was heard in camera.
>
> Because of the nature of that evidence those reasons continue to necessitate a departure from the principle of open justice after the conclusion of the trial and at the present time. (*Guardian News and Media Ltd. and ors. v R and Erol Incedol [2016] EWCA Crim 11 paras.73–74*; see also Cobain 2016)

Juries

The jury room of the Crown Court is an area of the court proceedings surrounded in secrecy. The deliberations of the jury in this room are confidential and the reporting of deliberations by a jury member will lead to swift sanctions. Having taken their oath as a juror, the judge gives all 12 jury members a warning about disclosures; these include the reminders that:

> Jurors should not discuss the case with anyone (including family and friends) whether face to face, or over the telephone, or over the internet (including on Facebook or Twitter).
> If jurors do talk to other people they would be breaching confidentiality. They might also listen to someone else's views about the case and let it affect their own opinion, even without realising it.

A notice on the wall of the jury room further makes the point:

> To members of the jury. Her Majesty's judges remind you of the solemn obligation upon you not to reveal, in any circumstances, to any persons, either during the trial or after it is over, anything relating to it which has occurred in this room while you have been considering your verdict.

The law in question is the Contempt of Court Act 1981. Section 8 of this Act makes it an offence to disclose or solicit any particulars of statements made, opinions expressed, arguments advanced or votes cast by members of a jury in the course of their deliberations. The idea is that jury members will be able to have more frank and open discussions if they know they are speaking in confidence. Breaches of confidentiality and of Section 8 can lead to custodial sentences.

Youth Courts

Youth courts are an exception to the 'public hearings' principle, and courts covering the criminal activities of 10–18 year olds are closed to the public. Youth courts are under a duty to 'have regard to the welfare of the child or young person' before them (Children and Young Persons Act 1933 s44). Part of this welfare duty is met by the closure of the court to the public. The press is allowed in to the youth court but press reporting of the proceedings is restricted and the press cannot, for example, report a child's name, address or school or any other information that could lead to their identification.

The protection of children from the glare of publicity in the criminal court has always been argued as allowing them to grow out of crime and not to be burdened later with youthful indiscretions. The 1989 UN Convention on the Rights of the Child supports the idea:

> Article 40 (1). States Parties recognize the right of every child alleged as, accused of, or recognized as having infringed the penal law to be treated in a manner consistent with the promotion of the child's sense of dignity and worth, which reinforces the child's respect for the human rights and fundamental freedoms of others and which takes into account the child's age and the desirability of promoting the child's reintegration and the child's assuming a constructive role in society.

And this includes the right:

> Article 40 2 (vii) To have his or her privacy fully respected at all stages of the proceedings.

The Council of the European Union published a Directive on safeguards for children in criminal proceedings on 26 April 2016. Article 14 offers them a further 'right to protection of privacy':

1. Member states shall ensure that the privacy of children during criminal proceedings is protected.
2. To that end, member states shall either provide that court hearings involving children are ordinarily held in the absence of the public or allow courts or judges to decide to hold such hearings in the absence of the public.
3. Member states shall, with respect to freedom of expression and information and freedom and pluralism of the media, encourage the media to take self-regulatory measures in order to reach the objectives set out in this Article (Council of the European Union 2016).

This reflects current human rights standards in Article 6 ECHR (e.g., see *T v. UK, No. 24724/94, 16 December 1999*). Once published in the EU Official Journal, member states have three years to transpose the provisions into their national laws. The UK, even before the result of their referendum to leave the EU was known, had opted out of the directive and will not be bound by it (ibid.: para. 69).

Legal Restrictions on Reporting in the Youth Court

The restrictions on reporting from the youth court were established in law by the UK in the Children and Young Persons Act 1933. It is this Act that allows only 'bonâ fide representatives of newspapers or news agencies' into the courts (s. 47 (2) (c)) and section 49 that imposes automatic reporting restrictions:

s.49 *Restrictions on reports of proceedings in which children or young persons are concerned.*

(1) The following prohibitions apply (subject to sub-section (5) below) in relation to any proceedings to which this section applies, that is to say:

(a) no report shall be published which reveals the name, address or school of any child or young person concerned in the proceedings or includes any particulars likely to lead to the identification of any child or young person concerned in the proceedings; and

(b) no picture shall be published or included in a programme service as being or including a picture of any child or young person concerned in the proceedings.

(2) The proceedings to which this section applies are:

(a) proceedings in a youth court;

(b) proceedings on appeal from a youth court (including proceedings by way of case stated);

(3) The reports to which this section applies are reports in a newspaper and reports included in a programme service and similarly as respects pictures.

Programme service refers to any broadcast medium including radio or TV. Identification would include the so-called jigsaw identification whereby people could put two and two together and realise who it was. The publishing of any such details which would allow the public to identify the child would make the editor or publisher of the newspaper or their equivalents in the broadcasting media liable to conviction and a fine (1933 Act s.49 (9)).

In the late 1990s politicians did discuss the opening up of the youth courts which they described as a 'secret garden', especially if a degree of shaming looked as though it might prevent further offending (BBC News 1998). The law does allow the magistrates of the youth court to lift reporting restrictions if it is believed to be in the public interest to do so:

If a court is satisfied that it is in the public interest to do so, it may, in relation to a child or young person who has been convicted of an offence, by order dispense to any specified extent with the requirements of this section in relation to any proceedings before it. (Children and Young Persons Act 1933 s49 (4A))

The youth court can only lift reporting restrictions if it has, firstly, taken into account any representations from parties to the proceedings (1933 Act s. 49 (4B)). The wordings of the s49 4A and 4B amendments were added by the Crime (Sentences) Act 1997 s45.

This does beg the question—what is meant by the 'public interest'? The defining of 'public interest' is problematic and it has always been said that 'public interest' is something different from matters that the 'public is simply interested in'. It might be related to the nature or seriousness of the crime, but how do you avoid it just being prurient interest?

Reporting restrictions may also be lifted if it would avoid an injustice to the child or young person or it would help apprehend a child unlawfully at large; the latter circumstances only apply if the offence alleged is a violent offence, a sexual offence or an offence punishable in the case of a person aged 21 or over with imprisonment for 14 years or more (1933 Act s.49 (5) as amended by Criminal Justice and Public Order Act 1994 s.49; Clarkson and Thomas 1995).

As the Children and Young Person's Act 1933 s.49 provides for automatic reporting restrictions on children and young people in the Youth Court, so section 39 of the same Act allowed reporting restrictions when children and young people were in other courts such as the magistrates and Crown Court. It gave judges the power to make an order imposing reporting restrictions. From 13 April 2015, section 39 of the Children and Young Person's Act 1933 no longer applied to criminal proceedings. Instead, the newly commenced section 45 of the Youth Justice and Criminal Evidence Act 1999 applied to all criminal proceedings involving children and young people whether in the Youth Court or any other court.

One of the anomalies of the Youth Court reporting restrictions was that they ended once a young person reached the age of 18. In theory, they could then be named in the press, although in practice it had never happened. The Criminal Justice and Courts Act 2015 s.78 (amending the Youth Justice and Criminal Evidence Act 1999 with a new section 45A) has resolved this anomaly by allowing the making of 'a reporting direction' that gives witnesses and alleged victims in the Youth Court a lifetime of anonymity; the new law commenced on 13 April 2015. Children and Young Persons who are defendants were not covered by this change.

The lifting of reporting restrictions on young people in the Courts inevitably leads to more extensive reporting. Throughout the trial of the two ten-year-olds charged with the murder of two-year-old James Bulger, they were referred to only as Child A and Child B. At the end of the trial, reporting restrictions were lifted and photographs of the two children given to the press where they appeared on one front page beneath the headline 'Freaks of Nature' (*Daily Mirror* 25 November 1993). This headline is taken from a police sergeant's statement to the press at the end of the trial:

Sergeant Phil Roberts said: 'These two were freaks who just found each other. You should not compare these two boys with other boys – they were evil'. (quoted in Pilkington 1993)

Police statements on the conclusion of trials have become almost a normal automatic event in the UK. It is not exactly clear when or why this practice started but it was probably about the time of the Bulger trial. It is interesting to note the far more prosaic tabloid headline, just four years before the Bulger case but of very similar circumstances, which reads 'The Murderer age 12' from a time when there was presumably no police spokesperson to voice a more colourful opinion (Kane 1988).

We might also note another case less than 12 months before Bulger, of another case of a child killing a child in the UK. This involved the man-slaughter of an 18-month-old boy by an 11-year-old girl who was 12 at the time of her trial in York. This child was not named and there are no photographs; the victim's name is not reported and the case is not remembered or imprinted on the public conscience in anything like the way the Bulger murder is. Even the arguably unusual detail that the defendant was a girl rather than a boy has not raised the level of the reporting (Pithers 1992).

Two boys, aged 10 and 11, who appeared in a South Yorkshire court for serious crimes of violence committed against two boys, aged 9 and 11, in Edlington near Doncaster were also not named and we have no pho-tographic images of them. In this case, the two boys had been brought up in the public care of the local authority which might have made some-thing of a 'public interest' case for them being identified (Wainwright 2009; Brooke and Martin 2010).

The Bulger killing was certainly newsworthy. As a crime, it was visible, spectacular, violent and graphic. As a news item the crime had all the attributes of a 'good' news story both in the UK and internationally (see Franklin and Petley 1996, for an account of the contemporary report-ing). With names and photographs, the British public had a clear identity to put to the narrative of the crime, and the result was an outpouring of aggression and support for a punitive response to them. This has been termed the 'Goldstein effect' after the character Emmanuel Goldstein in George Orwell's novel *Nineteen Eighty-Four*; Goldstein was the subject of the periodic 'Two Minute Hate' (Logan 2009: 96).

The European Court of Human Rights has also declared that the UK Crown Courts sitting as Youth Courts are improperly organised and incom-patible with 'a fair trial' as required by Article 6 of the ECHR. The decision was related to the buildings used, the structure and the children's lack of understanding (*V and T v UK [1999] 30 EHRR 121*). The response this time was a Practice Direction by the Attorney General on how the Crown Courts sitting as Youth Courts might be better organised, but another 2004 judgement in Europe declared the UK to still be defaulting on compliance with Article 6 (*SC v UK [2004] 40 EHRR 10*; Wolff and McCall Smith 2000).

More recently, a report to the Secretary of State for Justice has still described the UK Crown Courts sitting as Youth Courts in uncomplimentary terms:

> I spoke recently to a barrister involved in the trial of two girls accused of murder who described the atmosphere in the court – which is open to the public and reporters – as 'like a circus'. (MoJ 2016b: para. 105).

The Special Case of the ASBO

In 1998, the Crime and Disorder Act introduced the Anti-social Behaviour Order (ASBO) which allowed the publicising of young people, as young as ten, who had engaged in anti-social behaviour. This was encouraged in order that local communities knew who was subject to an ASBO and could therefore report breeches accordingly and was permitted by the fact that ASBOs were made in the civil courts rather than the youth criminal courts and applications were not subject to reporting restrictions. Local authorities went further and produced their own leaflets with photographs and details of children and the areas they lived in (see, e.g., Herbert 2005; Thomas 2005).

It is interesting to compare the campaign that started in 2000 to allow residents to know when an adult sex offender had moved into their area. The 'For Sarah' campaign fronted by the *News of the World* newspaper wanted a law comparable to the American 'Megan's Law' which allows such 'community notification' (see Fitch 2006). The government resisted the calls for fear of vigilantism and driving sex offenders 'underground'. Clearly what was acceptable for children on ASBOs was not acceptable for adult offenders.

In 2007, the United Nations conducted one of its regular audits of the UK's compliance with the UN Convention on the Rights of the

Child (UN 1989). The audit found the UK wanting on its provisions allowing publicity on children subject to ASBOs declaring that 'the State party has not taken sufficient measures to protect children, notably those subject to ASBOs, from negative media representation and public naming and shaming' (UNCRC 2008: para. 36 (b)). The audit went on to recommend that 'the State party conduct an independent review of ASBOs, with a view to abolishing their application to children' (ibid.: para. 80).

A review of ASBOs did take place after the 2010 change of government. The Anti-Social Behaviour, Crime and Policing Act 2014 eventually abolished ASBOs and replaced them with civil Injunctions. These had many of the attributes of the old ASBOs and were available for use with adults and children. They had the same negative prohibitions but now had positive requirements added to them such as attendance at alcohol awareness classes for alcohol-related problems. Breach of an Injunction was no longer an offence but a contempt of court (Anti-Social Behaviour, Crime and Policing Act 2014 ss. 1–21).

In cases of violence or risk of harm, adults could be excluded from their homes by an injunction (ASBCP Act 2014 s.13). Statutory guidance issued at the same time, however, reminded practitioners that they should bear in mind Article 8 of the ECHR:

> We do not expect the power of exclusion to be used often and the court will pay special attention to proportionality in light of the Article 8 (Right to respect for private and family life, European Convention on Human Rights) implications. As such, applications should only be made for exclusion in extreme cases. (Home Office 2015g: 24)

In terms of reporting, the same situation applies to young people as it did with ASBOs (ASBCP Act 2014 s.13), and the Children and Young Persons Act 1933 s49 offering automatic reporting restrictions does not apply to the youth court proceedings (s.23(8) (a)). The Children and Young Persons Act 1933 s39 may be used to impose restrictions but as has been pointed out the Act does not place responsibility on to any one particular agency to assess the need to apply for s39 (SCYJ 2015: 20). The Home Office guidance states that:

When deciding whether to publicise the injunction, public authorities (including the courts) must consider that it is necessary and proportionate to interfere with the young person's right to privacy, and the likely impact on a young person's behaviour. (Home Office 2015g: 25)

Other Restrictions on Press Reporting

Apart from 'reporting restrictions' on children and young people, there are laws to allow privacy to other groups of witnesses and defendants including adults.

Sexual Offences

In 1975, the case of *R v. Morgan ([1975] 2 All ER 347)* generated a wide debate on the definition of rape and the defence of the man believing he had consent; questions were also raised about the extent to which a woman's previous sexual behaviour could be admitted as a defence (see above) and to what degree there should be press 'reporting restrictions' in rape cases. A committee of inquiry was asked to formally look into these questions and recommend accordingly (Heilbron Committee 1975).

The question of 'restrictions on reporting' was resolved by the Sexual Offences (Amendment) Act 1976, s. 4, which introduced anonymity into rape proceedings for both complainant and defendant. The press could still report proceedings but not identify any of the parties involved during the trial. The Criminal Law Revision Committee in 1984 returned to the question of press reporting of sexual offence cases and recommended the removal of the right to anonymity from the defendant in a case of alleged rape (CLRC 1984). In 1988, this right was duly repealed, on the grounds that being accused of rape was no different from being accused of other serious crimes and did not warrant special treatment (Criminal Justice Act 1988 s158). The Sexual Offences (Amendment) Act 1992 ss.1–2 extended these provisions on court anonymity for complainants only to sexual offences hearings other than rape.

Trials continued to take place where defendants were found not guilty but felt their reputations remained damaged because they had had no anonymity protection (see, e.g., *R v Blackwell [2006] EWCA Crim 2185*). Inevitably, at these times, the anonymity debate would be restarted. The Coalition government announced within days of their election that they intended to reintroduce anonymity for defendants (HMG 2010a: 24) and the controversy took off again (see, e.g., Jones 2010). The Ministry of Justice acted with caution, however, and commissioned a review of the evidence before taking any action; the findings did not support the need for change, and the government dropped the proposal (MoJ 2010).

Anonymity for defendants continued to emerge as a point for discussion (see, e.g., Evans 2014). When Ched Evans was sentenced to custody for rape of a 19-year-old woman in 2012, his position as a professional footballer meant the case drew a good deal of media attention. Evans was given a five-year custodial sentence. People spoke up for him on social media and his victim was denigrated as 'crying rape' and 'money grabbing'; a number of people also reported the victims' name and found themselves in breach of the Sexual Offences (Amendment) Act 1976. A total of ten people were ordered to pay compensation to the named person (BBC News 2013b).

Anonymity is also usually available to public hearings applying for civil orders under the Sexual Offences Act 2003. Under Part 2 of the 2003 Act, the police can apply for these civil orders in the form of Sexual Risk Orders and Sexual Harm Prevention Orders. Both of these orders are applied for in open magistrates' courts and seek to impose prohibitions on behaviour that could lead to sexual harm; breach of the prohibitions is dealt with in the criminal courts as an offence.

Full reporting of such cases, giving names and addresses, could lead to the possibility of public disorder and vigilantism in the vicinity of the person subject to the orders, and any such increase in public disorder not only diverts police resources but could encourage and allow the defendant to abscond from the arrangements the police and probation have put in place to manage the risks he or she poses:

> Therefore, it has become normal practice in some police areas, when applying for an order of this type, for an application to be made to the court at

the outset of proceedings (in general with the support of the defendant) for an order under section 11 of the Contempt of Court Act 1981 prohibiting the publication of the defendant's name and address. It is for the court to decide whether such a prohibition is necessary. (Home Office 2016d: 29)

Modern Slavery Act 2015

Special measures are in place for witnesses in criminal proceedings under the Modern Slavery Act 2015. This Act was designed to deal with slavery, servitude and forced or compulsory labour and about human trafficking. It includes provisions for the protection of victims and the creation of the post of an Independent Anti-slavery Commissioner.

The Act's s46 amends the Youth Justice and Criminal Evidence Act 1999 ss.17, 25 and 33 to include references to the 2015 Act that are to replace references to the old Asylum and Immigration (Treatment of Claimants, etc.) Act 2004. This includes special measures for child witnesses and intimidated adult witnesses; it also includes offences where the court may direct evidence to be given in private.

Female Genital Mutilation

The Serious Crime Act 2015 s71, which came into force on 3 May 2015, introduced a new automatic reporting restriction for the victims of Female Genital Mutilation (FGM). The reporting restriction applies from the moment that an allegation has been made that an FGM offence has been committed against a person and imposes a lifetime ban on identifying that person as being an alleged victim of FGM. Section 71 amends the Female Genital Mutilation Act 2003 (s4A and Schedule 1), making it a criminal offence to publish anything regarding a victim or an alleged victim of this crime.

The court has the power to relax or remove the restriction if satisfied that the restriction would cause substantial prejudice to the conduct of a person's defence at a trial of an FGM offence or if the restriction imposes a substantial and unreasonable restriction on the reporting of the proceedings, and it is in the public interest to do so (Female Genital Mutilation Act 2003 Schedule 1 para. 1 (4–8)).

Pre-sentence Requirements

Pre-sentence Reports

In order to assist the court in making a sentencing decision, the Probation Service provides Pre-Sentence Reports (PSRs) to the magistrates or judge; some PSRs on young people may be written by officers of the local Children's Department. The idea is to give a more rounded picture of the person to be sentenced as well as an analysis of the crime that has been committed, the offenders' circumstances, likelihood of reoffending (a risk assessment) and possible sentencing options that may help the offender themselves to reduce their offending behaviour. PSRs have been in existence since the 1970s when they were known as Social Inquiry Reports, but a legal definition of a PSR can now be found in the Criminal Justice Act 2003 ss156–9. The law does not prescribe the content of a PSR but accompanying guidance states that it should at least contain:

- Offence Analysis and pattern of offending beyond a restating of the facts of the case
- Relevant offender circumstances with links to offending behaviour highlighted, as either a contributing factor or a protective factor
- Risk of harm and likelihood of reoffending analysis based on static predictors and clinical judgement
- An outcome of pre-sentence checks with other agencies or providers of probation services including if any checks are still outstanding
- Address any indications provided by the court
- Sentence proposals are commensurate with the seriousness of the offence and will address the offenders' assessed risks and needs (NOMS 2016e: para. 2.4)

The writer of the PSR is enabled to collate personal information on the offender from the CPS, the police and other professionals with knowledge of them; police information would include any previous criminal record history. The writer will also sit down with the offender and discuss their view of what has happened and include any personal information they are willing to share. There is no legal obligation to talk to the officer writing the report but it is usually a given that cooperation will be helpful. The offender must be interviewed in private for the purpose of preparing the PSR (ibid.: para. 1.12).

In the court itself, the PSR is only disclosed to the offender and their legal representatives, the judiciary and the CPS. It is not disclosed to the media but questions in court arising from it might be reported on. If the PSR contains particularly sensitive personal information, this should not be presented orally in the court and only be provided in written form (ibid.: para. 1.14).

Probation Officers also write other reports to the court such as Specific Sentence Reports (SSRs) proposing, as the name suggests, very specific forms of sentencing, and other professionals may write medical reports. People thought to be mentally disordered offenders can be remanded to a psychiatric hospital for the sole purpose of having reports to the court written on them (Mental Health Act 1983 s.35).

Other Pre-sentence Requirements

Courts may request other pre-sentence information with varying degrees of intrusion on privacy such as Pre-Sentence Drug Tests, if a treatment order is being considered, or Pre-Sentence Finance Information, if a fine is being considered. The police are expected to provide the offenders *Antecedents* to the court which consists of a list of his or her previous convictions to assist with the courts' sentencing decisions. In general terms, the courts pass lower sentences on a first-time offender and then work backwards to higher sentences for the more persistent offender.

Summary

In earlier chapters, we have considered the intrusion upon privacy coming in to the suspect's life from various agencies of the state and in various forms. Here we have inverted the concept of privacy to demonstrate how the preservation of a degree of privacy is meant to help people in courts when they have appeared as defendants or witnesses. Defendants in the

Youth Court are entitled to automatic privacy with only the more serious cases leading to a lifting of reporting restrictions. The intimidated or vulnerable witness is allowed 'special measures' to protect them from the worst rigours of the court. The courts are expected to be open and fair and any privacy protection must consider that whether it be 'witness anonymity', 'witness protection' or the withholding of a complainant's previous sexual history in a rape case.

8

Punishment and Privacy

Introduction

Punishment of offenders generally divides into time periods in custodial settings (prison) or time periods in the community subject to community orders; privacy issues arise in both these forms of punishment. The prison seeks to demarcate areas around the offender to restrict his or her liberty and require their lives to be lived by certain rules, while living in a designated place with other offenders that inevitably impacts on their privacy. The community-based sentence tries to do the same with forms of supervision (probation officers) that literally means having a superior form of vision over the offender in order to know their whereabouts and their behaviour patterns as best as the supervisor can. Technology in the form of electronic tagging, and other systems, has been put in place to assist the supervisor. This chapter considers both forms of punishment and their impact on privacy.

© The Author(s) 2017
D. Marshall, T. Thomas, *Privacy and Criminal Justice*,
https://doi.org/10.1007/978-3-319-64912-2_8

Prisons

Life in the closed society of a prison inevitably restricts opportunities for privacy and not least when prisons are overcrowded as they currently are in the UK. The prisoners meet each other on a regular basis and there is no avoiding action that can be taken. Bullying and violence are endemic within UK prisons. Prisoners may be subjected to searches of varying degrees of intensity, mandatory drug tests (MDT) and their phone calls and letters to the outside world may be monitored. A personal record of each prisoner is maintained and every prisoner is photographed on reception.

Critical to the safe running of a prison is the balance between free movement and association for prisoners within the establishment and the need for stability and security within the prison population. The National Security Framework (NSF) for prisons was developed in 2004 to offer guidance on how this might be achieved. The NSF is a series of Prison Service Instructions (PSIs) grouped together under subject-related functions. Individual prisons are then required to set out specific details of how security operates within their establishment in a Local Security Strategy (LSS).

Overcrowding

The number of people in prison in the UK has been rising inexorably since the end of the Second World War. The prison estate has struggled to keep pace with this rising figure which stood at 85,752 in May 2017 (MoJ et al. 2017) and the result has been prison overcrowding. Cells built originally for one person now take two or three prisoners which arguably impacts directly on matters of prisoner privacy (BBC News 2012b).

The Prison Act 1952 s.14 provides that no cell should be used for the confinement of a prisoner unless it is certified by an inspector that its size, lighting, heating, ventilation and fittings are adequate for health and that it allows the prisoner to communicate at any time with a prison officer. On space in cells, NOMS decrees that the underlying principle is that each prisoner place must provide sufficient space for furniture and normal in-cell activities. In-cell activities are classified according to whether a cell is 'uncrowded' or 'crowded'. For uncrowded conditions, the activities are:

> In-cell activities are classified according to whether a cell is designated 'uncrowded' or 'crowded'. For uncrowded conditions, the activities are sleeping, dressing and undressing, using a WC (in private) and using wash-basin and being able to pursue personal pursuits such as reading, writing and listening to TV/sound and music systems. For crowded conditions, the activities are similar but more restricted especially regarding personal pursuits and storage of personal possessions (NOMS 2012b: Appendix 1).

HM Prison Service decides what is the prison's Certified Normal Accommodation (CNA) which represents a decent standard accommodation for a particular prison and the Operational Capacity which is the total number of prisoners that an establishment can hold, taking into account control, security and the proper operation of the planned regime. Prison governors must ensure that the approved Operational Capacity is not normally exceeded other than on an exceptional basis to accommodate pressing operational needs. When it is exceeded the prison is officially overcrowded.

The following is taken from a routine HMIC report on Leeds Prison, illustrating general points of privacy infringements:

Case Study

HM Chief Inspector of Prisons Report on an unannounced inspection of HMP Leeds (2016), 30 November–11 December 2015: Reported examples of lack of privacy

2.2 Most residential areas were cramped and very old; overall, the prison was overcrowded and the majority of cells designed for one were occupied by two. The residential environment was reasonably clean, and there was a painting programme. However, the old buildings were subject to water penetration and some cells had mould; they also had graffiti on their walls. The furniture was inadequate in the majority of cells; many had lockers with no doors, very few had lockable cabinets and some had no table. Toilets in many cells lacked proper screening and did not have seats or lids; prisoners often rigged up makeshift curtains from sheets to screen the toilet. The communal showers were adequate, although those on the ground floor offered limited privacy.

2.43 Legal visits took place every day and could be booked by email 48 hours in advance. Facilities had not improved and interview booths still did not provide sufficient privacy.
2.62 Five locum GPs provided medical cover, but at the time of inspection there was no lead GP in place. There was a lack of confidential space in the health centre and clinical staff routinely left doors open during consultations, compromising prisoners' privacy.
4.24 On arrival, all prisoners had an assessment of their immediate needs through the basic custody screening tool part 1, completed by offender supervisors, and part 2 completed by Catch 22 staff. Assessments were conducted on busy wings, which compromised privacy.
(Available at: https://www.justiceinspectorates.gov.uk/hmiprisons/wp-content/uploads/sites/4/2016/04/Leeds-Web-2016.pdf accessed 18 November 2016)

The numbers of people sent to prison is clearly not a matter for the prisons themselves, and the long-term rise in prisoner numbers has a number of explanations. The courts sentence people to immediate custody and sentences have become longer. When an emergency arises, the government has to instruct prisons to accommodate the extra population. In June 2014, for example, reports suggested:

Forty prisons in England and Wales have been told to raise their 'operational capacity' in the next two months, according to documents seen by the BBC. All but six of these are running at full capacity or are overcrowded. Justice Secretary Chris Grayling said he was taking 'sensible steps to make sure we can accommodate everyone'. (BBC News 2014b)

Case Study

Mr Ahtsham Ali, Muslim Advisor, HM Prison Leeds (Armley)
I had worked as a youth worker, and I'd worked with ex-offenders, trying to resettle them in their communities. But when I started, I had a totally naïve view of prisons. I remember my first week in Armley, when I was on induction with the Muslim chaplain. I saw a young man, about 20 years old, who came after Friday prayers and said he wanted to speak to the Imam. He broke down in tears and said he just couldn't cope. 'Could you please have a word with my cell mate?' They share two to a cell and

there is no privacy. 'Every time I go to the toilet he switches off the TV and leans over and I have to put a newspaper around me'. Such basic things that you don't think of: lack of privacy and lack of personal space. Things that we take for granted are not there. This dispelled from my mind the picture we get in the media that it's 'a cushy number'. It's quite a harrowing experience and more harrowing depending on which prison you go to.

Minutes of the All-Party Penal Affairs Parliamentary Group, held on 24 January 2012, available at http://www.prisonreformtrust.org.uk/PressPolicy/Parliament/AllPartyParliamentaryPenalAffairsGroup/Prisonandcommunity chaplaincyJanuary2012 accessed 18 November 2016

Searches of Prisoners

The searching of prisoners is an ongoing activity in the interests of security. The Prison Rules allow for the searching of prisoners and state that this should be done in as seemly a manner as is consistent with discovering anything concealed; no prisoner shall be stripped and searched in the sight of another prisoner or in the sight of a person of the opposite sex (Prison Rules SI 1999 No. 728 Rule 41).

The officers conducting a search may use 'reasonable force' if necessary (ibid.: Rule 47). An exact definition of 'reasonable force' has not been attempted in law and is usually said to be 'reasonable' in relation to the degree of resistance or force being faced by the officer.

People visiting prisons may also be liable to a search to ensure they are not bringing prohibited items in for prisoners. Again the Prison Rules state that people and vehicles entering or leaving a prison may be searched and that those searches should be carried out in as seemly a manner as is consistent with discovering anything concealed (Prison Rules SI 1999 no 728: Rule 71).

Supplementary guidance on the searching of all parties—prisoners, staff and visitors—issued by NOMS lists four forms of search: (a) level A 'rub-down' searches for relatives and social visitors to the prison; (b) level B 'rub-down' searches for professional visitors to the prison; (c) full searches (formerly known as strip-searches) and (4) searches of other body areas (NOMS 2016a: para. 2.3).

The procedural guidance for a full search, for example, requires that:

1. Two officers will be present. No person of the opposite sex will be present.
2. You will not be required to be fully undressed at any stage.
3. You will be asked to remove clothes from one-half of your body and pass them to an officer so that they may be examined. Your body will then be observed briefly so that the officers can see whether anything is concealed. The clothes will then be returned to you without delay and you will be given time to put them on.
4. The procedure will then be repeated for the other half of the body.
5. The soles of your feet may be checked.
6. When your lower body is undressed, if you are a man, you may be required to position yourself in such a way as to enable staff to observe whether anything is hidden in the genital and anal areas. Your body will not be touched during this process.
7. If you have long hair, it may be necessary for an officer to search it. It may also be necessary for an officer to check your ears, nose and mouth (ibid.: 2016: Annex J).

A 2008 report into how to stop drugs getting into prisons noted the lack of technology being used in a consistent way (MoJ 2008a). Mechanical aids have subsequently been introduced that may be used to assist officers and include X-ray machines to search baggage, clothes, goods and so on and hand-held metal detectors that make a sound or light up if metal is detected; metal-detecting portals that people walk through setting off noise or light alarms may also be used, and Body Orifice Security Scanner (BOSS) Chairs' which prisoners have to sit on and which bleep if they have a phone—or any other form of metal—hidden inside them are also used.

Another form of technological aid is the so-called Mercury Intelligence System (MIS) developed by NOMS. The MIS effectively allows NOMS to collate personal data allowing prison officers to improve the reduction of drugs and mobile phones in prisons, the prevention of escapes and the managing of risks posed by extremism and radicalisation.

The Prison Service has developed a greater all-round capacity to collate and analyse intelligence in recent years. Prison Intelligence Officers have grouped together to form Regional Special Operations Units, and at a central level a new National Prison Intelligence Coordination Centre has come into being to help manage high-priority offenders:

> The National Prison Intelligence Coordination Centre was launched as a multi-agency response to better understand, manage, and disrupt the threat posed by high priority offenders in prison. It will lead a programme to strengthen regional and local prisons intelligence capabilities. (NCA 2016: para. 214)

The National Prison Intelligence Coordination Centre brings together counterterrorism and organised crime expertise and capabilities to develop a comprehensive picture of the threat; to identify and manage the cohort of offenders who represent the highest risk of harm to national security and public protection; and to ensure the effective collection, use and management of intelligence relating to that cohort of offenders (ibid.: see also MoJ 2016c: paras. 193–5).

The Corston Report into the position of women in the criminal justice system was particularly critical of the use of strip-searching in prisons:

> There is one particular aspect of entrenched prison routine that I consider wholly unacceptable for women and which must be radically changed immediately in its present form. This is the regular, repetitive, unnecessary use of strip-searching. Strip-searching is humiliating, degrading and undig-nified for a woman and a dreadful invasion of privacy. (Corston Report 2007: para. 3.18)

Officers interviewed said they rarely found anything during these searches and Corston recommended that the practice should be reduced to an absolute minimum compatible with security (ibid.: paras. 3.18–3.21).

In response to the Corston Report, the routine full searching (strip-searching) of women prisoners ended in April 2009, and current guidance states that:

> Women prisoners must not be full-searched as a matter of routine but only on intelligence or reasonable suspicion that an item is being concealed on the person which may be revealed by the search. (NOMS 2016a: para. 2.54)

Apart from searching the individual prisoners, the cell areas and other physical parts of the prison may be liable for separate searches such as internal and external perimeter areas, toilets, visiting rooms, chapels and multi-faith rooms. Vehicles coming into the prison area may also be searched including lorries delivering equipment and stores. The most serious items of contraband are considered to be drugs, arms and explosives. These searches are also seen as part of the National Security Framework requirements (NOMS 2016b).

In making searches of cell areas, officers complete two levels of search known as 'routine' or 'routine plus'; the 'routine plus' search includes a full search of the prisoner:

- Once the appropriate search of the prisoner has been completed, the prisoner(s) must vacate their accommodation.
- Search and clear a suitable surface (e.g., bed or table) on which to place all searched items.
- Use the door as a starting point and work your way around the accommodation, searching all of its contents systematically and thoroughly. Include all known voids, ventilators, ceilings, floors, walls, doors, windows (inside, and where possible, outside) grilles, pipes and fixed furniture and fittings (ibid.: Annex A).

The guidance on making prisoners leave their cell search while a search was carried out led some prisoners to believe that officers were going through normally confidential correspondence between the prisoner and his or her lawyers. A prisoner called Daly took a test case to the House of Lords saying it breached his Article 8 right to privacy. The Lords agreed with his claim. The Daly Judgement meant that prisoners must now, in normal circumstances, be present when legal correspondence is searched during a cell search unless it was an emergency (*R v Secretary of State for the Home Department, ex parte Daly [2001] UKHL 26* at para 23; NOMS 2016b: para. 2.34).

At the moment, governors can set local searching and security strategies to match their own particular security problems. Some prison areas have regionally based Dedicated Search Teams (DSTs) which can be used for specific prison operations. The High Security Estate has a DST within each prison who are organised, trained and equipped to undertake searches of prisoners, visitors, staff, accommodation and other areas. These teams can also be boosted to include active and passive search dogs with the ability to detect drugs, mobile devices, arms and explosives (MoJ 2016c: para. 210).

New CCTV technology is being piloted to help prison authorities detect people on prison perimeters to spot people likely to be throwing contraband over the prison walls (Weston 2016).

Mandatory Drugs Tests

The presence of illegal drugs in prison has been a long-standing problem. Smuggled in by visitors, thrown over the walls and sometimes taken in by staff, the use of drugs is clearly contrary to Prison Rules (Prison Rules 1999 Rule 51(9) and (24)) and may lead to violent and unpredictable behaviour among prisoners. A relatively new synthetic form of cannabis known as 'spice' has caused particular problems (Brown 2014) and according to HM Chief Inspector of Prisons, Peter Clarke, the advent of New Psychoactive Substances (NPS) has created major problems and:

> Prison staff have told me that the effect on individuals and prisons as a whole is unlike anything they have seen before. (quoted in Sample 2016; see also CSJ 2015)

In order to detect whether an individual prisoner has taken drugs the government introduced MDT in 1994. Powers to require prisoners to provide a sample of urine for drug-testing purposes were in the Criminal Justice and Public Order Act 1994 s.151 which inserted the following section 16A into the Prison Act 1952:

(1) If an authorisation is in force for the prison, any prison officer may, at the prison, in accordance with Prison Rules, require any prisoner

who is confined in the prison to provide a sample of urine for the purpose of ascertaining whether he has any drug in his body.

(2) If the authorisation so provides, the power conferred by sub-section (1) above shall include power to require a prisoner to provide a sample of any other description specified in the authorisation, not being an intimate sample, whether instead of or in addition to a sample of urine (Prison Act 1952 s16A).

The Divisional Court case of *Tremayne* in 1996 rejected the claim that MDT contravened Articles 6 or 8 of the ECHR since the provisions did not violate the presumption of innocence or amount to unnecessary interference with privacy (*R v Secretary of State for the Home Department, ex p Tremayne (1996) Unreported, 2 May 1996*).

MDT on its own would not reduce drug misuse in prisons and the Prison Service *Drug Strategy Tackling Drugs in Prison*, published in May 1998, recognised the need to provide a more balanced and consistent approach with greater emphasis on the provision of treatment and support programmes. This meant implementing MDT as part of a wider anti-drug misuse strategy.

Prison Rule 50 outlines the power to carry out MDT, and Rule 50(8) states:

A prisoner required to provide a sample of urine shall be afforded such degree of privacy for the purposes of providing the sample as may be compatible with the need to prevent or detect any adulteration or falsification of the sample; in particular a prisoner shall not be required to provide such a sample in the sight of a person of the opposite sex. (Prison Rules SI 1999 No. 728 Rule 50(8))

Prison Service guidance on conducting MDTs is conscious of the need to protect privacy. Article 8 (1) of the ECHR—the right to privacy—is marked out as a critical backdrop to testing:

Requiring a prisoner to provide a sample against their wishes is prima facie a breach of this article. However, given the significant problems experienced with drug misuse within prisons, it would be argued that the United

Kingdom Government have the power to interfere with the rights of prisoners under Article 8(1) using the provisions set out in Article 8(2). (PSO 3601 para. 2.21)

Article 8(2) being the qualifying:

There shall be no interference by a public authority with the exercise of this right except such as in … the prevention of disorder or crime, for the protection of health or morals, or for the protection of the rights and freedoms of others. (CoE 1950)

Prison Service Order 3601 on MDT for prisoners draws further attention to the need to safeguard prisoner's privacy:

Case

Prisoner privacy when providing an MDT sample

Article 3 of Schedule 1 to the Human Rights Act 1998 specifies that 'No one shall be subjected to torture or to inhuman or degrading treatment or punishment'. Legal advice received is that the requirement to provide a sample of urine, in the direct view of a prison officer of the same sex, would constitute degrading treatment. Indirect observation is however more appropriate.

When providing a sample, the privacy of a prisoner should not be infringed unnecessarily. The level of privacy allowable as standard should be approved by the governor, as should any variations from this level which may be considered necessary. The approved level of privacy should not be reduced where a particular prisoner is suspected of cheating, or has cheated on a previous occasion, or the level of cheating in the prison is such that samples have to be collected with less privacy allowed to all prisoners. However, for such prisoners staff may deem it appropriate to conduct a further full search following long periods of confinement.

In the absence of direct observation of the sample provision process, it may on occasion prove difficult to prevent interference with the sample.

Where staff are suspicious, the best safeguard is to conduct as thorough a search of the prisoner as is possible and to ensure that the sample is checked carefully after provision (temperature, smell, appearance). Where a prisoner repeatedly provides negative samples but is suspected of interfering with the sample, the best approach is to conduct an on-suspicion test at a time least expected by the prisoner (**HM Prison Service 2007: paras. 6.26–6.29**).

Separate guidance is provided in the same document on the safeguarding of privacy for women prisoners subject to MDT (ibid.: paras. 6.30 to 6.33).

Disclosing Information About Prisoners

People who were well known in the community or have committed serious high-profile offences continue to have press stories written about them while in prison. Prison officers are forbidden to pass information on these prisoners to the press despite there being a ready market for such stories; journalists and others commit offences if they try to obtain stories from prison officers.

When the England footballer Adam Johnson was imprisoned for child sex offences, *The Sun* newspaper obtained information that he was working as a barber in the prison. The story referred to an unnamed source who was providing the information:

> The player, on £60,000 a week at Sunderland, gets £20 a week for six-hour days at the jail's barber shop.
>
> A source said: 'Johnson is working full time while doing a training course. He seems to enjoy it and is getting on well'. …
>
> He is housed in a single cell in its sex offender unit after being sentenced to six years for grooming and sexual activity with a 15-year-old girl fan.
>
> The source said: 'Johnson is trying to keep his head down and avoid problems with other inmates. Some are slightly annoyed because he has landed quite a cushy job, does not have to work too hard and even gets two hours off for lunch. But no one has given him trouble about it.' (Hamilton and Sims 2016)

The Prison Rules are quite clear on prison staff communications with the press:

> 67 (1): No officer shall make, directly or indirectly, any unauthorised communication to a representative of the press or any other person concerning matters which have become known to him in the course of his duty.
>
> (2) No officer shall, without authority, publish any matter or make any public pronouncement relating to the administration of any institution to which the Prison Act 1952 applies or to any of its inmates.

Contact with Family and Friends

Maintaining contact with the outside world is considered of benefit to prisoners and aids their resettlement when they leave. Prisoners are allowed both written correspondence and telephone calls to assist them in this task as well as visits from family and friends. Letters and phone calls, however, can be read or listened to by prison officers, and visitors can be searched in the interests of prison security and public protection.

Letters

Normally, there is no limit on the number of letters that can be sent to a prisoner. The letters to and from a prison are checked by prison staff unless they are from solicitors and courts and contain matters of 'legal privilege'. These letters are supposed to be marked on the envelope as 'confidential' or 'Rule 39', the latter being the relevant Prison Rule covering confidential letters. Letters are read by officers on a random basis:

> A proportion of incoming mail (usually 5%) is read on a random basis. Prisoners who are subject to public protection restrictions, or who pose particular security concerns, may have all their incoming mail read. In both cases, these actions are logged. (HMIP 2015: para. 6.22)

The sort of contraband that will be removed from correspondence or parcels includes anything indecent or obscene or anything that threatens the security of the prison. It is a criminal offence to pass illegal drugs, alcohol, weapons, a camera or a mobile phone to a prisoner by correspondence or during a visit (Prison Act 1952 ss. 40A-D as amended by the Offender Management Act 2007 s22 and Crime and Security Act 2010 s45).

Telephone Calls

A prisoner may make external calls using a prison phone; they are unable to take incoming calls and are not permitted to have mobile phones. Outgoing calls are made using a Personal Identification Number (PIN) and prisoners can only make calls to a list of numbers that they have previously given to the prison that have been added to their prison PIN account; this list marks out the numbers that are confidential or privileged.

Prison staff can listen to and record most types of calls; an exception would again be when a prisoner calls a legal adviser or an MP or other authorised body. The law permitting the tape recording of a prisoner's calls is the Regulation of Investigatory Powers 2000 s.4 (4) and the Prison Rules 1999 Rules 34, 35, 35 A-D and 39. The Interception of Communications Commissioner's Office (IOCCO) provides oversight of these routine arrangements in prisons and conducts inspections of prisons (see also NOMS 2016c).

Concerns were raised in 2008 that prison officers were improperly listening in to and recording phone calls to MPs; one of the MPs was Sadiq Khan (BBC News 2008c). A later inquiry report from HM Prison Inspectorate revealed the prevalence of this activity:

> By early November 2014, NOMS, with the help of BT, concluded that a total of 358 calls to 32 separate MPs had been recorded and listened to between March 2006 (the earliest data for which data was available) and October 2014. (HMIP 2015: para. 1.4)

The Chief Inspector of Prisons did not believe this to be a deliberate attempt to monitor communications with MPs and put most of it down to error with a 'widespread ignorance about how the system was supposed to operate among both prisoners and staff' (ibid.: Foreword).

The problem of illicit mobile phone being smuggled in and used in prisons has continued. The Ministry of Justice reported that in 2015, nearly 17,000 mobile phones and SIM cards were found in prisons in England and Wales (the equivalent of 46 a day). This was an increase from around 10,000 in 2014 and 7000 in 2013 (MoJ 2016c: para. 206); some offenders had used these phones to organise crimes from within the prison.

The Prisons (Interference with Wireless Telegraphy) Act 2012 allows the Secretary of State, or Scottish Ministers, to grant an authorisation to prison governors/directors, permitting them to interfere with wireless telegraphy for the purpose of preventing, detecting or investigating the use of mobile telephones within a prison. The Serious Crime Act 2015

s.80 had given powers to the Secretary of State to force telephone operators to disconnect any one illicitly using a mobile phone in prison, and
NOMS reported that technology was available in prisons to track the
whereabouts of mobile phones when they are being used:

> Portable mobile phone signal detectors have been supplied to all prisons
> and are available for purchase through Procurement. These may be used in
> line with local security strategies for locating mobile phones throughout
> the prison. (NOMS 2016b: para. 2.4)

A White Paper published in November 2016 proposed taking even
further measures:

> We will build on what we have done already by
>
> • working with partners to implement new technology to stop illicit
>   mobile phones working in prisons;
> • using Telecommunications Restriction Orders to permanently discon-
>   nect mobile phones or SIM cards identified as operating within a
>   prison without the need to first take possession of a phone or to iden-
>   tify the user (MoJ 2016c: para. 208).

Provisions for the Telecommunications Restriction Orders were
included in the Prisons and Courts Bill (Clause 21 and Schedule 2) published 23 February 2017. The technology used to intercept a mobile signal and identify the user is referred to as an International Mobile
Subscriber Identity (IMSI) catcher also known as Covert Communications
Data Capture (CCDC) equipment; UK police forces are reportedly
already using it for other detection purposes albeit within a cloak of some
secrecy (Pegg and Evans 2016).

The CCDC technology creates a 'false' cell phone tower that the signal
to the mobile automatically seeks out as the nearest mobile tower. Placed
outside a prison it would pick up all the signals entering the prison. A
spokesman for Privacy International has pointed out that it would also
pick up other innocent messages in the same area:

> IMSI catchers, by their very nature, operate indiscriminately, gathering
> information from all individuals in the particular operating area. This

collateral intrusion into the private lives of many innocent individuals is deeply concerning in any context let alone one that is, almost deliberately, opaque. (quoted in Pegg and Evans 2016)

There has been little public debate on the use of this technology by either the police or the prison service although there are clear implications for matters of privacy.

Visitors

Prisoners are allowed visitors as the best way to maintain family contacts. Visitors are subjected to a search to ensure they are not bringing in contraband and, indeed, the visit is conditional upon there being a search.

The searching of visitors has not always gone smoothly. Mary Wainwright and her son Alan were the subject of a full strip-search while visiting a family member in HM Prison Leeds. Mrs Wainwright sought remedy in all the national courts and finally in the European Court of Human Rights (see case study).

Case Study

Mrs Mary Wainwright, aged 53, and her 31 year old son Alan attended HM Prison Leeds in Armley on 2 January 1997 to visit her other son Patrick O'Neill detained there on remand. Neither Mrs Wainwright nor Alan had ever visited a prison before. At the prison they were both taken to one side and informed they were to be strip searched by staff and that if they refused they would be denied their visit to Mr O'Neill.

Two female officers took Mrs Wainwright into a small room with windows overlooking the road outside and an administration block; the window roller blinds were not pulled down. Mrs Wainwright was asked to remove her upper clothing and while one officer went through the clothing the other walked around her examining her naked upper body. She was then instructed to remove her shoes, socks and trousers, leaving her standing naked apart from her underwear; by this time she was crying. On her request Mrs Wainwright was given her vest back.

Mrs Wainwright was told to pull down her underwear and to widen her legs. She was then told to widen her legs and take one leg out of her underwear so her legs could be spread wider. She was told to bend forward and

> her sexual organs and anus were visually examined. Mrs Wainwright was then asked to raise her vest until it was above her breasts; she asked why that was necessary as they had already inspected her top half. The officer ignored her and continued walking around her body. She was then told to get dressed.
>
> At the end Mrs Wainwright was shaking and visibly distressed. She believed that anyone looking through the windows could have seen her in a state of undress. After she had got dressed one of the officers asked her to sign the form to consent to a strip search. She did so without reading it.
>
> (taken from *Wainwright v UK European Court of Human Rights (Fourth Section) Application No. 12350/04, Strasbourg 26 September 2006 paras. 7–16)*

Leeds county court in 2001 had upheld a claim against the Home Office brought by Mary and Alan Wainwright, deciding that their privacy had been infringed. The Court of Appeal overturned that decision but the law lords refused to create a tort of privacy when the case reached them in 2003 (Dyer 2003a). The European Court of Human Rights in Strasbourg did, however, find in favour of the Wainwrights, ruling that the traumatic strip-searches had breached Article 8 of the European Convention and their right to respect for private life, awarding each £2000 compensation, plus £11,700 towards their costs (*Wainwright v UK European Court of Human Rights (Fourth Section) Application No. 12350/04, Strasbourg 26 September 2006*).

The Strasbourg judges accepted that searching visitors was a legitimate activity for prison officers, given that drugs were endemic in the prison in question, and Patrick Wainwright—the prisoner being visited—was suspected of having taken them. But the court emphasised that:

> the application of such a highly invasive and potentially debasing procedure to persons who are not convicted prisoners or under reasonable suspicion of having committed a criminal offence must be conducted with rigorous adherence to procedures and all due respect to their dignity. (ibid.: para. 44)

That had not happened in Leeds. The Wainwrights were not told their rights. Prison officers had been sloppy and the searches did interfere with the Wainwright's right to respect for their private and family life, guaranteed by Article 8. The court decided that this interference could not be justified as proportionate to the legitimate aim of stopping drugs entering the prison.

Women in Prison

There has been a belated realisation in HM Prison Service that women prisoners may require different services to male prisoners. David Ramsbotham, a former Chief Inspector of Prisons, was surprised to find that in December 1995, 'no one at [Prison Service] headquarters had overall operational responsibility for the oversight of women in prison' (Ramsbotham 2005: 11). That position has now been rectified but many issues still remain concerning women in prison. Here we consider two of them relating to women who are pregnant and who live in designated prison Mother and Baby Units (MBUs).

Pregnant Women in Prison

Women in custodial settings who are pregnant have in the past presented difficulties for prisons. Concerns rose to a peak in the mid-1990s when the press revealed that pregnant women in prison, far from being given extra privacy, were being shackled in chains and handcuffed for periods of time when they were in hospital. Kathleen Mackay was chained for 24 hours a day in hospital when she was 22 weeks pregnant, Sue Edwards had been handcuffed throughout the birth of her baby girl and Annette Walker had been shackled for 10 out of the 12 hours she was in labour.

The *Daily Mirror* published photographs of Holloway prison inmate Kathleen Mackay, heavily pregnant and chained to a guard in Whittington Hospital, North London. *Channel 4 News* showed secret film of another Holloway prisoner, identified as Annette Walker, chained in the hospital during the early stages of a 12-hour labour.

Prisons Minister Ann Widdecombe told the Commons that it was Prison Service policy not to keep women handcuffed during labour and childbirth:

I am grateful to have the opportunity to clarify both Prison Service policy in general and the practice in Holloway. It is our policy to secure all prisoners under escort for whatever reason, but where medical treatment is concerned we remove restraints for both male and female prisoners as and when requested by medical staff. However, it is the policy of the Prison Service not to keep women handcuffed while in labour and childbirth. It has never been Prison Service policy to keep women handcuffed during labour and childbirth. (*Hansard House of Commons Debates 9 January 1996 vol. 269 col. 19*)

Chains were removed when doctors confirmed labour had started and forms had been filled in. She insisted that Annette was not in labour when she was secured. The opposition was not satisfied:

Mr. Straw: Is the Minister aware that the statement that she has just made is completely unacceptable, and that in a civilised society it is inhuman, degrading and unnecessary for a prisoner to be shackled at any stage of labour? (*Hansard House of Commons Debates 9 January 1996 vol. 269 col.20*)

Nearly ten years on, a former Chief Inspector of Prisons recalled a meeting he had had with a woman in Holloway Prison in London in 1995:

[she] described how humiliated she had felt when attending an antenatal clinic in chains. She had been trying to keep herself to herself when a small boy came up, peered at her, and shouted to his mother to come and look at this woman in chains. The whole room turned round. (Ramsbotham 2005: 19)

Mother and Baby Units

Prisoners who are mothers of babies can apply to have their child with them for the first 18 months of life in prison Mother and Baby Units (MBUs). Of the 12 women's prisons in England, some 6 of them have such units that can accommodate 54 women. Admission is by application through an Admissions Board and the 'Secretary of State may, subject to any conditions he thinks fit, permit a woman prisoner to have her baby with her in prison, and everything necessary for the baby's maintenance and care may be provided there' (Prison Rules SI 1999 no.728: Rule 12(2)). Supplementary guidance states that 'babies and their mothers must not be locked in their rooms' and:

> It is part of the ethos of the Units that they are quiet, orderly places with a calm atmosphere primarily for the benefit of the children. (NOMS 2014a: para. 3.1.18)

Former Prime Minister David Cameron called for a review into the treatment of pregnant women in prison in February 2016. In a wide-ranging speech to the Public Policy Exchange think tank on prison reforms, the prime minister said: 'It is absolutely terrible to think that some babies are spending the earliest months – even years – of their lives behind bars':

> Think of the damage done to the life chances of these children. I believe we've got to try to break this cycle. So I want us to find alternative ways of dealing with women offenders with babies, including through tagging, problem-solving courts and alternative resettlement units. (Cameron 2016)

A more positive initiative came from the organisation Birth Companions who launched 'The Birth Charter for women in prisons in England and Wales' on 26 May 2016. The Birth Charter is intended to help inform the government's review to improve current practice across prisons, on aspects ranging from antenatal care and birthing partners to breastfeeding, family visits and counselling. At present, it is reported that babies in prison are more likely to become autistic and suffer from ADHD (Birth Companions 2016; Fenton 2016).

Transgender Prisoners

HM Prison Service has been criticised for being slow off the mark to cater for transgender prisoners; these are men or women who have chosen to live their lives as the opposite gender to which they were biologically assigned. They are people who are born with typical male or female anatomies but feel as though they have been born into the 'wrong body'. Some women, for example, may have typical female anatomy but feel like a male and seek to become male by taking hormones or electing to have sex reassignment surgeries. The problem for transgender prisoners was their allocation to an appropriate prison and everyday issues of privacy concerning sharing a cell, showers and other toileting facilities.

The Gender Recognition Act 2004 allows people across the UK to apply to the Gender Recognition Panel for legal recognition of their acquired gender. Applicants who fulfil the legal requirements will receive a full Gender Recognition Certificate (GRC) (Gov.uk 2017b).

In the latter end of 2015, a number of cases of transgender women being placed in male prisons came to light. Tara Hudson, 26, who was born male but lived her entire adult life as a woman, was sent to HMP Bristol a week after admitting assault over a Boxing Day bar fight (Gayle 2015). Vicky Thompson, aged 21, a transgender woman from Keighley, West Yorkshire, was sent to Leeds jail for men (November 2015) after a conviction at Bradford Crown Court but was found dead a week or so later (*Yorkshire Evening Post* 2015). Joanne Latham, 38, another transsexual woman, was found hanged by a prison officer at HMP Woodhill, a men's prison in Milton Keynes in December 2015 (Buchanan 2015).

In response to questions, Andrew Selous, the then Parliamentary Under-Secretary at the Ministry of Justice, told the House of Commons that:

> Prisoners are normally placed according to their legally recognised gender, which means either the gender on their birth certificate or the gender on their gender recognition certificate. However, the guidelines allow some room for discretion, and senior prison staff will review the circumstances of every case in consultation with medical and other experts in order to protect the physical and emotional wellbeing of the person concerned, along with the safety and wellbeing of other prisoners. (*Hansard House of Commons 20 November 2015 col.975*)

He added that the existing NOMS policy was outlined in the Prison Service Instruction (PSI) 'Care and Management of Transsexual Prisoners' (NOMS 2011) which states that female-to-male transgender prisoners cannot be refused location in the male estate. A male-to-female transgender prisoner may be refused location in the female estate only on security grounds (and would then be held as a female prisoner in the male estate) but this provision relates only to those male-to-female transgender prisoners who have a GRC.

A review of this 2011 policy was already in progress, and revised guidance was to be issued and implemented 'in due course', and the exact number of transgender prisoners would be counted. The only number currently available was put at 'around 80', provided in evidence to a Women and Equalities Committee report (House of Commons 2015e: Oral evidence Q284).

It was to be another year before the review was completed. It was only eight pages long when it did appear but among other things it stated that an underlying principle for the care of transgender prisoners should be 'the maintenance of appropriate levels of decency and privacy' (MoJ 2016d: 5); the official number of transgender prisoners was revised down to 70 in an accompanying paper (MoJ 2016e: 5).

The new NOMS PSI guidance also appeared in November 2016 outlining how transgender prisoners should be treated. An innovation in this PSI was the introduction of the Voluntary Agreement that transgender prisoners were encouraged to sign to record all the things both staff and prisoners agree will happen to help the prisoner live in the gender they feel is right for them:

> The provision of a Voluntary Agreement for transgender prisoners is to support consideration of privacy, dignity, well-being, and arrangements for searching and personal care whilst living in a communal environment. All transgender prisoners covered in this policy, including prisoners who have applied for or gained legal recognition of the gender they identify with, should be encouraged to enter into a Voluntary Agreement, subject to risk, security and operational assessments, whether located in the male or female part of the estate. (NOMS 2016d: para. 6.20)

Another transgender woman remanded into a male prison in Doncaster was subsequently found in her cell; Jenny Swift, aged 49, was found dead at HMP Doncaster in December 2017 (BBC News 2017b).

Leaving Prison

The use of electronic tags to enable early release from prison is known as the Home Detention Curfew (HDC) scheme. It was introduced by the Crime and Disorder Act 1998 and allows certain prisoners to leave early if they are willing to wear an electronic tag that will police any curfews placed on them. Sex offenders and violent offenders are not allowed to be considered for the HDC scheme.

Child sex offenders have their homes checked out before leaving prison—a social worker from the local authority Children's Department visits the address the prisoner says he is going to live at to see if there are any children living there and any potential child protection issues likely to arise if he goes there. The origins of these home circumstances checks can be traced back to the 1960s when a Home Office circular confirmed that the police would notify local authorities whenever a person convicted of incest, a child sexual offence or any offence involving cruelty or ill-treatment of a child was leaving prison and there were possible concerns for a child living at his address; a social worker would visit the home and report to the police (Home Office 1964: para. 6–7).

These arrangements were not foolproof. John Auckland from South Yorkshire was imprisoned in Durham Prison after killing his 15-month-old daughter in 1968. On his release, Auckland had gone on to kill a second daughter, only nine weeks old, in 1974. The resulting inquiry into what had gone wrong focused on the lack of communication between the prison and community-based services, which could have alerted practitioners that a child was potentially at risk.

The new arrangements now entered into consisted of a social work visit to the address the offender said he was going to live at and a triangular exchange of information between prison, probation service and the then social services departments (now redesignated as Children's Departments) to identify any possible child protection questions (DHSS 1978). These arrangements were revised in 1994 and are now to be found in the Public Protection Manual (Gov.uk 2009).

Community Orders

Most convicted offenders do not receive custodial sentences but rather they receive community-based sentences and in particular Community Orders. Community Orders were introduced by the Criminal Justice Act 2003 and any such Order made by the criminal courts had a 'requirement' included in it for the recipient. The sort of 'requirements' that could be imposed included an unpaid work requirement, an activity requirement, a mental health treatment requirement or a drug rehabilitation requirement (for the complete list see Criminal Justice Act 2003 s.177).

The 'unpaid work requirement' was explained in more detail as being based on a number of hours the offender had to work and be over 40 hours but less than 300 hours spread over a number of weeks to be completed within 12 months. The court must be satisfied that the offender is fit enough to do the work in question which usually included such tasks as removing graffiti, clearing wasteland or decorating public places and buildings (see Criminal Justice Act 2003 ss199–200). The National Probation Service produced guidance on how the 'unpaid work' was to be supervised by the probation service and suggested the arrangements should be called 'Community Payback' (NPS 2005).

Community Payback

The Cabinet Office report *Engaging Communities in Fighting Crime* drawn up by Louise Casey in 2008 made a number of recommendations to make these 'known' offenders doing 'unpaid work' even more visible and demanding; this visibility was not for public protection reasons but to give the public greater confidence that a punishment was being administered:

> In particular, there was a real public appetite for community penalties that provide a visible punishment for offenders where they carry out demanding work to 'payback' to the community. (Cabinet Office 2008a: 53 and Proposals 13–14)

The Government's response was specific. They were in favour of high-visibility jackets for community sentences involving 'unpaid work' or 'community payback'—and offenders were to wear signifying clothing or tabards (Home Office 2008). High-visibility orange jackets duly came in from 1 December 2008, and according to Secretary of State for Justice Jack Straw:

> The public, the taxpayer, has an absolute right to know what unpaid work is being done to payback to them for the wrongs the offender has committed. These high visibility jackets with the distinctive logo 'community payback' are one way in which I am trying to open up this part of the criminal justice system. (quoted in Ministry of Justice 2008b)

At this point, it is perhaps worth restating the views of two international declarations on the implementation of non-custodial sentences where public knowledge of sentences was viewed with caution. The United Nations had produced its *Standard Minimum Rules for Non-custodial Measures* often referred to as 'the Tokyo Rules' in 1990:

> In the application of non-custodial measures, the offender's right to privacy shall be respected, as shall be the right to privacy of the offender's family. (Tokyo Rules 1990: para. 3.11)

and two years later the Council of Europe published its own version as the *Rules on Community Sanctions and Measures* which stated that:

> The nature, content and methods of implementation of community sanctions and measures shall not jeopardise the privacy or the dignity of the offenders or their families, nor lead to their harassment. Nor shall self-respect, family relationships, links with the community and ability to function in society be jeopardised. Safeguards shall be adopted to protect the offender from insult and improper curiosity or publicity. (CoE 1992: Rule 23)

Neither of these rules could be said to have been applied with any rigour in the introduction of distinctive clothing for those in the UK completing community sentences, and the immediate experiences of offenders recorded by the National Association of Probation Officers

(NAPO) would suggest that a high degree of intrusion into privacy and a demeaning nature of 'self-respect' were experienced. NAPO reported incidents of 'abuse, threats, and taunting from members of the public' and:

> In one area a group of youths chanted 'nonces, smackheads, low lifes' at a work group, in another they were called 'fucking criminals' and in another, cans were thrown at individuals on placements. Some offenders have refused to wear the vests and have reacted aggressively and abused supervisors. (NAPO 2008)

Such exposure had a clear resonance with the stocks of the middle ages built in public areas.

NAPO also raised the legal matter that non-compliance with wearing the high-visibility jackets was not seen as contempt of court because neither the courts—nor the law—had ever said it was part of the sentence; in turn, this raised real problems of enforcement when offenders refused to wear the jackets (ibid.). A Ministry of Justice spokesman tried to calm the situation saying the government had reportedly bought 10,000 labelled vests and they were being widely used and 'there are hundreds of projects across the country complying with the requirement to wear these jackets' (Russell 2008).

Today tabards are taken as an accepted part of 'community payback':

> The purpose of the tabards is to make the work visible to the public and to improve awareness of Community Payback Their use supports the policy objective of making Community Payback visible to the public. Visibility is intended to increase public awareness of the sentence and to provide tangible evidence that community sentences are being carried out, so improving public confidence in those sentences.
>
> The purpose of the tabards is not to stigmatise or humiliate offenders. Experience of their use by probation trusts since 2008 suggests they are now an accepted component of Community Payback delivery. (NOMS 2014b: paras. 3.1–3.2)

Undeterred, the UK government went on to try and bring more details of offenders and their criminal records home to their local communities.

The *Engaging Communities in Fighting Crime* report found the public to be distant from the criminal justice system and in particular 'they do not see enough visible action being taken to challenge, catch and punish criminals' (Cabinet Office 2008a: 6). One member of the public expressed the concern:

> Why do criminals suddenly become invisible when they are caught? We have a right to know about what happens to them, but the powers that be all conspire to keep us in the dark! (ibid.: 48)

The Report wanted better dissemination of criminal conviction information to local communities so they could see what was being done; the local press often only reported on the high-profile cases and then just added a court list of other sentences collected from the clerk to the court at the end of the day (Home Office 1989). Some researchers on local newspapers at that time had concluded that 'most courts in the areas we surveyed sit with their press benches empty' (Franklin and Murphy 1991; see also Robins 2016). *Engaging Communities in Fighting Crime* felt more was needed if people were to fully know about the less serious cases.

The 2008 Cabinet Report was followed up by the announcement that the government was going to trial a system of dissemination of the convictions and sentencing on adults for a period of one month after sentencing; this was going to be done by a possible use of leaflets, public meetings, local newsletters or on-line availability. Addresses would not be released in full, presumably to try and avoid vigilantism; the government was enthusiastic about using photographs (OCJR 2009: 4; see also MoJ et al. 2009: section 3B). In the event and with the change of government in 2010, these proposals were not implemented and have not reappeared (see also Thomas and Thompson 2010).

Electronic Tags

We have encountered electronic monitoring at the pre-trial stage to support bail curfew conditions (Chap. 7) and to enable early release from prison (see above). The idea that agencies of the criminal justice system should be allowed to put electronic tags on people to enable their whereabouts in the community to be tracked has clear implications for the privacy of those people. An initial withdrawing from the very thought of tagging because of its association with tagging animals and livestock was balanced against the counter idea that at least it would avoid the use of prison which would be worse.

As the technology became more possible, the use of electronic monitoring began to take a hold in political circles and the Home Office:

[politicians] found it an irresistible aid in trying to cajole and reassure an electorate which had become increasingly sceptical about the power of any politician to make an impact on crime. Tagging has some very reassuring features which, in addition to the promise of a 'quick fix' solution make it all too appealing. (Whitfield 1997: 10)

Tags promised straight control and compliance rather than the more difficult area of trying to change people through supervision. The main opposition came from probation officers:

These new sanctions were not popular with sections of the probation service who regarded themselves as a profession whose aim is to help or care for offenders, rather than to supervise or control them. (Davies et al. 2010: 23)

Some probation officers were said to just be confused as to how the new arrangements would work and which people should be put forward for tagging (Whitfield 1997: 21).

As we noted in Chap. 7, the first UK pilot schemes of electronic monitoring started in August 1989 and were used on people remanded on bail. The tag worn on an ankle or a wrist was in radio contact with a fixed device in the wearer's home. The results of the pilots were not very good, and the technicians went back to the drawing board (Mair and Nee 1990).

A second attempt was made in 1995. By this time, laws had been passed to support the use of electronic monitoring in conjunction with court-made curfew orders—the monitoring being to ensure compliance with the order (Criminal Justice Act 1991 ss. 12–13; Criminal Justice and Public Order Act 1994 Schedule 9 para. 41). The implication was that tagging was not a punishment in itself but a means of incapacitation and knowing where someone was at a given time; just as a prison wall marks out a spatial area around someone, so too would the electronic tag for someone living in the community. Three pilot schemes started July 1995 in Norfolk, Manchester and Reading, and this time the results were more positive (Mair and Mortimer 1996).

The arguments about invasion of privacy started to fade as the use of electronic monitoring started to spread. The implementation of the monitoring was given to the private sector and not to the probation service who had been so critical in the early days. Developments in technology have suggested that a new form of electronic monitoring may become available using GPS satellite tracking to know exactly where a person is even if not under curfew (Shute 2007). Progress, however, has not always been as smooth as expected as the Under-Secretary for Justice told the House of Commons in February 2016 (*Hansard House of Commons 26 February 2016 cols.21WS–22WS*).

Electronic monitoring in the UK has had an unfortunate history with the private companies who implement the monitoring. The companies G4S and Serco in 2014 were found to have falsely claimed money from the Ministry of Justice for providing spurious tags on criminals, some of whom were dead, back in prison or had fled the country. The overcharging is believed to have started in 2005 and to have included billing for monitoring the movements of 3000 'phantom' offenders. G4S repaid £109 million and SERCO repaid £70.5 million (Travis 2014). The contracts were withdrawn from the companies and given to Capita where different allegations were made. This time the allegations were that offenders bribed Capita security staff to deliberately fit electronic ankle tags loosely in order that they could evade their curfews and leave home while creating the illusion that they were still at home; some 32 offenders reportedly paid £400 a time for this illicit service (Sabur 2017).

Voice Verification

A variation on electronic tagging is that of voice verification. An initial voice recording is taken from the offender, which is used as a blueprint for all future communication by telephone. The technology enables the monitoring company to check the unique voice of the subject against the recorded and stored version each and every time the subject calls through. Voice verification is based on biometrics which measures distinctive characteristics derived from spoken phrases. These characteristics are based on the physiology of the vocal tract combined with unique behavioural aspects of speaking to enable verification of the identity of the person who is speaking (G4S 2017).

Sobriety Tags

A different form of electronic monitoring is provided by tags that can monitor a person's blood-alcohol levels. These so-called Sobriety Tags are used on people who have committed crime where alcohol consumption was an element of the offence or contributed to the commission of the offence; they are generally not used on people with severe alcohol problems. This included offences such as common assault, actual bodily harm, grievous bodily harm, affray and violent disorder. The person concerned can be regularly tested, via a transdermal alcohol monitoring device in the form of a 'tag' fitted around the ankle, which detects consumption of alcohol through sweat. The tags are said to be bulkier and more obvious than the standard electronic tag.

The idea was first put forward in the Government's *Alcohol Strategy* published on 23 March 2012 (Home Office 2012b: paras. 319–20) and in the consultation paper *Punishment and Reform: Effective Community Sentences* also published in March 2012 (MoJ 2012). The proposed Alcohol Abstinence and Monitoring Requirement (AAMR) also known as 'sobriety tags' was to be available as part of Police Conditional Cautions or Community or Suspended Sentence Orders made in court.

The consultation paper spelt out the new intervention which was based on an idea from South Dakota, the USA:

the Government is taking forward provisions in the Legal Aid, Sentencing and Punishment of Offenders Bill to give courts a new power to impose an Alcohol Abstinence and Monitoring Requirement as part of a community or suspended sentence order on an offender who has committed an alcohol-related offence.

Under the new requirement:

- Offenders will be required to abstain from drinking for a period specified by the court (up to 120 days).
- They will either be required to attend a police station or test centre to be monitored by breathalyser equipment or to wear an alcohol tag around their ankle. We are in the process of testing alcohol tagging technology for this purpose.
- The test for imposing a requirement would be a link between alcohol consumption and the offending behaviour (MoJ 2012: paras. 178–9).

The AAMR duly appeared in the Legal Aid, Sentencing and Punishment of Offenders Act 2012 s76, which inserted a new s212A into the Criminal Justice Act 2003. The offender was not to be completely dependent on alcohol but the consumption of alcohol was to be an element of the offence or contributed to the commission of the offence for which the order was to be imposed and that monitoring by electronic means or by other means of testing was in place. The AAMR was to last a maximum of 120 days. Arrangements for trials and pilot schemes were made (Home Office 2013e).

Northamptonshire Police trialled the use of sobriety bracelets as part of Police Conditional Cautions with generally positive results (Northamptonshire Police 2014). In London, an evaluation of the trials in four south London boroughs (Croydon, Lambeth, Southwark and Sutton) found that offenders were largely unhappy about the appearance and 'wearability' of the alcohol tag. Many felt that the tag was bulky and not comfortable to wear, and some felt it disturbed their sleep and limited their clothing choices; concerns were also expressed about not being able to bath while wearing it.

Some National Probation Service/Community Rehabilitation Companies and judiciary interviewees and survey respondents also saw this as a negative of the AAMR, raising health and safety concerns for offenders with an active or very visible job or lifestyle wearing the tag. (Pepper and Dawson 2016: 6)

The AAMR scheme was rolled out across London in February 2016 with the:

MOJ [Ministry of Justice] … contributing £400,000 towards the cost of extending the scheme past its initial four pilot boroughs to the whole of the capital from April 2016. The initiative will be run by the London Mayor's Office for Policing and Crime (MOPAC), which is contributing £450,000 to the extension. (MoJ 2016f)

Summary

It is only possible here to give a flavour of life in prison or on a community sentence and the extent to which matters of privacy are impacted. All entrants to prison have records opened up on them and have their photograph taken. Prisoners may have DNA samples taken from non-intimate body samples, using reasonable force if necessary, and officers use various techniques of control and restraint to maintain order in prisons. It should be noted that Article 8 of the European Convention has been interpreted as protecting not just privacy but the right to physical integrity and is capable of protecting individuals against forms of involuntary ill-treatment (*Storck v Germany 16 September 2005 ECHR Application no. 61603/00 para. 143*). As a general point, we might add that electronic monitoring in particular, for all its invasion of privacy, and the stigma-inducing visibility of the tag, does provide a more economic and 'normal' existence for the wearer compared to a custodial sentence in prison.

9

Counterterrorism

Introduction

The widely held notion is that the 2001 terrorist attacks in the USA 'changed the world' (see, e.g., Chomsky 2016; Stohl 2008b). Terrorism has long been used as a tool of political violence since the nineteenth-century European revolutions (Bloss 2009), but 9/11 marked a rapid shift to a new national security-focused era in which Islamic terrorism was perceived as an immediate threat to national security and public safety. The then Prime Minister Tony Blair declared that the UK was 'at war with terrorism' (BBC 2001). This led to the introduction of multiple and wide-ranging anti-terrorism legislation in the UK, further expedited by the 2005 attacks in London and post-9/11 terror attacks around the world. UK security agencies deem terrorism the most immediate threat to the UK (see, e.g., HMG 2016b). The validity of such threats cannot be fully addressed here, but this chapter explores counterterrorism policy in the UK and issues for the privacy and liberty rights of citizens.

© The Author(s) 2017
D. Marshall, T. Thomas, *Privacy and Criminal Justice*,
https://doi.org/10.1007/978-3-319-64912-2_9

Terrorism

Terrorism is not unique to contemporary societies and the term can be found dating back to the eighteenth century (Lacquer 1987). In modern times, there has been a shift from domestic or localised terrorism, such as that experienced in the UK with the troubles in Northern Ireland since 1969 (for an overview see O'Leary and McGarry 2016) to the 'new international terrorism' typified by extremist Islamic fundamentalist groups such as al Qaeda and Daesh (see HM Government 2016a; Lacquer 2000; Morgan 2004). Daesh is currently identified as the predominant terrorist threat to the UK and overseas interests (HM Government 2016a), and the seriousness of the threat can be seen in the mass deaths from attacks in Belgium, France, Germany, Tunisia and Turkey during 2015 and 2016 (Yourish et al. 2016).

Bobbit (2002) asserts that this shift to a more global terrorism will lead to a fundamental reworking of the state; this appears to have been the case in the UK since 2000. Stohl (2008a) has further argued that developments in information technology have enabled some terrorist organisations to communicate between secure cells on a global scale, presenting new challenges to the non-terrorist states to work collaboratively to combat this. The declared *war on terror* presents further issues of defining what exactly *terrorism* is (for further discussion of state terrorism and violence see Chomsky 2016; Stohl 2008a, b).

The definition of *terrorism* remains the subject of continuing international debate; there is no universally accepted definition. The UK statutory definition of *terrorism* has been criticised for its 'dangerous' and 'excessive breadth' (see, e.g., Liberty 2016c; Anderson 2016a). The Terrorism Act 2000 provides a definition—subsequently updated by the Terrorism Act 2006 and the Counter-Terrorism Act 2008—which applies to the use or threat of action 'made for the purpose of advancing a political, religious, racial or ideological cause … designed to influence the government or an international governmental organisation or to intimidate the public or a section of the public' anywhere in the world (Terrorism Act 2006 s1). *Action* is defined as involving:

> serious violence against a person, serious damage to property, endangers a person's life, other than that of the person committing the action, creates a

serious risk to the health or safety of the public or a section of the public, or is designed seriously to interfere with or seriously to disrupt an electronic system. (Terrorism Act 2006 s.1)

All subsequent powers for the police and courts flow from this definition, and the broad scope of the definition encompasses many offences, opening the potential for large numbers of people to be criminalised.

In the case of *R v Gul* (2013), Lord Neuberger and Lord Judge asserted that 'the definition of terrorism in section 1 in the 2000 Act is, at least if read in its natural sense, very far reaching indeed'. In January 2016, the Court of Appeal gave judgement in the case of David Miranda. Miranda, the spouse of Glen Greenwald—one of the journalists to break the NSA leaks by Edward Snowden in 2013 (see Chap. 4 of this book)—was stopped by officers of the Metropolitan Police on 18 August 2013 at Heathrow Airport under the Terrorist Act 2000 Schedule 7. Miranda was in possession of encrypted material, taken from the NSA by Snowden, which he was carrying from Berlin to Rio de Janeiro via the UK allegedly to assist in the journalistic activity of Greenwald. As in *R v Gul*, the Court of Appeal held that the power had been used for a lawful purpose. But, it rejected the interpretation of the word 'terrorism', reinterpreting and trimming the scope of the definition, which the court said, on its literal interpretation, 'involves according to the word "terrorism" a meaning which is far removed from its ordinary meaning' and 'potentially gives rise to unpalatable consequences' (*R (Miranda) v Secretary of State for the Home Department and Commissioner for the Metropolitan Police* [2016] EWCA 6).

In an independent review[1] of terrorism laws in 2013, QC David Anderson warned against 'excessive breadth', recommending changes to the definition to narrow the focus. He repeated this call in his annual reports through to the most recent in 2016 (Anderson 2016a). In response to the *Miranda* Court of Appeal judgement, Anderson welcomed the changes proposed but cautioned against the limited interpretation by the Court which still left the possibility that 'campaigning journalism with a religious, political or ideological purpose may class as terrorism, with all the ancillary consequences that this could imply'(ibid.:25 4.5). In November 2016 Home Secretary Amber Rudd responded to Anderson's review:

Having given this matter consideration in the light of developments over the last year, and of the judgment handed down by the Court of Appeal on 19 January 2016 in *Miranda*, I maintain the view that it would not be appropriate to make changes to the statutory definition at this stage. The complexity and fluidity of the terrorist threat, and its ability to evolve and diversify at great speed, demonstrate the importance of having a flexible statutory framework – with appropriate safeguards – to ensure that the law enforcement and intelligence agencies can continue to protect the public. (HMG 2016b: 6)

The statutory definition remains broad in scope and there remains no agreed-upon international definition; this arguably provides a wider net for intrusion of privacy and less concern shown for civil liberties. Since 2000, there have been numerous terrorism laws introduced in the UK. Ignatieff (2002) refers to the Roman adage to justify measures for emergency procedures; *salus populi primus lex*—the safety of the people is the ultimate law:

In these circumstances, law itself should be no barrier to the ultimate safety of the people. In the name of that principle, the UK (and other societies faced with terrorist threats) have curtailed rights to political participation. Groups that do not dissociate themselves from terrorist activity are not allowed to compete for votes or hold office. People suspected of association with terrorist organizations may be interned or held without trial. These abridgements of rights may appear justified by *salus populi primus lex*, but they conflict with the idea that rights are either unconditional or they are worthless. (Ignatieff 2002:1144)

Countering Terrorism

Human rights law requires that the State protect the right to life, including measures to prevent terrorism. Important factors in counterterrorism efforts have been identified as the rights to freedom of speech and thought, freedom of action, non-self-incrimination, privacy, life and rights not to be tortured (Miller 2009). The protection of privacy and liberty is also a key requirement under the ECHR and human rights law in the UK; it is the perceived violation of these rights which attracts criticism of counter-terrorism legislation (for a detailed discussion of civil liberties and human rights, see Stone 2014). Safeguarding human rights is shown to characterise ethical and effective counterterrorism (Walsh and Piazza 2010; Jones 2012). The key elements of legislation introduced in the UK since 2000 are now explored further.

Countering Terrorism Before the '9/11' Attacks on New York

In 1996, Lord Lloyd of Berwick led an inquiry to advise the government on the need for permanent terrorist legislation, following the Irish Republican Army (IRA) ceasefire, to replace the temporary statutes which had been subject to annual parliamentary renewal since 1974: the Prevention of Terrorism (Temporary Provisions) Act 1989, the Northern Ireland (Emergency Provisions) Act 1996 and parts of the Criminal Justice (Terrorism and Conspiracy) Act 1998. The report advised that despite the ceasefire, a permanent anti-terrorism law was needed (Berwick Report 1996).

The Terrorism Act 2000 was the first permanent counterterrorist legislation in the UK 'to make provision about terrorism; and to make temporary provision for Northern Ireland about the prosecution and punishment of certain offences, the preservation of peace and the maintenance of order' (Terrorism Act 2000: Introductory Text). As previously discussed, the 2000 Act included a broad definition of terrorism—to apply to domestic and international terrorism and terrorism related to Northern Ireland—which has been widely criticised.

One effect of this wide definition was the alleged overuse of stop and search powers in section 44 of the Terrorism Act 2000. This resulted in it being disproportionately used against peaceful protesters and ethnic minority groups (Liberty 2016d; see Chap. 3 of this book). In 2009/2010, there were 101,248 stop and searches under section 44 resulting in 506 arrests representing 0.5% (or 1/200) of section 44 stop and searches (Home Office 2010). Of all terrorism-related stops in 2009/2010 (which included using the Terrorism Act 2000, Anti-Terrorism Crime and Security Act 2001, Prevention of Terrorism Act

2005 and the Terrorism Act 2006), 173 terrorism arrests were made, resulting in 12 charges (7% of arrests) under terrorism legislation. This suggests that the use of stop and search for terrorism-related offences was overly intrusive to individual privacy—93% resulting in no charge. This suggestion was further confirmed when the ECHR ruled that section 44 violated Article 8 of the ECHR (*Gillan and Quinton v UK (application no. 4158/05)* 2010).

In May 2012, section 44 was repealed and replaced the Act with section 47A by the Protection of Freedoms Act—an improvement welcomed by civil liberties groups which 'allows a senior police officer to authorise an area for stop and search without suspicion in a specified area where she or he reasonably suspects an act of terrorism is about to occur. With tougher time limits and other safeguards aiming to ensure the power is only used in genuine emergencies' (Liberty 2016d).

Another power in the Terrorism Act 2000 criticised for being too broad and intrusive is that contained in Schedule 7 of the Act, which allows a constable, immigration or customs officer to stop, search and detain individuals at ports, airports and international rail stations. In addition, without reasonable suspicion, the police (at a police station) can take DNA and biometric data of anyone entering or leaving the UK and remove and download the contents of the individual's mobile phone to determine whether they are 'used in the commission, preparation or instigation of acts of terrorism' (Schedule 7 (9)(1)). Officers can detain the person and question them for up to nine hours and retain their belongings for up to seven days. The person commits an offence if they wilfully obstruct the exercise of the functions under Schedule 7. While limited in geographical terms, Schedule 7 has been criticised for being a more intrusive power than the repealed section 44 of the Terrorism Act 2000 (see Liberty 2016e). In addition, due to its broad definition, Schedule 7 could be used in a discriminatory fashion, potentially based on stereotype rather than genuine suspicion.

Statistics from 2010–2016 suggest that those who self-define as Asian were proportionately more likely to be examined under Schedule 7 (Anderson 2016a). The international travelling public is not the same as the general population of the UK, so it is difficult to draw strong conclusions from these statistics alone about discriminatory practice. Hurrell (2013) conducted an experimental analysis of examinations and detentions under Schedule 7 and found that black and Asian or other ethnic groups experienced high levels of race disproportionality in 2010/2011, particularly Pakistani people. This data further showed that while only 1 in 25 of total examinations took over one hour, those self-defined as Asian or other formed 65.2% of these examinations and detentions. In addition, the main increase over time was the percentage of people with ethnicity 'not stated'. Hurrell suggests a four-fold increase between 2011/2012 (1.9%) and 2012/2013 (8.5%), which may account for the overall decrease in examinations of white people and Asian/Asian British people in the same time period, rather than there being genuine decreases. Hurrell's analysis support the trends identified by Anderson (2016a).

Schedule 7 is not supposed to be a randomly applied power. If this was the case, the figures above would suggest strong unlawful discrimination. According to the Codes of Practice, officers using the power 'must be informed by the threat from terrorism to the United Kingdom and its interests posed by the various terrorist groups, networks and individuals active in, and outside the UK' and 'take into account considerations that relate to the threat of terrorism' (Home Office 2015h: 11) such as known or suspected current or past involvements in acts or threats of terrorism. While this provides guidance, it is broadly defined, and the potential for unnecessary and/or discriminatory intrusion of an individual or group's privacy remains.

Case Study

The case involving Faizah Shaheen highlights concerns of the use of Schedule 7 and its intrusion of privacy. Shaheen was travelling back home to the UK from Turkey on 25 July 2016. A *Thomson Airways* cabin-crew member had reported Shaheen for suspicious behaviour on her outbound flight two weeks earlier; this suspicious behaviour was that Shaheen was reading the book *Syria Speaks: Art and Culture* from the Frontline. On landing at Doncaster airport, police officers detained and questioned Shaheen for 15 minutes under Schedule 7; she was subsequently released without charge (Cain 2016).

Countering Terrorism After the '9/11' Attacks on New York 2011

Terrorism legislation had been overhauled by the Terrorism Act 2000, but a year, later the events of 9/11 in the USA prompted the government to again amend existing terrorism legislation. Emergency legislation—the Anti-Terrorism, Crime and Security Bill 2001—was introduced in parliament on 12 November 2001. The government issued a derogation from Article 5 of the ECHR (the right to liberty and security), provided by Article 15 (derogation in time of emergency). A Statutory Instrument (SI 2001/3644) contained the derogation and came into force on 13 November 2001 and the Act was implemented from 14 December 2001. Part 4 of the Act allowed for a foreign national suspected of involvement in terrorism to be imprisoned indefinitely without charge or trial or deported (if safe to do so, e.g., the person would not be tortured or killed if returned to their home country).

A challenge to this law was brought about in *A v Secretary of State for the Home Department [2004] UKHL 56* after a group of nine foreigners were detained at Belmarsh prison in London for almost three years. The nine men were each appointed a 'special advocate' that had access to the information held about them—seen only by the Home Secretary and the Special Immigration Appeals Commission (SIAC) which had initially reviewed the case—but not to the men themselves. The SIAC found that the powers were discriminatory (Article 14 ECHR), but this decision was reversed by the Court of Appeal taking account of the derogation from Article 5. The appeal was heard by a nine-member panel of the House of Lords on 16 December 2004, which held that detaining foreign terrorist suspects without trial was discriminatory and broke human rights laws. Lord Hoffman stated:

> The real threat to the life of the nation, in the sense of a people living in accordance with its traditional laws and political values, comes not from terrorism but from laws such as these. That is the true measure of what terrorism may achieve. It is for Parliament to decide whether to give the terrorists such a victory. (*A v Secretary of State for the Home Department*, para. 97.)

In response, the government repealed Part 4 of the 2001 Act and replaced it with a system of Control Orders in the Prevention of Terrorism Act 2005 (these have since been further replaced by Terrorism Prevention and Investigation Measures (TPIM) notices in 2011—discussed below).

Counterterrorism Strategy

In 2003, the UK Government established a strategy, in secret, for countering international terrorism, known as CONTEST; details of this cross-departmental government strategy were made public in 2006 (see HMG 2006a), forming part of the UK's *National Security Strategy* published for the first time in March 2008 (Cabinet Office 2008b). The aim of CONTEST is 'to reduce the risk to the UK and its interests overseas from terrorism so that people can go about their lives freely and with confidence' (HMG 2016a: 9). The strategy remains complex and multi-faceted, aiming to identify radicalised individuals and also challenge the violent extremist ideology through empowering resilient communities. In particular, targeting the perceived principal threat to the UK from radicalised individuals using 'a distorted and unrepresentative interpretation of the Islamic faith to justify violence' (HMG 2006a: 6), the programme sought to partner with Muslim organisations to support integration of British Muslims and challenge violent extremism.

CONTEST is organised around four strands, known as the '4Ps':

(1) *Pursue,* to stop terrorist attacks by reducing the terrorist threat to the UK and to UK interests overseas by disrupting terrorists and their operations;

(2) *Prevent,* to stop people from becoming terrorists or supporting violent extremism by tackling the radicalisation of individuals;

(3) *Protect,* to strengthen UK protection against terrorist attacks, reducing the vulnerability of the UK and UK interests overseas; and,

(4) *Prepare,* where an attack cannot be stopped, to mitigate its impact, ensuring that the UK is as ready as it can be for the consequences of a terrorist attack.

This '4P' structure remains in place almost 15 years since its creation. CONTEST has divided opinion. Some support this strategic approach to develop 'systematic processes to identify desirable and achievable ends and help all those concerned reach agreement on the strategic campaigns necessary to bring them about' (Omand 2005:107). Others have criticised the strategy for its disproportionate use towards Muslim communities (see Pantazis and Pemberton 2009; Ragazzi 2016) and as representing a move towards a surveillance state (see Nyst 2014; BBC News 2006). Criticism has also focused on the lack of analysis of CONTEST as a strategy; suggestions are that the strands of CONTEST appear underdeveloped or not as strategic as they are claimed to be (see Gearson and Rosemont 2015). In addition, the lack of access to government-held, primary data is claimed to have led to the stagnation of terrorism research and scholarly speculations with little empirical grounding (Sageman 2014).

The *Prevent* strand of CONTEST, for example, remained undeveloped until its formal introduction in 2007 by the then Labour government in response to the 7/7 bombings of July 2005 (DCLG 2007). Due to its failure to address the underlying issues of extremist ideology and perceived 'securitised integration', the Coalition government revised the strategy in 2011, formally separating the promotion of community cohesion and the prevention of terrorism (HMG 2011). There was suggestion that this separation was not possible and that the coalitions' revised strategy actually increased securitisation, as cohesion and prevention remained intertwined at the local level (Thomas 2012).

The Counter-Terrorism and Security Act 2015 placed *Prevent* on a statutory footing, requiring colleges, schools, prisons and councils to prevent terrorism. Previous narratives of the *Prevent* programme were embedded in community responsibility, whereas now it has become a legal obligation for a range of public sector institutions (Counter-Terrorism and Security Act 2015 s26 and Schedule 6).

Criticism of *Prevent* has highlighted concerns regarding individual privacy. In particular, the statutory requirement that frontline professionals report to—'Channel'—a police-coordinated, multi-agency partnership that focuses on providing support at an early stage to individuals at risk of being drawn into terrorism (including violent and non-violent *extremism*)—creates a serious risk of violations of the right to privacy (see HMG 2015). The processing of personal data (which could include an individual's name, address, date of birth and national insurance number) presents potential interference with the right to respect for private life of the data subject. In the case of *S. and Marper v. The UK*, the ECHR stated that:

> the protection of personal data is of fundamental importance to a person's enjoyment of his or her right to respect for private and family life, as guaranteed by article 8 of the Convention. The domestic law must afford appropriate safeguards to prevent any such use of personal data as may be inconsistent with the guarantees of this article. (*S. and Marper v. The UK 2008*, para. 103)

The requirements on public sector organisations to report to 'Channel' and the targeting of Muslim people raise concerns about the right to privacy regarding religion and philosophical conviction. The European Court observed in the case of *Folgerø and Others v. Norway*:

> that information about personal religious and philosophical conviction concerns some of the most intimate aspects of private life. It agrees with the Supreme Court that imposing an obligation on parents to disclose detailed information to the school authorities about their religions and philosophical convictions may constitute a violation of Article 8 of the Convention and, possibly also, of Article 9. (2007: para. 98)

Case Study

Criticisms of securitising integration and uncertainty of public institutions on what should be reported to 'Channel' were highlighted in the recent case of two brothers, aged five and seven, who were reported to the police, for being at risk of radicalisation, after one of them told his teacher he had been given a toy gun as a present (see Anonymous 2017). The police concluded there was no cause for concern, after the boys were kept apart from their mother for almost two hours while being questioned in March 2016. The local education authority admitted racially discriminating against the two boys, of mixed Indian and Middle Eastern heritage, and breaching their human rights (see Addley and Topping 2017).

The ECHR Article 8(2) protects the right to enjoy family relationships without interference by a public authority. Any interference, such as taking a child into care or restricting contact between parents and their children, must be in accordance with law, pursue a legitimate aim and be necessary in a democratic society (see *Olsson v. Sweden, [1988] ECHR 2*).

Figures released by the National Police Chiefs Council under the Freedom of Information Act revealed that 3955 people were referred to the 'Channel' programme in 2015, a rise of 235% from 2014 (1681 referrals) (see NPCC 2016a, b). These were the first figures released since the statutory duty was placed on public institutions to report to the Channel programme, suggesting an increased vigilance of public bodies in reporting individuals believed to be at risk of extremism (Halliday 2016).

The definition of *extremism* raises further concern. The 2011 Prevent strategy document defines extremism as:

> vocal or active opposition to fundamental British values, including democracy, the rule of law, individual liberty and mutual respect and tolerance of different faiths and beliefs. We also include in our definition of extremism calls for the death of members of our armed forces, whether in this country or overseas. (HMG 2011:107)

This definition is broad in scope. In particular, defining British values is problematic and raises concerns for freedom of speech in universities (see Garton Ash 2016b). In addition, some universities are warning students that their e-mails may be retained and monitored (Weale 2017). The consistent theme in counterterrorism legislation is that it undermines the principles of UK justice, innocent until proven guilty, and treating individuals as criminal suspects. The statutory obligations placed on public institutions may do more harm than good (see O'Toole et al. 2013; Versi 2016).

The 'Encouragement of Terrorism'

Other counterterrorism legislation has raised concerns about freedom of expression. Section one of the Terrorism Act 2006 introduced the offence of 'encouragement of terrorism'. This includes the glorification of terrorist acts (s. (1) (3)) and is punishable by up to seven years' imprisonment (s. (1) (7) (a)). The legislation is broadly worded, and it is an offence even if the individual or group making the statement did not intend to encourage terrorism. Given the broad definition of terrorism, discussed above, this encouragement of terrorism offence could criminalise anyone speaking out against any regime anywhere in the world. As human rights lawyer Geoffrey Bindman highlighted, this:

> becomes a very dangerous inroad on freedom of speech, because people may wish to express views about a repressive regime which may involve suggesting that ultimately it may be necessary to use violence to bring an end to that regime. (see Tempest 2006)

The United Nations Human Rights Committee also criticised this as too 'broad and vague', recommending that the government:

> should consider amending that part of section 1 of the Terrorism Act 2006 dealing with 'encouragement of terrorism' so that its application does not lead to a disproportionate interference with freedom of expression. (UNHRC 2008:7)

While freedom of expression caused concern for academics and universities, the Terrorism Act 2006 did not require that they monitor students' political activities or beliefs and 'police' campus extremism; nine years later, the Counter-Terrorism and Security Act 2015 did require that they monitor and report such activity (as discussed above).

Pre-charge Detention

Pre-charge detention is the period that a person can be detained by the police between being arrested and being either charged with a criminal offence or released. Powers of arrest and detention for people suspected of direct involvement in criminal activity are covered by PACE 1984 Code C with a maximum detention without charge limit of 96 hours (see Chap. 3 of this book). Under anti-terror laws a person can be detained without charge for up to 14 days beyond an initial period of 48 hours

(Terrorism Act 2000 s.41; 36(3)(b)(ii) of Schedule 8; Home Office 2017c).

The initial period of detention without charge was fixed at 7 days but was increased to 14 days by the Criminal Justice Act 2003. Following the London bombings on 7 July 2005, the government (on the advice of the police) sought to extend the pre-charge detention period to 90 days; this was defeated in the Commons but extended to 28 days by the Terrorism Act 2006 s.23(7) (see BBC News 2005). Despite this 28-day detention period rarely being used, in 2008, the government was defeated in a further attempt to extend the detention limit to 42 days as part of the Counter Terrorism Bill 2008 (see Watt 2008b). In 2011, the Coalition government did not renew the extension to 28-day limit, and the order lapsed on 25 January 2011 reverting to a 14-day pre-charge detention limit (Horne and Berman 2012). The 14-day limit still leaves a significant difference between the most serious non-terrorist offences (4 days) and terrorism offences (14 days) and remains the longest period of pre-charge detention of any comparable democracy (e.g., in the USA and Germany, the limit is 2 days; see Liberty 2010b).

In addition, it is possible for a person to be detained and questioned if they have information about an offence but without direct involvement in that offence (Terrorism Act 2000 s.19). This raises serious implications for issues of privacy and civil liberty rights, undermining the UK's democratic principles of justice, fairness and equality. There is clear interference with Article 8 ECHR, the right to a private life, and intrusion on personal privacy without any charges being brought against the person.

Other Anti-Terrorism Laws

The Prevention of Terrorism Act 2005

The Prevention of Terrorism Act 2005 introduced derogating and non-derogating Control Orders, with only the latter ever being used (Stone 2014). Due to the speed and controversial nature of the Prevention of Terrorism Act 2005, the government agreed that Control Orders would automatically lapse after one year unless renewed through a vote in parliament each year. Control Orders—civil orders made by the Home Secretary—were less intrusive to human rights than indefinite detention but placed very real constraints on an individual's freedom of movement, interaction with others, and in the life of society such as house arrest, electronic tagging, rules about who the accused could contact and curfews. As with indefinite detention, this power was exercised outside of the criminal justice system and without due attention to the principles of justice in the UK. There was no requirement for a trial and the accused and their lawyers had no right to see or rebut the evidence against them—security-cleared advocates would represent their interests.

Fifty-two Control Orders were imposed upon men suspected of terrorism-related activity between 2005 and 2011 (Anderson 2013). Twenty-four had British Citizenship and 23 out of the 52 were involuntarily relocated to different parts of the UK at the Home Secretary's choosing and were subject to additional restrictions on their movements, communications and association (ibid.).

There were multiple cases challenging the extent of these powers. In *Secretary of State for the Home Department v JJ* [2007] UKHL 45, [2007] 3 WLR 642, the Law Lords quashed the non-derogating Control Orders of six individuals, who were not allowed to leave their respective one-bedroomed flats save for a period between 10 am and 4 pm, as they were deprived of their liberty as guaranteed by Article 5 ECHR. In a very intrusive order to personal privacy, in the *Secretary of State for the Home Department v GG* [2009] EWCA Civ 786, the Court of Appeal held that a power contained in a Control Order which made the subject of it liable to personal searches, including intimate searches, whenever requested by the police, went beyond what was permitted by s. 1(3) of the Prevention of Terrorism Act 2005. This was:

> insufficient to authorise the inclusion in a control order of a general requirement to submit to searches of the person, whether on the demand of anyone authorised by the Home Secretary or only of a police officer. (*Secretary of State for the Home Department v GG* para. 22)

The issue of Article 6 ECHR, the right to a fair trial, was raised in *Secretary of State for the Home Department v AF* [2009] UKHL 28. The

House of Lords ruled that the Control Order was incompatible with Article 6 due to the individual and his legal team not having access to some of the evidence and the use of special advocates to represent the accused in a closed hearing. Drawing heavily on *A v United Kingdom* (2009) 49 EHRR 29—in which the ECHR had ruled on the case of indefinite detention under the Anti-Terrorism, Crime and Security Act 2001 as discussed above—the Lords followed this approach when ruling on Control Orders that each case should be reconsidered on an individual basis.

The Coalition government in 2010 committed itself to reviewing counterterror laws and abolishing Control Orders. They renewed Control Orders in March 2011 but replaced them in the TPIM 2011. For two moving accounts of what life is like under a Control Order, see Liberty (2010c) *The story of Cerie Bullivant* and Al Jnidi (2009) *Life with a control order: a wife's story.*

The Counter-Terrorism Act 2008

Part 4 of the Counter-Terrorism Act 2008 introduced notification requirements for people convicted of terrorism offences from 1 October 2009. This register, maintained by the police in a similar way to the sex offender register (see Chap. 10), required convicted terrorists who had served custodial sentences of over 12 months to provide personal details to the police, such as date of birth, national insurance number, change of home address (s47(2)) and to report foreign travel plans (s52). These notification requirements are required between 10 and 30 years, depending on the sentences received (s.53). Schedule five of the Act allowed for Foreign Travel Restriction Orders, which prohibit the person from travelling. These orders must be made applied for by a chief officer of police (Schedule 5 3 (1)) to a magistrate's court (Schedule 5 3 (3)). Guidance emphasises the need to get information to the offender manager in the case:

> because of Part 4 Terrorism Notification Requirements, offenders will be required to notify the police of their address on release and of any subse-

quent changes of address or travel plans. In these cases, the police must ensure that they provide this information to the Offender Manager. Such cases should be recorded on ViSOR. The Police are responsible for the management of the record during sentence, licence and beyond. (NOMS 2012a, b: para. 24.19)

There has been one attempt to challenge these requirements as a breach of Article 8 of the ECHR (right to respect for family and private life). In October 2012, the Court of Appeal dismissed the appeal and upheld an earlier finding of the High Court that the notification requirements do not constitute a disproportionate interference with Article 8. The Court concluded that terrorism offences by their nature fall into a special category of offences and that the requirements constitute a 'relatively modest intrusion', which cannot be said to be disproportionate. The appellant sought permission to appeal his case to the Supreme Court but permission was refused (*R, on the application of Mohamed Irfan v The Secretary of State for the Home Department [2012] EWCA Civ 1471*).

The purpose of the requirements is said to be:

- to provide information about the whereabouts and identities of individuals who have been convicted of terrorist crimes, providing a helpful tool to the police in managing the risks that they may pose to public safety;
- to allow the police to maintain accurate records of individuals who have been convicted of terrorism and terrorism-related offences; and
- to play a part in deterring convicted terrorists from reoffending and ensuring that the police have accurate and up-to-date information to assist with terrorism investigations (Home Office 2014g: para. 8.10.4).

As on 30 September 2013, 58 individuals were required to comply with the Part 4 requirements and to date no one has been prosecuted for non-compliance. There have been minor problems in a few cases but they have been dealt with without recourse to the courts. 'In each case, soon after the alleged breach, the police have been able to contact the subject and seek an explanation' (ibid.: para. 8.10.5).

The Terrorist Asset-Freezing Act 2010

Similar to Control Orders and TPIMs (see below), the Terrorist Asset-Freezing Act 2010 provided powers which could be applied to people who had never been convicted of any offence, allowing the Treasury to freeze the assets of anyone it suspected or believed was involved in terrorism. This would prevent a person and their family having access to their finances, essentially 'financial imprisonment'. The Act provided powers to government, not the courts, operating independently of the criminal justice system, raising further issues of the undermining of the principles of justice in the UK and potential unnecessary intrusion of personal and information privacy and the right to a private and family life.

The Terrorism Prevention and Investigation Measures Notices Act 2011

The TPIM 2011 finally abolished Control Orders and replaced them with TPIMs. TPIM notices have been described as 'control order-lite' and replicating the worst aspects of the Control Order regime (Liberty 2016f), providing only limited improvement on the original Control Orders. They allow for similar restrictions as Control Orders under more limited conditions, usually needing permission from a court (Stone 2014). The Home Secretary initiates TPIM notices and the system retains much of the same controls, such as electronic tagging and curfews and restricting movement and association; Schedule 1 of the Act states the restrictions which can be imposed.

The time limit of a TPIM notice is one year, which can be extended only once to a total of two years (s.5); any subsequent notice must be based on new evidence. The Home Secretary must be satisfied that five conditions (from A to E) are met before issuing a TPIM notice:

A. the Secretary of State reasonably believes that the individual is, or has been, involved in terrorism-related activity—broadly defined in s. 4—(the 'relevant activity').

B. some or all of the relevant activity is new terrorism-related activity. 'New' here means since the most recent TPIM notice issued against the individual or if there has been no notice.

C. the Secretary of State reasonably considers that it is necessary, for purposes connected with protecting members of the public from a risk of terrorism, for TPIM to be imposed on the individual.

D. the Secretary of State reasonably considers that it is necessary, for purposes connected with preventing or restricting the individual's involvement in terrorism-related activity, for the specified TPIM to be imposed on the individual.

E. either the court gives the Secretary of State permission under section 6 or the Secretary of State reasonably considers that the urgency of the case requires TPIM to be imposed without obtaining such permission. (Terrorism Prevention and Investigation Measures Notices Act 2011 s.3)

Section 6 states the prior permission of the court, which must quash the notice if conditions A–C are not met (s.6(7)) and may give directions to the Home Secretary in relation to the measures to be imposed on the individual (s.6(9)).

TPIMs are part of the state's attempt to provide its statutory obligation to protect the right to life of its citizens, including measures to prevent terrorism. But, if an individual is suspected of being a terrorist and there is sufficient evidence to support this, the individual should arguably be charged and detained securely by way of protection to the public and to provide a fair and open trial for the individual, adhering to the principles of UK justice, within the criminal justice system. Anonymity orders have been provided to the individual's subject to TPIMs except in two cases where the individuals absconded. Herein lies an important lack of safeguards. The lack of secure detention means that potentially dangerous terrorists could escape, as in the cases of Ibrahim Magag (Malik 2013) and Mohammed Mohamed (Doyle 2013), and pose a threat to the public.

In addition, if there is insufficient evidence to charge and convict an individual suspected of terrorism, then TPIMs—operating outside of the criminal justice system—are a significant intrusion on the privacy of the individual and potential associates of the individual, placing dehumanising sanctions on people based on suspicion rather than evidence, further reversing the UK principle of justice—innocent until proven guilty.

In 2014, the House of Commons Joint Committee on Human Rights stated that TPIMs appeared to be 'withering on the vine as a counterterrorism tool of practical utility' (House of Lords/House of Commons 2014: 25) in response to only eight TPIM notices being in force as of 30 November 2013; these were all British citizens. Only ten had been made in total since TPIMs were introduced—nine were transferred from Control Orders—and all had now lapsed (Anderson 2014). No new TPIMs were imposed between 2012 and 2014, until mid-2014 when one new TPIM was in force (Anderson 2015b). As of 31 May 2016, only one TPIM was in force (*Hansard House of Commons 14 July 2016 WS 92*). As Anderson (2016a) has stated, the use of TPIMs has been modest, but this should not justify the intrusive powers they provide.

The Counter-Terrorism and Security Act 2015

At the time of writing (May 2017), the most recent counterterrorism legislation is the Counter Terrorism and Security Act 2015. Section 16 of this Act reintroduced *involuntary relocation* which had been removed by the TPIM Notices Act 2011. This allows the Home Secretary to order individuals subject to a TPIM notice to move to a new specified location. Previously viewed as the most draconian part of the Control Order regime, involuntary relocation or *internal exile* has been criticised. In 2010 the Joint Parliamentary Committee on Human Rights were 'alarmed' at the increasing use of relocation in which 'British citizens who have grown up in a particular community [had] to uproot themselves from that community and move to a new and unfamiliar location' and the subsequent effects on individuals and their families who were 'treated with contempt'. Giving evidence to the committee, Human Rights solicitor Gareth Peirce said 'this may affect only a small group of people but in terms of its contribution to what one might call the folklore of injustice it is colossal' (House of Lords/House of Commons 2010: para. 41).

Nonetheless, the Counter-Terrorism and Security Act 2015 reintroduced the measures, with the requirement of a higher standards of proof, amending TPIM Measures Notices Act 2011 s3 (1) from 'reasonably believes' to 'is satisfied, on the balance of probabilities'. In addition, the Counter-Terrorism and Security Act 2015 doubled the penalty of a person subject to a TPIM breaching a travel ban by leaving the specified area from five to ten years' imprisonment (Counter-Terrorism and Security Act 2015 s.17(4)).

Temporary Exclusion Orders (s.2) were also introduced by the Counter-Terrorism and Security Act 2015, under which suspected terrorists with British passports can be excluded from entering the UK for two years (s.2(4)). Similar to previous counterterrorism legislation, these orders can be signed off by the Home Secretary on the basis of 'reasonable suspicion of involvement in terrorist activity'. The individual may return to the UK under controlled conditions imposed by the Secretary of State (s.2 (9)). Non-compliance with these obligations is punishable by up to five years in prison (s.2 (10)).

Schedule One of the Counter-Terrorism and Security Act 2015 provided new powers for police or border officials to temporarily confiscate the passports of suspected terrorists on the spot. Previously, the Home Secretary had to personally authorise this. Passports can be held for 14 days (Schedule one (5) (3)) which can be extended up to a maximum of 30 days with judicial authority (Schedule one (8) (7)). As with previous counterterrorism legislation, this is broadly defined and could result in unnecessary intrusion of personal privacy and disproportionate ethnic profiling similar to that of stop and search laws (see *Gillan and Quinton v UK (application no. 4158/05)*—discussed in Chap. 3) and the use of pre-charge detention discussed above.

The Counter-Terrorism and Security Act 2015 (s. 21) further contained data retention measures which obliged internet and mobile phone service providers to retain information to be handed over to the authorities on request, allowing the security services to match specific IP addresses to individual computers. This was repealed by the Investigatory Powers Act 2016 which consolidated and updated the existing law on the interception of communications (discussed in Chap. 4).

The Counter-Terrorism and Security Act 2015 also placed an obligation on airlines to disclose advance passenger data; failure to do so could
result in landing rights being denied. These data retention powers have
been criticised for mirroring the blanket powers sought under the DRIPA
2014 (Liberty 2016g), which were ruled unlawful and in violation of
privacy rights in 2014 by the ECJ *(Digital Rights Ireland (C-293/12) and
Seitlinger and Others (C-594/12))* and again in 2015 by the High Court
(*Davis and Watson v Secretary of State for the Home Department [2015]
EWHC 2092 (Admin)*; for more on DRIPA see Chap. 4).

Section 46 of the Act allowed the Secretary of State to establish a
Privacy and Civil Liberties Board (PCLB) to assist the Independent
Reviewer of Terrorism Legislation in 'the discharge of their functions'
(s.24 (1)). The Conservative government elected in May 2015 decided
not to establish the PCLB but instead to make an annual £50,000 available to fund research and assistance; three special advisors were subsequently appointed (Anderson 2016b).

The Counter-Terrorism and Security Act 2015 provided further
restrictions to the already broad and intrusive counterterrorism powers
available. The prevention of travel and reintroduction of involuntary
relocation presented enhanced interference with the rights of those subjected to the powers, in particular the increased potential for intrusion to
personal and information privacy and the right to a private and family
life.

Summary

The introduction of UK counterterrorism legislation since the 9/11 terror attacks in New York has been vast and wide ranging. Counterterrorism
remains high on the political agenda, presenting significant challenges for
the privacy and liberty of citizens. The legal definition is broad and far
reaching—notwithstanding the legal duty of government to protect the
right to life—and this broad definition combined with numerous legislation have cast a wide net to intrude upon the privacy of individuals who
have not committed any offences. Indeed, the Human Rights Act 1998,
which provides this legal protection, divides opinion over its power to

protect the privacy rights and civil liberties of individuals, often used as justification to attack civil liberties. It has not been possible to assess the validity of the threat posed by terrorism in this chapter, but few would disagree that there is a real threat to be countered; the methods adopted by the government to achieve this remain contentious.

Notes

1. Commonly referred to as 'Independent Reviewer'; this role is appointed and renewed by the Home Secretary and funded by government (see Prevention of Terrorism Act 2005, sections 14(2) and 14(7) and https:// terrorismlegislationreviewer.independent.gov.uk/about-me/)

10

Rehabilitation After Punishment

Introduction

The difficulties of defining privacy are clearly manifest in looking at how information on the people who have completed sentences is used. On the one hand, there are restrictions on the disclosure of this personal information in the interests of helping people rehabilitate themselves in the community but on the other hand it is distributed relatively freely in the interests of crime prevention, public protection and employment screening. This chapter is divided into these two competing ways of looking at information and rehabilitation.

Restrictions on Disclosing Personal Information

Most punishments are time restricted. Prisoners talk about 'doing time' and moralists exhort us all: 'don't do the crime if you can't do the time'. Custodial sentences are for a given length of time. Periods of probation supervision are determined by reference to time. Punishments have a beginning and an end. In practice, the exact location of the end point of

© The Author(s) 2017
D. Marshall, T. Thomas, *Privacy and Criminal Justice*,
https://doi.org/10.1007/978-3-319-64912-2_10

punishment is not so easily defined and time periods of resettlement or rehabilitation are built into finding that point in time when punishment ends. It is within this grey area of time that attempts have been made to offer some privacy to the person whose punishment has ended to enable them to fully rejoin the civic society they were denied for the time of their punishment.

The Rehabilitation of Offenders Act 1974

One of the major obstacles to former offenders gaining employment has been the existence of a criminal record that lasts way beyond the end of any time period of punishment. The original UK arguments for restricting knowledge of criminal records to assist the former offender are to be found in the Gardiner Report. The proposal was made that people with less serious criminal convictions and who had not reoffended could regard their record as having been 'spent' after a given period of time. The time periods would be 5 years for a community sentence, 7 years for a custodial sentence of less than 6 months and 10 years for a custodial sentence up to 24 months; these time periods would be halved for juveniles. After the prescribed time and with no further offending, the person with the record could 'legally lie' about that record's existence and say they had no record to increase their chances of employment or insurance applications (Gardiner Report 1972).

The resulting Rehabilitation of Offenders Act 1974 adopted these proposals but with the qualifying length of custodial sentence being raised from 24 months to 30 months before the privacy conditions were allowed to fall. The criminal record is not literally expunged by the police, who hold all the records on the PNC, and a criminal record could still be revealed if the person was ever in court again or if the employment sought was designated as an 'exempted' or 'excepted' occupation. These 'exemptions'—or 'exceptions'—were initially listed in the Rehabilitation of Offenders Act 1974 (Exceptions) Order 1975 SI 1975/1023. Over the following years, the list of 'exceptions' grew steadily as more and more employers claimed that they could not allow job applicants to withhold any information on their criminal convictions.

The 1974 Act was implemented from 1 July 1975. The growing number of exceptions—and the possibility of new offending occurring during a rehabilitation period—soon made it quite difficult to follow the provisions of the Rehabilitation of Offenders Act. Critics said the 30-months condition was too short and the time periods before a record was 'spent' could also be shortened. One unintended consequence of the Act was that it drew attention to criminal records and employment in a more direct way than had been the case in the past (Breed 1987: 52).

Amidst continuing criticism (see, e.g., Haskins Report 1999; SEU 2002) the government completed a review of the 1974 Act in July 2002. The review proposed replacing the existing 'rehabilitation periods' with new time periods—to be known as 'disclosure periods'—based on the length of sentence plus a so-called buffer period (Home Office 2002). There was overall agreement with the proposals with some differences of opinion on individual points (Home Office 2003). The 1974 Act has now been amended, with changes to the rehabilitation periods described in Table 10.1 (for details of the changes, see the Legal Aid, Sentencing and Punishment of Offenders Act 2012: Chap. 8); the amended 1974 Act was implemented from 10 March 2014 (MoJ 2014).

The campaign group Unlock has devised the Disclosure Calculator which is a web tool that can be used to find out when a criminal record becomes spent under the Rehabilitation of Offenders Act; it operates using the rehabilitation periods as they apply in England and Wales (Unlock 2017).

Despite the criticisms of the Rehabilitation of Offenders Act, it did establish the principle that a veil of confidentiality and privacy could, in law, fall over information about old, less serious, criminal behaviour, in the interests of rehabilitation.

Anonymity to Assist Rehabilitation

Having established this principal of confidentiality and information privacy for old criminal records with the 1974 Act, a school of thought has developed that some former prisoners might need a degree of more general anonymity to assist them with their successful rehabilitation back into the community.

Table 10.1 The 2012 review of the Rehabilitation of Offenders Act 1974

Under the reforms the rehabilitation periods will change to:
For custodial sentences:

Sentence length	Current rehabilitation period (applies from date of conviction)	New rehabilitation period is period of sentence plus the 'buffer' period below which applies from end of sentence)
0 - 6 months	7 years	2 years
6 - 30 months	10 years	4 years
30 months - 4 years	Never spent	7 years
Over 4 years	Never spent	Never spent

For non-custodial sentences:

Sentence	Current rehabilitation period (applies from date of conviction)	Buffer period (will apply from end of sentence)
Community order (& Youth Rehabilitation Order)	5 years	1 years

Sentence	Current period	New period
Fine	5 years	1 years (from date of conviction)
Absolute discharge	6 months	None
conditional discharge, referral order, reparation order, action plan order, supervision order, bind over order, hospital order	Various – mostly between one year and length of the Order	Period of order

As with the current scheme, the above periods are halved for persons under 18 at date of conviction (except for custodial sentences of up to 6 months where the buffer period will be 18 months for persons under 18 at the date of conviction).

For many years, it had been common practice that the press published photographs of high-profile offenders when they left prison. In February 2008, the High Court in Northern Ireland made a temporary injunction preventing the Belfast *Sunday Life* newspaper from publishing pictures of a convicted murderer—Kenneth Callaghan—on his day release from prison after 21 years ('Callaghan ruling could set dangerous precedent' *Belfast Telegraph* 11 February 2008). In January 2009, the High Court made the temporary injunction in the Callaghan case permanent (Sweney 2009).

The chief psychologist for the Northern Ireland Prison Service, Professor Jackie Gaston, told Belfast High Court that she believed:

it would be detrimental to efforts to discourage Callaghan from re-offending if he was publicly identified. She said there is evidence to suggest that public identification of a sex offender could encourage them to move house, leave employment or change their identity – which could increase the likelihood of them re-offending. (Smyth 2008)

Counsel for the newspaper group argued that it wished to publish the photographs so that members of the public could identify the former prisoner and were therefore enabled to take precautions in respect of the risk that he posed. They also argued that it was entitled to publish the photographs in the interests of freedom of expression as long as it did not publish the detailed location of where he was living.

The judge granted the injunction on the grounds of Callaghan's Article 8 privacy rights to protect him from harassment. The judge also ordered, at the request of the Northern Ireland Office, that nobody should publish any photograph which identified any serving prisoner who was being assessed at the unit without giving the Northern Ireland Office 48 hours' notice of intention to publish it (*Callaghan v Independent News and Media Ltd [2009] NIQB 1*; see also Ponsford 2009).

At about the same time in England, the West Yorkshire Police refused to release a photograph of Michael Scully to a local newspaper because it might hamper his subsequent monitoring and rehabilitation following custody. Scully had previously terrorised a neighbourhood in Halifax and left one housing worker with 'mental scars' from the threats he made (*Halifax Evening Courier* 2008).

The Divisional Commander in West Yorkshire explained that they would be managing this offender on his release and the local community needed to know the full picture:

To publish this man's face on the front of the *Courier* prior to his release, would, in my opinion, do nothing to persuade him to work with us. My officers have already met with him in advance of his release, to explain the program and his options. Remember, not only will he be released on licence but he is also subject of an Asbo – plenty for us to intrusively monitor and manage. (*Halifax Evening Courier* 2008)

Anonymity to 'Protect Life'

Other legal provisions have been made for people to have a veil of anonymity fall over their names and not just their criminal records. These arrangements have been there to protect the physical safety of the person who had been involved in serious and high-profile crime rather than just trying to improve their employment opportunities.

In 1968, Mary Bell was found guilty of the manslaughter of two small boys when she herself was aged just 11 years old; she is said to have strangled the boys, aged four and three, solely for the pleasure and excitement of killing. Mary Bell was released on licence in 1980 and given a new identity. Her case raised controversy again when her biography was published in 1998 and it emerged she had been paid for contributing to the book (Sereny 1998). When Bell's daughter reached 18 in May 2002, their right to anonymity could have been lifted, but the High Court granted them both life-long anonymity citing Article 8 of the ECHR, in May 2003, on the grounds they were entitled to a private and family life (*X, A Woman Formerly Known As Mary Bell -and-Y v Stephen O'brien -and- News Group Newspapers Ltd. -and- Mgn Ltd. [2003] EWHC 1101 (QB) 21 May 2003*).

Case

The identities and whereabouts of the two boys who murdered two-year-old James Bulger in 1993 are to be kept secret for the rest of their lives, the High Court ruled in 2001. Lawyers for Jon Venables and Robert Thompson—who were both aged 10 when they committed the murder—successfully argued that their anonymity should be protected by law after their release. The decision was based on fears that the boys would become victims of revenge and vigilante attacks if information about their new identities became known. As Lady Butler Sloss said in her judgement awarding the 'necessary' anonymity injunction, 'the claimants are uniquely notorious (and) their case is exceptional' (*Venables and Thompson v NG Newspapers Ltd., [2001] 1 WLR 1038*).

The *Manchester Evening News* was found guilty of contempt of court over an article about the boys' whereabouts published just hours after the Parole Board ruled they could be released. The newspaper was fined £30,000 in the High Court for contempt of court for publishing material which included details likely to identify, to someone with local knowledge, the secure units in which Venables and Thompson were then being held. The court accepted that the material was not published deliberately to identify them (*Attorney General v. Greater Manchester Newspapers Ltd [2001] All ER (D) 32 (Dec)*). When Venables was later recalled to prison, the anonymity injunction prevented reporting of the reasons why he had been recalled (Whitehead 2010).

Karen Matthews was released from Foston Hall prison, near Derby, in April 2012, with a new identity as she tried to rebuild her life. Matthews had been sentenced to prison in 2008 for the crime of kidnapping her own daughter Shannon in the hope of making some money. The very nature of the crime was thought to put her safety at risk. Matthews was smuggled out of prison, halfway through her eight-year sentence, to start a new life. Stringent measures needed to protect her on the outside were imposed including conditions that mean she can never go back to the estate in Dewsbury Moor in West Yorkshire, where she had lived (Wainwright 2008; PA 2012).

A final example is that of Maxine Carr, the then girlfriend of Ian Huntley, the man who had killed two children in the Cambridge village of Soham in 2002. The former classroom assistant served 21 months in prison for providing Huntley with a false alibi after he murdered Holly Wells and Jessica Chapman, both aged ten; Carr was released in 2003. The anonymity order prevents any reporting about her (*Maxine Carr v News Group Newspapers Limited & others [2005] EWHC 971 (QB)*; Rozenberg 2005).

The Disclosure of Personal Information

In the first part of this chapter, we considered the restrictions on dissemination and disclosure of information on old offenders in the interests of their rehabilitation, and here we consider the opposite—dissemination for purposes of crime prevention, public protection and employment screening.

Crime Prevention

Crime prevention is a broad term and can take many forms. The police circulation of photographs of convicted offenders has taken place in the interests of crime prevention. The idea is that staff in, for example, shops, swimming pools or sports centres will be able to identify them and take appropriate action should they venture on to their premises. Other attempts at crime prevention have involved publicity of ASBOs and Injunctions and publicity of sentences in the interests of 'shaming' or deterring' others from committing crime.

Information Exchange

Crime prevention may involve just the simple exchange of personal information on individuals between criminal justice agencies. The idea is that several agencies might have separate information on families or individuals that once put together provided the bigger picture of what was needed to help those families and individuals avoid further offending behaviour.

The earliest model of agencies working together came in the field of child abuse and child protection where different professionals would sit around a table at case conferences or child protection conferences to share information and draw up intervention plans (DHSS 1976; DoH 1991). Later, the same practice grew up to help young offenders (Home Office 1980) and Juvenile Bureaux became the forerunners of multi-agency Youth Offending Teams.

One of the groups of offenders that has caused most public disquiet has been the child sex offender. In spring 1997, the police in North Wales gave information directly to members of the public that two convicted child sex offenders were living close to them. As a precaution, the police did this by using press cuttings of their original trial and sentence that meant police were not disclosing confidential police information. The two offenders challenged the police's right to do this in the courts but the courts agreed that it was the correct thing for the police to do, using common law powers in the interests of crime prevention, and if the offenders in question could be shown to pose a serious risk (*R v. Chief Constable of North Wales Police, ex p. Thorpe (1998) Times, 23 March* and *R v Chief Constable of North Wales ex p Thorpe [1999] QB396*).

In the past, there had been fears that some agencies had been reluctant to share information they held in the name of confidentiality. The Crime and Disorder Act was meant to free up this exchange of information by empowering any relevant authority to disclose information 'necessary or expedient for the purposes of any provision of this Act' (Crime and Disorder Act 1998 s115).

This was the same Crime and Disorder Act 1998 that had introduced ASBOs and allowed the press reporting of the courts, making them on children and young people (see Chap. 7). It also started the process of allowing local authorities to distribute leaflets with photographs of those (including juveniles) who had been given ASBOs so that members of the public could report any breaches of the conditions imposed; in Middlesbrough, the authorities went so far as to put details of an adult subject to an ASBO across the back of local buses (Watson 2006). A legal challenge to this sort of information disclosure by local authorities was lost (*R (Stanley, Marshall and Kelly) v Metropolitan Police Commissioner [2004] EWHC 2229 (Admin)* at para. 21).

Organised arrangements for information exchange involving criminal justice agencies include Multi-Agency Risk Assessment Conferences (MARACs) and Multi-Agency Safeguarding Hubs (MASH). MARACs were first piloted in Cardiff in 2003 to share information and coordinate local responses to domestic abuse; by 2009 there were over 200 local MARACs across England and Wales (Groves and Thomas 2014: 135). Information sharing guidance has been issued to MARACs by the Department of Health (DoH 2012).

MASH, sometimes known as Central Referral Units or Joint Action Teams, are arrangements bringing together agencies dealing with 'child sexual exploitation' (CEIS n.d.). This is the criminal activity of men targeting young girls for purposes of sexual abuse and child prostitution and in the past has been referred to as 'localised grooming'. The Home Office has noted that 'the need for effective multi-agency working and information sharing in order to secure improved safeguarding outcomes is clearly stated in a number of reviews, policy documentation and statutory guidance' (Home Office 2014h: 4). Five Secretaries of State subsequently wrote a joint letter to health and local authorities, the police and GPs across the country emphasising the point:

> Let's be absolutely clear – a teenager at risk of child sexual exploitation is a child at risk of significant harm. Nothing should stand in the way of sharing information in relation to child sexual abuse, even where there are issues with consent. (DoH et al. 2015)

Police Circulation of Photographs

Shopkeepers in Derbyshire asked the police for photographs of thieves and shoplifters so that the staff would recognise them should they come into their shops. The police provided photographs provided that they were only seen by shop staff and not the public. One person whose photograph had been handed out decided to complain but the courts upheld the police's right to do this in the name of crime prevention and detection or the apprehension of suspects unlawfully at large (*Hellewell -v- Chief Constable of Derbyshire QBD [1995] 1WLR 804*)

People committing offences in public houses may be given an additional exclusion order by the courts on top of their sentence (Licensed Premises (Exclusion of Certain Persons) Act 1980). The voluntary organisation Pubwatch has taken this practice of exclusion further and been given police photographs of people subject to such orders. Pubwatch then includes the photographs in their posters that are distributed to pubs that might be effected. The Licensed Victuallers' Association claimed that the first such poster campaign of this kind was carried out in Bedford when a man was barred from some 107 pubs in the town. It was stated that 'the police, who support the initiative, provided the photograph' (Kelsey 1992).

This would be an extension of the police's right to disseminate information for crime prevention purposes. Pubwatch personnel obtaining the photographs would need to deal with the images sensitively. Today the Pubwatch website confirms the practice is still in place:

> The Police may also be willing to provide you with police photographs of banned individuals, but this will be at their discretion and will be for a police purpose e.g. prevention of crime and disorder. It will also be subject to a locally agreed data sharing agreement. Police forces deal with this issue in different ways. Some will produce a folder of police photographs which has to be signed for by the Watch member; others will share them by using a system such as Pubwatch Online where the member has to use a secure password to access the site and the photograph is given a watermark to show who has downloaded an image. (Pubwatch 2017)

Public 'Shaming' and 'Deterrence'

The publicising of convictions and sentences in the interests of 'shaming' or 'deterring' others from committing crime has a chequered history. The Essex Police in 2002 had put posters of custody photographs they had taken of offenders who had gone on to be convicted. The scheme was known as the 'Offender Naming Scheme' and posters were placed in public areas like railway stations and other transport locations. Gary Ellis, whose picture had been put up, challenged the right of the police to do this and the High Court had some sympathy for him. The court accepted that an offender naming scheme operated by a police force was devised to assist them in performing their statutory duty under the Crime and Disorder Act 1998 to formulate and implement strategies for reduction of crime in their area, but the court ruled that it needed further information to adjudicate:

> On the material which is before us, we are not prepared to grant a declaration that the Scheme is not capable of being operated lawfully during a trial period. Whether it is can only be answered when the properly investigated circumstances of a specific individual's position is before the Court to adjudicate upon. The outcome will then turn on the facts of that case. (*R (Ellis) v Chief Constable of Essex Police [2003] EWHC 1321 (Admin)*; Dyer 2003b)

The Essex police put their scheme on hold. The court had made reference to Article 8.

A More Transparent System

Another proposal for 'shaming' and 'deterrence' came from the final years of the Labour government and in particular the Cabinet Office report *Engaging Communities in Fighting Crime* published in June 2008. This was the same report that had called for visible community payback schemes in order that the public would know that offenders were being punished (see Chap. 8). The criminal justice system was seen as a 'privatised' system—not in the financial sense but because the public did not know what went on after the prisoner left the dock and everything seemingly went behind closed doors. The report noted that 'the public ... don't believe they are told enough about what happens in the system' (Cabinet Office 2008a).

The press reporting of the criminal courts was one feature seen to be failing the public. The press only seemed interested in the big sensational cases and not the lesser criminality that went on all the time. The press gallery in many courts was often empty with no journalists around (Franklin and Murphy 1991). The best the public got from many local papers was just a list of convictions and sentences under the name 'court briefs' or something similar. The list in question would usually be collected from the Clerk to the Courts office at the end of the courts working day (Home Office 1989).

To make the offender and his or her sentence more visible, it was now proposed to create more ways of disseminating this information. The proposal was for an Offender Naming Scheme and the dissemination of the convictions and sentencing on adults for a period of one month after sentencing; the practicalities of how that process would be implemented had yet to be worked out in detail. The possible use of leaflets, public meetings, local newsletters or on-line availability had all been suggested and more guidance was to be issued later (OCJR 2009: 4; Home Office 2009; Thomas and Thompson 2008).

The West Yorkshire Police started a pilot on-line scheme in 2009 known as 'In the Dock' that still runs today. The West Yorkshire Police website states its purpose:

> In the Dock' informs the public of the work of the criminal justice system across West Yorkshire. Following a risk assessment, adults given custodial sentences at the county's crown courts will have their names, photographs, details of the crime they have committed and the court's sentence published on these pages. Additionally, adult convictions at Magistrates courts which are of significant public interest may also be included. (West Yorkshire Police 2017b)

With the change of government in 2010, new guidance was published (MoJ et al. 2011). A national version of 'In the Dock' on the police.uk website was also flagged up (Barrett 2012) but a check of the website in 2017 shows no sign of it.

Public Protection

Public protection is one of those hard-to-define concepts that has evolved into our consciousness over the years. Once confined to the work of probation officers and the medical profession, it has gradually included other agencies into its work and from having once been something that was 'more or less carried on behind closed doors, public protection has now spread its tentacles across the public sector' and grown into 'a huge industry' (Nash 2006: 2). Sexual offenders have been prime candidates for public protection measures, and here we consider the work of the sex offender register, policies of 'community notification', the Multi-Agency Public Protection Arrangements (MAPPA) and restrictive orders that can be placed on sexual offenders and potential sexual offenders.

Sex Offender Registration

The USA, the UK, Australia and Canada were among the first jurisdictions to introduce sex offender registers as a form of assisting public protection policies. Under the registration arrangements people convicted of sexual offences and living in the community were required to notify their whereabouts and provide other specified information to the police as well as any other significant changes in their circumstances as and when they took place; if there were no changes, an annual verification exercise (or 'periodic notification') might take place. The requirement to notify lasted for different time periods based on the severity of the original sentence administered including a requirement for life-long registration. Failure to comply with providing this information was to become an offence in itself. Overall, this would keep police databases up to date and allow for a form of police management of these sex offenders in the community. Registration was not an additional punishment but a public protection measure (Logan 2009; Thomas 2011). The law on the UK register can be found at Sex Offender Act 1997 Part One, later to be replaced by the Sexual Offences Act 2003 ss. 80–93.

An individual reporting to the police in the UK must provide information about his or her address, their National Insurance number, passport details, travel plans, whether any child resides in the same house, bank account details along with credit and debit card details. This information would include details of bank account numbers, sort codes, card validation numbers and expiry dates (see The Sexual Offences Act 2003 (Notification Requirements) (England and Wales) Regulations 2012 No.

1876 and Home Office 2016d: Chap. 1). One person has tried to challenge the states right to request this private information but without success (*R on the application of Christopher Prothero v Secretary of State for the Home Department [2013] EWHC 2830 (Admin)*).

The police for their part:

> may require the offender to allow them to take fingerprints and photograph any part of that offender (i.e. photographs may be taken of an offenders face as well as distinguishing features, such as a tattoo). This definition also means that iris scanning technology may be used. However, the purpose for taking fingerprints and photographs must be to verify the identity of the sex offender. (Home Office 2016d: 15)

A sex offender register was introduced in the UK in 1997 and now, almost 20 years later, has 52,770 names on it (MoJ 2016g: 6). The register has been subjected to legal challenge including its compliance with the ECHR and not least Article 8 of the Convention and the right to privacy. The courts quickly established that the sex offender register did 'engage' Article 8 but did *not* necessarily 'breach' it; the sex offender register was deemed 'necessary and proportionate' (*Adamson v UK (1999) Application 22293/98; see also Massey v UK (2003) Application 14399/02*).

In the case of *Forbes v the Secretary of State for the Home Department*, the Court of Appeal was asked to rule on the matter of registration being an automatic process and whether or not this made it incompatible with Article 8 because the form and extent of the interference would vary with different individuals. The court agreed that automatic registration would bear more heavily on some individuals than others but 'to be viable the scheme must contain general provisions that will be universally applied to all within its purview' and therefore automatic registration was a 'necessary and reasonable element of the scheme' (*R (Forbes) v Secretary of State for the Home Department [2006] EWCA Civ. 962* para. 18).

In the spring of 2010, the UK Supreme Court was asked to rule on the sex offender register and its indefinite registration of people who had served more than 30 months in prison for their sexual crimes. This lifetimes' registration was appealed against by Angus Thompson, a 58-year-old man from Newcastle and an unnamed juvenile referred to as 'F'.

Thompson, and 'F' argued that indefinite registration under the Sexual Offences Act 2003 s80 (1) was incompatible with Article 8 of the ECHR because there was no right of review to consider whether continued registration was required. It was contended that some people should doubtless be on the register for life but that equally some offenders were able to change and should be able to come off it if they posed little or no risk. As it stood the absence of any right to a review made the notification requirements disproportionate to their stated purpose.

The question of indefinite registration had been considered before with respect to Article 8 in the Northern Ireland High Court where it had been found 'unquestionably an inconvenience' but nonetheless acceptable in the interests of public protection (*re Gallagher [2003] NIQB 26*). The court at this time had not looked at the question of a review mechanism for those on the register for an indefinite period.

In the *Thompson* case, the Divisional Court had initially granted the respondents claims' and made a declaration of incompatibility with the Convention in December 2008 (*F and Angus Aubrey Thompson v. Secretary of State for the Justice [2008] EWHC 3170*), and the Court of Appeal had later dismissed the Home Office appeal against that decision (*23 July 2009 [2010] 1 WLR 76*). In February 2010, the case had reached the UK Supreme Court where the engagement of Article 8, the right to privacy, was accepted. The Supreme Court then raised the following three questions:

- what was the extent of the interference with Article 8 rights?
- how valuable was the register in achieving its legitimate aims? and
- to what extent would that value be eroded if registration were made subject to review?

The Supreme Court found registration to be proportionate but did agree that there should be some form of appeal available in order to review the position and to end the requirement to notify should the time come when that is appropriate. The Home Office appeal was dismissed (*R (on the application of F (by his litigation friend F)) and Thompson (FC) (Respondents) v. Secretary of State for the Home Department (Appellant) [2010] UKSC 17*).

The Scottish Government, bound by the same Supreme Court decision, responded with its Sexual Offences Act 2003 (Remedial) (Scotland) Order 2010 no. 370. Another Remedial Order was made for England and Wales (Sexual Offences Act 2003 (Remedial Order) 2012 no.1883), and an Appeal arrangement was duly built into the registration requirements (Sexual Offences Act 2003 new ss.88A-I and ss.91A-F).

The police were charged with carrying out the reviews which were carried out in private (Home Office 2012c). A right of appeal from the police decision was allowed but this was to a magistrate's court which meant it would all be heard in public. Having the gaze of the press on them again was a natural deterrent for some offenders although some were prepared to risk it (see, e.g., *Yorkshire Post* 2013). By 2016, some 700 applicants had been reviewed and removed from the register (BBC News 2016c).

The French sex offender register known as FIJAIS (Fichier Judicaire automise des Auteurs d'Infractions Sexuelles) has also been challenged as breaching Article 8 of the European Convention in the cases brought by Bernard Bouchacourt, Fabrice Gardel and a person known only as MB. The European Court ruled that the aims of FIJAIS in terms of crime prevention could not be questioned and that inclusion on the database was not disproportionate especially given the opportunity to have the inclusion reviewed by a tribunal. The court also commented on the clear duty of confidentiality surrounding the database and declared that the register struck a fair balance between the competing private and public interests; it held unanimously that there was no violation of Article 8 (*Bouchacourt v. France (Application no. 5335/06, Gardel v France (Application 16428/05)) and MB v France (Application no. 22115/06) (2009))*.

Community Notification

'Community notification' is an adjunct to sex offender registration. In the USA, the argument was made that if the professionals such as police officers and probation officers could know where sex offenders lived through the register, then why should the general public not have access to the register for them to know where they lived. That way, the public could take their own precautions against coming into contact with these former offenders and—possibly more importantly—take precautions to ensure their children avoided contact with them. Sex offenders assessed as 'high risk' and therefore thought likely to reoffend were the most likely to have information disseminated on them.

The system of 'community notification' used in the USA is the most comprehensive arrangement for getting personal information on offenders to local neighbourhoods. Washington State was the first state to introduce 'community notification' in 1990 with its Community Protection Act. Other states started to take an interest, and following the rape and murder of a seven-year-old girl in New Jersey, by a resident of the same street she lived in with her family, that state passed its 'Megan's Law' in 1994 (New Jersey Statute 2C: 7-1-7-11); the law was named after the child victim Megan Kanka and brought 'community notification' to New Jersey. Two years later 'Megan's Law' was made a Federal Law requiring all states to put in place some form of 'community notification' or risk losing federal funding for criminal justice programmes. President Clinton declared that:

> From now on, every State in the country will be required by law to tell a community when a dangerous sexual predator enters its midst. We respect people's rights, but today America proclaims there is no greater right than a parent's right to raise a child in safety and love. Today America warns: If you dare to prey on our children, the law will follow you wherever you go, State to State, town to town. Today America circles the wagon around our children. (Clinton 1996; see also Logan 2009: 74–80)

The result was a variety of different forms of 'community notification' from proactive leaflets through doors and public meetings in local schools to information only given out when people applied for it in person at police stations. The Adam Walsh Act of 2006 tried to tighten up the various forms and to ensure that all local registers were available to the public on-line (Adam Walsh Child Protection and Safety Act 2006 Public Law 109–248 Stat. 120; Logan 2009: 62–66).

In the UK, community notification is not so 'universal' as to include whole neighbourhoods and populations and instead a more 'selective' approach has been adopted offering information to individuals. As we noted above, the courts had approved the dissemination of information on child sex offenders to people living near them in North Wales. That has not stopped periodic demands for the UK sex offender register to be opened to the public and most infamously in the 'For Sarah' campaign in 2000 led by the *News of the World* newspaper.

Sarah Payne was an eight-year-old girl sexually assaulted and killed in Sussex. While the police searched for the perpetrator, the *News of the World* demanded a form of community notification comparable to the arrangements in the USA in order for parents to better protect their children. The essence of the 'For Sarah' campaign was the newspapers' intent to publish photographs and details of sex offenders in lieu of the authorities doing it ('Named and Shamed' *News of the World* 23 July 2000). The result was numerous demonstrations across the country in favour of the idea with the most far-reaching being in Paulsgrove, a suburb of Portsmouth. Eventually, the protests subsided and the Home Secretary Jack Straw declared there would be no American-style 'community notification' in the UK (Bennetto 2000).

The 'For Sarah' campaign continued in a more subdued form, and eventually, a 'Sarah's Law' was launched in 2011. The Child Sex Offender Disclosure Scheme (CSOD) is referred to as 'Sarah's Law' even though it is not actually a law at all—only an administrative arrangement that allows individuals to ask the police if there is anything they should know about adults in regular and close proximity to their children (Home Office 2010). It is not comparable to the American 'community notification' scheme. It is reported that some 4754 applications to the police had been made by 2013 with as many as 700 child sex offenders having been identified by the Scheme (BBC News 2013c).

A similar scheme known as the Domestic Violence Disclosure Scheme provides a framework for the release of information about the violent past of partners. Informally, it is known as 'Clare's Law', named after 36-year-old Clare Wood who was murdered in Salford by her former boyfriend in 2009.

Every request under Clare's Law is thoroughly checked by a panel made up of police, probation services and other agencies to ensure information is only passed on where it is lawful, proportionate and necessary. Trained police officers and advisers are then on hand to support victims through the difficult and sometimes dangerous transitional period. (Home Office 2013f)

Multi-agency Public Protection Arrangements

Multi-Agency Public Protection Arrangements (MAPPA) were formed in 2001 to bring agencies together to help jointly manage sexual offenders who were on the sex offender register (Criminal Justice and Courts Services Act 2000 ss66–68). Other dangerous offenders were later included under their auspices. MAPPA is not an agency in itself but an arrangement that brings separate agencies together. The three main agencies or 'responsible authorities' are the police, probation and the prison service with others, such as health and local authorities involved under a duty to cooperate. Section 325(4) of the Criminal Justice Act 2003 expressly permits the sharing of information between these agencies for MAPPA purposes. Current guidance explains the significance of information exchange within MAPPA:

> The purpose of sharing information about individuals ('data subjects') is to enable the relevant agencies to work more effectively together in assessing risks and considering how to manage them. This points towards sharing all the available information that is relevant, so that nothing is overlooked and public protection is not compromised. On the other hand, agencies must respect the rights of data subjects, which will tend to limit what can be shared. In order to strike the right balance, agencies need a clear understanding of the law in this area. (MoJ et al. 2012: para. 9.5)

The same guidance draws the MAPPA agencies attention to the significance of Article 8 of the ECHR (ibid.: para. 9.9–9.10) and also to the *Data Sharing Code of Practice* published by the Information Commissioners Office (ICO 2011). MAPPA is equally a public protection exercise as well as a crime prevention arrangement (see below).

MAPPA officers have oversight of such systems as the CSOD Scheme and the provisions of the Criminal Justice Act 2003 327A (as amended by the Criminal Justice and Immigration Act 2008 s140). This is the law that requires the police or other MAPPA 'responsible bodies' to disclose information to members of the public who may be endangered by the unknown presence of a sex offender. The law places a *presumption to disclose* on the 'responsible authority' implying they should take the initiative and not wait to be asked for the information.

MAPPA arrangements about themselves are not so transparent. In the event of anything going wrong and, for example, someone getting seriously hurt by a known offender under supervision, a MAPPA Serious Case Review (SCR) will be undertaken. This SCR, however, 'must not be widely distributed or published' (MoJ et al. 2012: para. 20.21) and even a shortened summary known as an Overview Report should only be circulated 'on a limited basis' (ibid.: 20.25).

Restrictive Orders

In the opening paragraph of this book, we reported on the case of a man in Yorkshire who has been told by police officers that he must inform them some 24 hours before he has sex with anyone and he must name the person concerned. We saw this as an extreme invasion of privacy but others might see it as a proportionate public protection measure. SRO that he is subject to is a civil order to restrict behaviour; the man in question has no previous convictions.

A number of civil orders (comparable to ASBOs and Injunctions) have been introduced to contain the sex offender. Originally there were Sex Offender Orders, Sexual Offences Prevention Orders, Risk of Sexual Harm Orders, Foreign Travel Orders and so on but in 2014 these were all replaced and consolidated into just two Orders—the SRO and the Sexual Harm Prevention Order (SHPO) (Anti-social Behaviour Crime and Policing Act 2014 Part 9 and Schedule 5 amending the Sexual Offences Act 2003 ss103A-K and 122A-K). The SRO 'prohibits the defendant from doing *anything described in the order*' (Sexual Offences Act 2003 s122A (7) (a)—emphasis added).

The two new civil orders (SRO and SHPOs) started in 2015 and both require the subject of the Orders to notify the police of any changes to their address within three days of the Order being made or whenever the information changes (Sexual Offences Act 2003 s122 F (4)). The Home Office has made it clear that in the case of the SRO this form of notification *does not make the individual subject to the notification requirements for registered sex offenders* (Home Office 2016d: 48); this is presumably because an SRO can be imposed on someone with no convictions.

Employment Screening

The police disclosure of criminal records to employers to assist them to screen job applicants has a long history going back to the 1950s. At that time, this was a relatively discreet process aimed at vetting a few applicants for senior security or defence positions. Today the disclosure of this criminal record information held on the PNC takes place on an industrial scale and over four million disclosure certificates are issued each year. The turning point was the mid-1980s.

Starting in 1986, the disclosure system was based on individual police forces who used to disclose criminal record information directly to relevant employers in their catchment area. Relevant employers were those like health and local authorities who employed staff working with children and vulnerable people in such settings as schools, children's homes, day nurseries and children's wards in hospitals. An estimated 100,000 disclosures a year was anticipated (Home Office/DHSS 1985: para. 6.21) but the service was free and employers readily availed themselves of what was effectively a child protection service. Other employers sought the same service and by 1993, an estimated 1,000,000 disclosures a year were being made (Home Office 1993: paras. 23–26). Apart from disclosing criminal records to employers, these disclosure arrangements also gave employers soft information in the form of non-conviction information (Marshall and Thomas 2015a).

The Home Office decided to change the system to cope with the rising disclosure figures. A new centralised body was planned to take this work off the local police forces. The new arrangement was going to be partly delivered by a private company who would have direct access to the PNC and would charge a set fee for each disclosure they made. In the long run, it was hoped they would become a self-funding organisation (Home Office 1996). The Police Act 1997 Part V provided the legal foundation and the new centralised body was to be known as the CRB which started operations in Liverpool on 11 March 2002 (for a general history of these times see Thomas 2007: Chaps. 6–7). In 2012, the CRB itself was replaced by the Disclosure and Barring Service (DBS).

Before May 2013, all cautions and convictions were automatically disclosed on standard and enhanced criminal records checks. However, this system was judged to be disproportionate and in breach of Article 8 ECHR in the case of *R (T) v Greater Manchester Police*, in which Liberty intervened. In response to this judgement, the government brought in a new system that allows for some convictions and cautions to be filtered from DBS checks after a certain period of time, which means they will not be disclosed. More information can be found on the website (Gov.uk 2017c).

Parole Conditions

People leaving prison may be the subject of parole conditions for varying lengths of time. This requires them to report to probation officers at regular intervals and to comply with various forms of conditions imposed upon them; failure to comply may lead to a readmission to prison. These conditions might include an address they must live at, people and places they must stay away from and restrictions on their use of the internet. All of these conditions and the questions posed to them by probation officers are potentially invasive of the individual's privacy.

In 2003, the probation service began testing polygraphs on volunteer supervisees with a view to introducing them for people being supervised on parole; this was referred to as Post Conviction Sex Offender Testing (PCSOT) and probation officers reported back favourably on their impact (Grubin 2006). The Labour government introduced the necessary legal provisions in the Offender Management Act 2007, ss. 28–30, allowing for people over 18 convicted of sexual offences and on post-custody licences to have conditions written into those licences requiring them to attend for polygraph testing. Section 30 of the Act prevented any information obtained from a polygraph test from being used in criminal proceedings against the offender or for any recall or breach proceedings.

Mandatory polygraph testing for post-custodial sexual offenders was piloted between April 2009 and October 2011 in the East and West Midlands' probation regions. Equipment and training were provided by the University of Newcastle and an evaluation was commissioned from the University of Kent. New statutory rules were published to guide the practitioners (The Polygraph Rules 2009 SI no. 619). The evaluation study found that of the 300 sex offenders who took the tests, twice as many made 'clinically significant disclosures' to probation staff such as admitting to contacting a victim or entering an exclusion zone or thoughts that could suggest a higher risk of reoffending (Gannon et al. 2012: 12). It was also found that many of the sex offenders 'made disclosures because they believed so strongly in the powers of the polygraph'; in other words, it was not the test at all that made them disclose, and many of these disclosures even took place during the pre-polygraph interview before the test itself was carried out (Gannon et al. 2014).

Under-Secretary of State for Justice, Jeremy Wright, explained:

> As part of the supervision of sex offenders, it is not the detection of decep-tion that is the critical factor. It is the information disclosed by the offender before, during or after the polygraph test, which is used to inform decisions about their supervision. In other words, it is less about detecting lies and more about gathering useful information to properly manage risk. (*Hansard HC Debates, Third Delegated Legislation Committee 2 July 2013 col. 5*)

Compulsory lie detector testing started from October 2014 (Bowcott 2014; Marshall and Thomas 2015b).

Summary

Personal information held on people who have completed a period of punishment find that information is subject to movement in opposite directions. The information may be restricted in disclosure in the inter-ests of aiding rehabilitation and the future safety of the former offender or it may be disclosed widely in the interests of crime prevention and public protection. Information in the form of criminal record histories may also be disclosed to employers wishing to screen applicants for work in order to safeguard children or vulnerable adults that the employment involves working with or to safeguard financial arrangements that also need safeguarding. Former prisoners may be required to comply with parole conditions and be subject to continuing supervision by probation officers and such other restrictions on their privacy as exclusion zones, non-contact orders, curfews, internet restrictions and requirements to periodically submit to polygraph testing.

11

Conclusions

This book arose from our belief that 'privacy matters' and should be taken seriously and not least when it is intruded upon by the agencies of the criminal justice system. We accept the difficulties of defining privacy and we also accept the need for these agencies to be able to carry out their work preventing and detecting crime and protecting the public. We would argue that there needs to be a greater proportionate understanding in how this work is approached and not least when it is carried out using some of the most sophisticated information technology now available.

The idea of the book is that it takes the angle of 'privacy' as a starting point rather than something incidental to a study of surveillance and other law enforcement techniques. We hope the book will also act as a 'source book' to enable readers to go into further details on any of the subjects covered should they wish to do so. The bibliography at the back of the book lists the essential reading that gives the interested reader greater detail on the subjects explored.

In an interview with *The Guardian* in 2015, Edward Snowden stated that:

> People who say they don't care about privacy because they have got nothing to hide have not thought too deeply about these issues. What they are

© The Author(s) 2017
D. Marshall, T. Thomas, *Privacy and Criminal Justice*,
https://doi.org/10.1007/978-3-319-64912-2_11

really saying is I do not care about this right. When you say I don't care about the right to privacy because I have nothing to hide, that is no different than saying I don't care about freedom of speech because I have nothing to say, or, freedom of the press because I have nothing to write. (Rusbridger et al. 2015)

Have you got something to hide? In 2016, the campaign group Liberty produced a short film highlighting the intrusiveness of collecting data from members of the public. A woman approached members of the public asking to see their mobile phones—text messages, call history and emails—even going so far as entering the Home Office building in London and declaring that she was trying to hack their server and collect their communications data. Home Office staff were not willing to allow this, and members of the public were not happy about sharing their private information. The point being made by Liberty was that the Investigatory Powers Bill was proposing to do just this (enacted as the Investigatory Powers Act 2016, discussed in Chap. 4 of this book). The message from the public and the Home Office security staff seemed to be that 'privacy matters' (Liberty 2016h).

Would you be willing to show anyone the content of your mobile phone? No? Have you got something to hide? Probably not; rather, you wish to retain a sense of privacy. Private text messages may be just that, 'private' between you and the recipient(s). But, as we have shown throughout this book, these messages may not remain 'private'. For example, the police may gain access to this data in the interests of a criminal investigation, even though you may not have committed an offence.

A further illustration of just how much 'privacy matters' comes from an interaction between one of the authors of this book and a student. The student had not been alone in declaring in a seminar that privacy was not that important and that anyway, 'if you are innocent, what have you got to fear?' This is a current familiar refrain often heard about law enforcement agencies knowing things about you that are not in the public domain. The question was then put to the student, 'Can I see your mobile [telephone] to see who you have been phoning?' The answer was a clear (and shocked) 'no'. 'But if you are innocent, what have you got to fear?' The answer was still 'no'. The student appeared to be hanging on to information that he considered 'private', despite knowing he was 'innocent' and even though he was not being accused of any criminal intent or criminal conduct. Privacy and personal information arguably remains 'private' to the individual it 'belongs' to, regardless of its significance to anybody else.

We are not alone in suggesting that 'privacy' is something that needs to be 'balanced' when it comes to law enforcement and the activities of the criminal justice system. In the debate on the Investigatory Powers Bill, it was suggested that:

> the interference must be proportionate to the aim pursued. That is determined via a balancing exercise, which may for example require 'the interest of the … state in protecting its national security' to be balanced against 'the seriousness of the interference with the applicant's right to respect for his private life'. (Anderson 2015a: para. 5.22)

and

> the Bill must balance protecting the law-abiding majority from the criminals and terrorists against protecting the very democratic freedoms these terrorists are seeking to undermine. The right to privacy, embodied in the Human Rights Act 1998, is at the heart of this balance. It is not an absolute right, but one which is qualified to allow for proportionate legal intrusion in order to protect the wider interests of a democratic society. This balancing act will be central to the scrutiny by the Joint Committee on the Draft Investigatory Powers Bill. (House of Commons 2016a: para. 9)

There is a need for *intrusion* (protection of life, crime prevention and investigation) and for *protection* in the form of the integrity of individuals (both informational and physical) and criminal justice. Privacy needs safeguarding but there remains a need to control crime and other activities of people.

The problem has always been to measure the nature of this balance in particular circumstances, given the difficulties of defining 'privacy' in the first place. As long as there is discretion there will be debates as to where the line falls to make it a proportionate rather than disproportionate and abusive intervention. In the case of the European Convention on Human Rights Article 8, the courts will be the final arbiters. The threat of terrorism and child sexual offenders will always be used to counter those who try to protect privacy, as we noted in Chap. 1:

> While we recognise privacy concerns about bulk interception, we do not subscribe to the point of view that it is acceptable to let some terrorist attacks happen in order to uphold the individual right to privacy – nor do we believe that the vast majority of the British public would. (House of Commons 2015a: 36)

In more general terms, the nature of privacy also changes over time. Personal information once considered private may become much more freely available. Nearly 45 years ago, Home Secretary Robert Carr told the House of Commons:

> The supply of police information will continue to be governed by the general principle that no information is given to anyone, however responsible, unless there are weighty considerations of public interest which justify departure from this rule. (*Hansard House of Commons Debates 14 June 1973 col.1681*)

The only exceptions to this in 1973 were to be disclosure to the courts by way of antecedents and for the use of the police themselves in carrying out their investigative duties. Today, the Disclosure and Barring Service with their direct access to the PNC could report that they were disclosing personal information on some four million people annually by way of criminal conviction records and associated police intelligence for employers to screen applicants for designated work in the interests of public protection (DBS News 2016: 1; see also Chaps. 5 and 10 of this volume).

What becomes important is the nature of the regulatory regimes that law enforcement and other agencies of the criminal justice system are subjected to. Such regulation needs to be efficient, and there must be effective oversight to ensure a legal basis in every aspect of criminal justice; at present, we would argue that there is a lack of adequate policy/ frameworks in particular for safeguarding and storing the data and personal information. In practice, implementation may be difficult and complexities added to human decision-making will always make for a difficult compromise that leaves someone dissatisfied.

When the rapidly changing and ubiquitous use of digital technology lends itself to ever new forms of criminality, the criminal justice agencies are faced with challenges they have not met in the past. The old adage that the police are running to catch up with the new offenders with outdated police systems that cannot keep pace is repeatedly heard. Some of the examples noted in this volume would contest that the police and others are not that far behind and in some instances are ahead of the game; to quote Edward Snowden again, 'I don't want to live in a world where everything that I say, everything I do, everyone I talk to, every expression of creativity or love or friendship is recorded' (Greenwald et al. 2013).

Criminal justice data collection, for example, is increasing and there is an apparent global trend to this. Sometimes it does appear the state (CJS) is overly keen to collect everything but does not know why they are doing so. In the future, we can already see improved methods of data collection and retention particularly through the UK's Investigatory Powers Act 2016. Just prior to the general election campaign of May 2017, the UK Home Secretary gave her ideas for the future:

> Amber Rudd has called for the police and intelligence agencies to be given access to WhatsApp and other encrypted messaging services to thwart future terror attacks, prompting opposition politicians and civil liberties groups to say her demand was unrealistic and disproportionate. (Sparrow 2017)

Social media has presented more problems for the police and others in its short life. In our introductory chapter, we noted Wacks' argument that information privacy was becoming more important than a traditional spatial concept of privacy:

> Instead of pursuing the false god of 'privacy', attention should be paid to identifying what specific interests of the individual we think the law ought to protect. And it is submitted that at the core of the preoccupation with the right to privacy is the protection against the misuse of personal, sensitive information. (Wacks 1989: 10)

Wacks was writing before the growth of social media which has become, in its own right, the epitome of personal information exchange with new offences such as 'sexting' and new uses such as 'tweeting' directly from the courts.

'Privacy matters; privacy is what allows us to determine who we are and who we want to be' (Edward Snowden quoted in Castle 2013). It is important, now more than ever, that the criminal justice system is held to account for the safeguarding, collection and storage of private data. The lack of an adequate definition of privacy, combined with a rapidly changing world, will ensure that the courts continue to struggle in balancing public security with public rights to privacy. Criminal Justice processes must remain under constant review, if the right to privacy is to remain. Perhaps many more of us will become suspects, as the criminal justice surveillance net widens.

Bibliography

ACPO (Association of Chief Police Officers) (1987) *Code of Practice for Police Computer Systems*, London.

ACPO (Association of Chief Police Officers) (1995) *Code of Practice for Data Protection*, London.

ACPO (Association of Chief Police Officers) (2000) *General Rules for Criminal Record Weeding on Police Systems Version 5*, November, London.

ACPO (Association of Chief Police Officers) (2002) *Code of Practice for Data Protection*, London.

ACPO (Association of Chief Police Officers) (2004) *Driving Down Crime: Denying Criminals the Use of the Road*, London.

ACPO (Association of Chief Police Officers) (2010) *Criminal Use of Firearms: Briefing Paper – Anonymity in Investigations, Investigation Anonymity Orders, Coroners and Justice Act 2009*, London.

ACPO (Association of Chief Police Officers) (2013) *The Police Use of Automatic Number Plate Recognition*, January, London.

ACPO (Association of Chief Police Officers) (2014) *National Policing Position Statement: The Use of the Polygraph in Investigations*, May, London (available at: http://library.college.police.uk/docs/APPREF/National-Policing-Position-Statement-use-of-Polygraph-May-2014.pdf accessed 23 March 2017).

ACPO (Association of Chief Police Officers)/Centrex (2006) *Guidance on the Management of Police Information.*

© The Author(s) 2017
D. Marshall, T. Thomas, *Privacy and Criminal Justice*,
https://doi.org/10.1007/978-3-319-64912-2

Addley E and Topping A (2017) Council Admits Racially Discriminating Against Two Boys over Prevent Toy Gun Referral. *The Guardian*, 27 January.

Al Jnidi D (2009) Life with a Control Order: A Wife's Story, *The Independent*, 2 July.

Alford S (2012) *The Watchers: A Secret History of the Reign of Elizabeth I*, London: Allen Lane/Penguin Press.

Anderson D (2013) *Terrorism Prevention and Investigation Measures in 2012: First Report of the Independent Reviewer on the Operation of the Terrorism Prevention and Investigation Measures Act 2011* (available at https://www.gov.uk/government/uploads/system/uploads/attachment_data/file/228684/9780108512285.pdf accessed 27 January 2017).

Anderson D (2014) *Terrorism Prevention and Investigation Measures in 2013: Second Report of the Independent Reviewer on the Operation of the Terrorism Prevention and Investigation Measures Act 2011* (available at https://www.gov.uk/government/uploads/system/uploads/attachment_data/file/298487/Un_Act_Independent_Review_print_ready.pdf accessed 2 February 2017).

Anderson D (2015a) *A Question of Trust: Report of the Investigatory Powers Review*, Independent Reviewer of Terrorism Legislation, London.

Anderson D (2015b) *Terrorism Prevention and Investigation Measures in 2014: Third Report of the Independent Reviewer on the Operation of the Terrorism Prevention and Investigation Measures Act 2011* (available at https://www.gov.uk/government/uploads/system/uploads/attachment_data/file/411824/IRTL_TPIMs_2014_final_report__web_.pdf accessed 2 February 2017).

Anderson D (2016a) *The Terrorism Acts in 2015: Report of the Independent Reviewer on the Operation of the Terrorism Act 2000 and Part 1 of the Terrorism Act 2006* (available at https://terrorismlegislationreviewer.independent.gov.uk/wp-content/uploads/2016/12/TERRORISM-ACTS-REPORT-1-Dec-2016-1.pdf accessed 12 January 2017).

Anderson D (2016b) *Moving In – Moving On*, 31 March (available at: https://terrorismlegislationreviewer.independent.gov.uk/moving-in-moving-on/#more-2716 accessed 14 February 2017).

Anderson R, Brown I, Dowty T, Heath W, Inglesant P and Sasse A (2009) *Database State: A Report Commissioned by the Joseph Rowntree Reform Trust Ltd Nation*, York: Rowntree Trust.

Andrew C (2009) *The Defence of the Realm: The Authorized History of MI5*, London: Penguin.

Anonymous (2017) My Little Children Were Detained Because of a Toy Gun. Prevent Has Gone Too Far. *The Guardian*, 1 February.

Ariel B, Farrar WA and Sutherland A (2014), The Effect of Police Body-Worn Cameras on Use of Force and Citizens' Complaints Against the Police: A

Randomized Controlled Trial. *Journal of Quantitative Criminology*, 31(3): 509–535.

Bailey S (2011) Boscombe Police Apologise for 'Unlawful' Detainment of Woman. *Daily Echo*, 1 October (available from http://www.bournemouthecho.co.uk/news/9282303.Boscombe_police_apologise_for__unlawful__detainment_of_woman/ Last accessed 23 August 2016).

Bakir V, Cable J, Dencik HA and McStay A (2015) *Public Feeling on Privacy, Security and Surveillance*, ESRC, Bangor University and Cardiff University (available at https://sites.cardiff.ac.uk/dcssproject/files/2015/11/Public-Feeling-on-Privacy-Security-Surveillance-DATAPSST-DCSS-Nov2015.pdf accessed 16 April 2017).

Barr R (1962) *The Scotland Yard Story*, London: Hodder & Stoughton.

Barrett D (2012) Criminals to Be Named and Shamed by Home Office. *Daily Telegraph*, 14 October.

Barrett D (2015) Police Search Home of Lord Bramall as Part of Paedophile Sex Abuse Inquiry. *Daily Telegraph*, 8 March.

BBC News (1998) Young Offenders to Be 'Named and Shamed', 11 June (available at http://news.bbc.co.uk/1/hi/uk/110762.stm accessed 14 February 2017).

BBC (2001) Britain 'at War with Terrorism', 16 September (available at http://news.bbc.co.uk/1/hi/uk_politics/1545411.stm accessed 12 January 2017).

BBC News (2003) Spy Pictures of Suffragettes Revealed, 3 October (available at http://news.bbc.co.uk/1/hi/magazine/3153024.stm accessed 31 October 2016).

BBC News (2005) Blair Defeated over Terror Laws, 9 November, available at: http://news.bbc.co.uk/1/hi/uk_politics/4422086.stm accessed 3 February 2017).

BBC News (2006) Britain Is 'Surveillance Society,' 2 November (available at http://news.bbc.co.uk/1/hi/uk/6108496.stm accessed 27 January 2017).

BBC News (2008a) Warning on New Anti-Knife Powers, 24 May (available at http://news.bbc.co.uk/1/hi/uk/7418134.stm accessed 23 August 2016).

BBC News (2008b) Spy Law 'Used in Dog Fouling War', 27 April (available at: http://news.bbc.co.uk/1/hi/uk/7369543.stm accessed 6 December 2016).

BBC News (2008c) Call for Prison Bugging Inquiry, 9 February (available at http://news.bbc.co.uk/1/hi/uk_politics/7236536.stm accessed 25 November 2016).

BBC News (2011) Police Trial Lie Detectors on Sex Offender Suspects, 31 December 2011 (available at http://www.bbc.co.uk/news/uk-16371043 accessed 23 March 2017).

BBC News (2012a) Manchester Airport's Body Scanners Scrapped, 17 September (available at http://www.bbc.co.uk/news/uk-england-manchester-19620981 accessed 23 August 2016).

BBC News (2012b) Most Prisons Are Overcrowded – Prison Reform Trust, 28 August (available at http://www.bbc.co.uk/news/uk-19395427 accessed 24 November 2016).

BBC News (2013a) Christopher Jefferies Told 'Sorry' by Police over Arrest Distress, 16 September (available at http://www.bbc.co.uk/news/uk-england-bristol-24104834 accessed 8 March 2017).

BBC News (2013b) Ched Evans Rape Case: Tenth Person Fined for Naming Victim, 21 January (available at http://www.bbc.co.uk/news/uk-wales-north-east-wales-21123465 accessed 1 February 2017).

BBC News (2013c) 'Sarah's Law' Sees 700 Paedophiles Identified, 23 December (available at http://www.bbc.co.uk/news/uk-25489541 accessed 15 August 2016).

BBC News (2014a) Leicestershire Police Trial Facial Recognition Software, 15 July (available at http://www.bbc.co.uk/news/uk-england-leicestershire-28307938 accessed 31 October 2016).

BBC News (2014b) Full Jails Told to Take in More Prisoners, 13 June (available at http://www.bbc.co.uk/news/uk-27836961 accessed 18 November 2016).

BBC News (2015a) Dorset, Devon and Cornwall Police Forces to Trial Drones, 2 November (available at http://www.bbc.co.uk/news/uk-england-34700588 accessed 3 March 2017).

BBC News (2015b) Met Police Pay Men over Racism in 2007 Arrest, 2 October (available at http://www.bbc.co.uk/news/uk-england-london-34430530 accessed 2 February 2017).

BBC News (2015c) 'Innocent People' on Police Photo's Database, 3 February (available at http://www.bbc.co.uk/news/uk-31105678 accessed 31 October 2016).

BBC News (2016a) Man Ordered to Tell Police If He Plans to Have Sex, 22 January (available at http://www.bbc.co.uk/news/uk-england-york-north-yorkshire-35385227 accessed 25 July 2016).

BBC News (2016b) 24-Hour Sex Ban Man John O'Neill 'Lost Touch with Children,' 19 July (available at http://www.bbc.co.uk/news/uk-england-york-north-yorkshire-36833018 accessed 25 July 2016).

BBC News (2016c) Hundreds of Rapists and Child Abusers Taken Off Sex Offenders Register, 21 March (available at http://www.bbc.co.uk/news/uk-35833760 accessed 18 December 2016).

BBC News (2017a) Is It OK to Watch Porn in Public? 14 January (available at http://www.bbc.co.uk/news/magazine-38611265 accessed 17 January).

BBC News (2017b) Transgender Woman Found Dead in Cell at HMP Doncaster, 5 January (available at http://www.bbc.co.uk/news/uk-england-south-yorkshire-38518833 accessed 18 March 2017).

BBW (Big Brother Watch) (2010) *The Grim RIPA: Cataloguing the Ways in Which Local Authorities Have Abused Their Covert Surveillance Powers* (available from: http://www.bigbrotherwatch.org.uk/TheGrimRIPA.pdf accessed 6 December 2016).

BBW (Big Brother Watch) (2012) Doncaster Joins the Audio-CCTV Club (Press Release) 31 July, London: BBW.

BBW (Big Brother Watch) (2013) *Online Privacy Survey: International Findings* BBW/ComRes, London (available at https://bigbrotherwatch.org.uk/2013/06/new-research-global-attitudes-to-privacy-online/ accessed 16 April 2017).

BBW (Big Brother Watch) (2014) *Surveillance Transparency Is Now More Important than Ever*, London: BBW.

BBW (Big Brother Watch) (2015) *Body Worn Video Cameras*, London: BBW.

BBW (Big Brother Watch) (2016a) *Safe in Police Hands?* London (available at: https://www.bigbrotherwatch.org.uk/wp-content/uploads/2016/07/Safe-in-Police-Hands.pdf accessed 9 November 2016).

BBW (Big Brother Watch) (2016b) Reaction to the Publication of the Biometrics Commissioner's Annual Report (Press Release) 11 March, London (available at https://bigbrotherwatch.org.uk/all-media/reaction-to-the-publication-of-the-biometrics-commissioners-annual-report/ accessed 20 March 2017).

BBW (Big Brother Watch) (2017) *Smile While You Are on Body Worn Camera: Part 1 – Local Authorities*, February, London (available at https://bigbrotherwatch.org.uk/wp-content/uploads/2017/02/Smile-you-are-on-Body-Worn-Camera-Part-1-1.pdf accessed 14 March 2017).

Beavan C (2001) *Fingerprints: The Origins of Crime Detection and the Murder Case that Launched Forensic Science*, New York: Hyperion.

Bennetto J (2000) Straw Refuses to Allow Public Access to Sex Offender Register. *The Independent*, 16 September.

Bernstein C and Woodward B (1974) *All the Presidents Men*, New York: Simon and Schuster.

Berwick Report (1996) *Inquiry into Legislation Against Terrorism*, Cm 3420, October.

Best, S (2016) The Dog that Sniffs Out Paedophiles: K9 Finds Hidden Child Pornography by Detecting Chemicals in Digital Storage Devices. *Daily Mail*, 24 June.

Bichard Inquiry (2004) *Report* HC 653, June, London: TSO.

Bingham J (2008) Anti-Terror Powers Used to Spy on Paperboys. *Daily Telegraph*, 5 December.

Birkett Report (1957) Report of the Committee of Privy Councillors Appointed to Inquire into the Interception of Communications, Cmnd. 283, October, London: HMSO.

Birth Companions (2016) Birth Charter for Women in Prisons in England and Wales, March, London (available at http://www.birthcompanions.org.uk/media/Public/Resources/Ourpublications/Birth_Charter_Online_copy.pdf accessed 24 November 2016).

Blackledge, S (2013) Metal Detectors on Plymouth Streets from Tonight in Bid to Crack Knife Crime. *The Herald*, 19 April (available at http://www.plymouthherald.co.uk/metal-detectors-plymouth-streets-tonight-bid/story-18744758-detail/story.html accessed 27 February 2017).

Blair T (2002) Rebalancing the Criminal Justice System (Speech), 18 June (Reproduced in *The Guardian* available at https://www.theguardian.com/politics/2002/jun/18/immigrationpolicy.ukcrime1 accessed 28 January 2017).

Blake M (2011) Policemen Sacked After Posing for 'Inappropriate' Photo During Raid. *The Independent*, 4 August.

Bloss WP (2009) *Under a Watchful Eye: Privacy Rights and Criminal Justice*, Santa Barbara, CA: Praeger.

Bobbit, P (2002) *The Shield of Achilles: War, Peace and the Course of History*, New York: Alfred A. Knopf.

Boffey D (2012) Police Are Linked to Blacklist of Construction Workers. *The Guardian*, 3 March.

Boffey D (2013) Police Colluded in Secret Plan to Blacklist 3,200 Building Workers. *The Guardian*, 12 October.

Bonino S and Kaoullas L (2015) Preventing Political Violence in Britain: An Evaluation of over Forty Years of Undercover Policing of Political Groups Involved in Protest. *Studies in Conflict and Terrorism*, 38(10): 814–840.

Bowcott O (2008) Police Will Use New Device to Take Fingerprints in Street. *The Guardian*, 27 October.

Bowcott O (2014) Lie Detector Tests Begin on Sex Offenders. *The Guardian*, 8 August.

Bowling B and Phillips C (2007) Disproportionate and Discriminatory: Reviewing the Evidence on Police Stop and Search. *Modern Law Review*, 70(6): 936–961.

Breed B (1987) *Off the Record*, London: John Clare Books.

Brenner DJ (2011) Are X-Ray Backscatter Scanners Safe for Airport Passenger Screening? For Most Individuals, Probably Yes, but a Billion Scans per Year Raises Long-Term Public Health Concerns. *Radiology*, 259(1): 6–10.

Britten N (2004) Couple Shot Dead in Gang Revenge at the Seaside. *Daily Telegraph*, 10 August.

Brooke C and Martin A (2010) Name the Devil Boys – We Must Not Let Them Hide. *Daily Mail*, 23 January.

Brown S (2014) Synthetic Cannabis Causing Serious Health Problems in English Prisons. *The Guardian*, 15 May.

BSB (Bar Standards Board) (2015) *Handbook* (2nd ed.), London.

Buchanan RT (2015) Transgender Woman Joanne Latham Dies in Milton Keynes Male Prison. *The Independent*, 1 December.

Bud TA (2016) The Rise and Risks of Police Body-Worn Cameras in Canada. *Surveillance and Society*, 14(1): 117–121.

Bunyan T (1977) *The History and Practice of the Political Police in Britain*, London: Quartet Books.

Butcher L (2011) *Aviation: Security*, London: House of Commons Library (available from http://researchbriefings.parliament.uk/ResearchBriefing/Summary/SN01246#fullreport last accessed 23 August 2016).

Cable J (2015) UK Public Opinion Review – Working Paper – An Overview of Public Opinion Polls Since the Edward Snowden Revelations in June 2013, 18th June ESRC and Cardiff University (available at https://sites.cardiff.ac.uk/dcssproject/files/2015/08/UK-Public-Opinion-Review-180615.pdf accessed 16 April 2017).

Cabinet Office (2008a) *Engaging Communities in Fighting Crime*, London.

Cabinet Office (2008b) *The National Security Strategy of the United Kingdom: Security in an Interdependent World*, Cm 7291, March, London.

Cain S (2016) British Woman Held After Being Seen Reading Book About Syria on Plane. *The Guardian*, 4 August.

Calcutt Report (1990) *Report of the Committee on Privacy and Related Matters*, Cm1102, June, London: HMSO.

Cameron D (2016) Prison Reform: Prime Minister's Speech, 8 February (available at: https://www.gov.uk/government/speeches/prison-reform-prime-ministers-speech accessed 22 November 2016).

Campbell A (2011) *Scottish Fingerprint Inquiry Report*, Scotland: APS.

Campbell D (1979) Keeping Tabs on Everyone. *New Statesman*, 10 August.

Campbell D (1980) Society Under Surveillance, in Hain P (ed.) *Policing the Police Volume 2*, London: John Calder.

Campbell D (2012) Why Dawn Raid Works for the Police. *The Guardian*, 13 March.

Campbell D and Connor S (1986) *On the Record: Surveillance, Computers, and Privacy*, London: Michael Joseph.

Campbell D and Norton-Taylor R (2014) Murder in Hampstead: The Author, the Dissident and a Trial Held in Secret. *The Guardian*, 23 January.

Campbell D, Norton-Taylor R and Bowcott O (2014) Trial of AB and CD Part of Creeping Move Towards Secret Justice. *The Guardian*, 12 June.

Campbell D, Norton-Taylor R and Bowcott O (2015) Jailed MI6 Informant Blocked from Taking Case to Court of Human Rights. *The Guardian*, 16 December.

Castle S (2013) TV Message by Snowden Says Privacy Still Matters. *The New York Times*, 25 December.

CCRC (Criminal Cases Review Commission) (2016) Commission Refers the Murder Conviction of Wang Yam to the Court of Appeal (Press Release) 28 April.

CEIS (Centre of Excellence for Information Sharing) (n.d.) Multi-Agency Safeguarding Hubs (available at http://informationsharing.org.uk/wp-content/uploads/2014/10/P0075-MASH-briefing.pdf accessed 12 February 2017).

Channel 4 News (2013) Stephen Lawrence Family 'Targeted in Police Smear Campaign,' 24 June (available at https://www.channel4.com/news/stephen-lawrence-undercover-police-officer-smear-campaign accessed 23 March 2017).

Chomsky N (2016) *Who Rules the World?* New York: Penguin.

Choongh S (1998) Policing the Dross: A Social Disciplinary Model of Policing. *British Journal of Criminology*, 38: 623–634.

Clark D (2007) Covert Surveillance and Informer Handling, in Newburn T, Williamson T and Wright A (eds.) *Handbook of Criminal Investigation*, Cullompton: Willan.

Clarke JS (2014) Metropolitan Police Strip Searched More than 4,500 Children in Five Years. *The Guardian*, 16 March.

Clarkson M and Thomas T (1995) Press Reports of Young Offenders Under s49. *Childright*, 113 Jan/Feb: 5–6.

Clinton W (1996) *Remarks on Signing Megan's Law and an Exchange with Reporters* in Public Papers of the Presidents of the US, William J Clinton, Government Publishing Office, 17 May, Washington DC (available at https://www.gpo.gov/fdsys/granule/PPP-1996-book1/PPP-1996-book1-doc-pg763 accessed 10 February 2017).

Clout L (2007) Talking CCTV Gives Big Brother a Voice. *Daily Telegraph*, 4 April.

Cobain I (2016) Erol Incedal Trial: Media Groups Lose Appeal over Reporting Restrictions. *The Guardian*, 9 February.

CoE (Council of Europe) (1950) *European Convention on Human Rights*, Strasbourg.

CoE (Council of Europe) (1981) *Convention for the Protection of Individuals with Regard to Automatic Processing of Personal Data*, (Convention No. 108), Strasbourg.

CoE (Council of Europe) (1992) Recommendation no. R (92) 16 of the Committee of Ministers to Member States on the European Rules on Community Sanctions and Measures, Strasbourg.

CoE (Council of Europe) (2010) Parliamentary Assembly Prohibiting the Marketing and Use of the 'Mosquito' Youth Dispersal Device (Press Release) 12 July.

College of Policing (2013) Guidance on Relationships with the Media, May, APP Reference Material (available at: http://www.npcc.police.uk/documents/reports/2013/201305-cop-media-rels.pdf accessed 6 September 2017).

College of Policing (2014a) Code of Ethics: A Code of Practice for the Principles and Standards of Professional Behaviour for the Policing Profession of England and Wales, July (available at http://www.college.police.uk/What-we-do/Ethics/Documents/Code_of_Ethics.pdf accessed 29 January 2017).

College of Policing (2014b) *Police Trial Body-Worn Video Begins* (available from http://www.college.police.uk/News/archive/2014jan/Pages/news-Trial-BWV.aspx accessed 23 August 2016).

College of Policing (2014c) *Information Management: Management of Police Information*, APP, 24 October (available at https://www.app.college.police.uk/app-content/information-management/management-of-police-information/ accessed 29 January 2017).

College of Policing (2014d) *Body-Worn Video*, Coventry: College of Policing (available at http://www.college.police.uk/News/archive/2014aug/Documents/Body_worn_video_guidance.pdf accessed 20 March 2017).

College of Policing (2015a) *Stop and Search* (available at: https://www.app.college.police.uk/app-content/stop-and-search/?s=stop accessed 6 May 2017).

College of Policing (2015b) *Detention and Custody – Buildings and Facilities* (available at https://www.app.college.police.uk/app-content/detention-and-custody-2/buildings-and-facilities/ accessed 23 August 2016).

College of Policing (2015c) *Detention and Custody – CCTV* (available at https://www.app.college.police.uk/app-content/detention-and-custody-2/buildings-and-facilities/cctv/ accessed 23 August 2016).

College of Policing (2016a) *Covert Policing* (available at: https://www.app.college.police.uk/app-content/covert-policing/undercover-policing/ accessed 6 December 2016).

College of Policing (2016b) *Public Order – Command AAP* (available at https://www.app.college.police.uk/app-content/public-order/command/#considerations-and-principles accessed 24 March 2017).

College of Policing (2016c) *Information Management* – APP (available at http://www.app.college.police.uk/app-content/information-management/?s accessed 24 October 2016).

College of Policing (2016d) *Public Order: Tactical Options APP* (available at: https://www.app.college.police.uk/app-content/public-order/planning-and-deployment/tactical-options/ accessed 6 May 2017).

College of Policing (2016e) *Investigation: ANPR* (available at https://www.app.college.police.uk/app-content/investigations/investigative-strategies/investigative-strategiesanpr/#top accessed 14 February 2017).

Commissioner of Police for the Metropolis (1925) Annual Report for the Year 1924, Cmd. 2480, London: HMSO.

Commissioner for the Retention and Use of Biometric Material (2014) *Annual Report 2014*, March, London: Office of the Biometric Commissioner.

Commissioner for the Retention and Use of Biometric Material (2016) *Annual Report 2015*, March, London: Office of the Biometric Commissioner.

Corera G (2015) *Intercept: The Secret History of Computers and Spies*, London: Weidenfeld & Nicolson.

Corston Report (2007) *A Report by Baroness Jean Corston of a Review of Women with Particular Vulnerabilities in the Criminal Justice System*, London.

Council of the European Union (2016) *Proposal for a Directive of the European Parliament and of the Council on Procedural Safeguards for Children Suspected or Accused in Criminal Proceedings* Brussels, 16 March 2016 *PE-CONS 2/16*.

Court of Justice of the European Union (2014) The Court of Justice Declares the Data Retention Directive to Be Invalid (Press Release) No. 54/14 Luxembourg, 8 April 2014.

CLRC (Criminal Law Revision Committee) (1984) Sexual Offences (15th report), Cmnd. 9213, London: HMSO.

CPS (Crown Prosecution Service) (2009) The Director's Guidance on Witness Anonymity, December (available at http://www.cps.gov.uk/publications/directors_guidance/witness_anonymity.html accessed 1 February 2017).

CRAE (Children's Rights Alliance for England) (2014) *State of Children's Rights in England – Review of Government Action on United Nations' Recommendations for Strengthening Children's Rights in the UK*, London: CRAE.

Creedon M (2013) Operation Herne: Report 1 Use of Covert Identities, Derbyshire Constabulary (available at: http://www.derbyshire.police.uk/About-us/Operation-Herne/Operation-Herne.aspx accessed 16 March 2017).

Creedon M (2014a) Operation Herne: Operation Trinity Report 2 Allegations of Peter Francis, Derbyshire Constabulary (available at: http://www.derbyshire.police.uk/About-us/Operation-Herne/Operation-Herne.aspx accessed 16 March 2017).

Creedon M (2014b) Operation Herne: Special Demonstration Squad Reporting: Mentions of Sensitive Campaigns, Derbyshire Constabulary (available at: http://www.derbyshire.police.uk/About-us/Operation-Herne/Operation-Herne.aspx accessed 16 March 2017).

Crystal G (2016a) *Consequences for Refusing a Full Airport Body Scan*, Cheshire: Civil Rights Movement (available from http://www.civilrightsmovement.co.uk/consequences-for-refusing-full-airport-body-scan.html accessed 23 August 2016).

Crystal G (2016b) *Airport Body Scanners a Breach of Privacy?* Cheshire: Civil Rights Movement (available from http://www.civilrightsmovement.co.uk/airport-body-scanners-breach-privacy.html accessed 23 August 2016).

CSJ (Centre for Social Justice) (2015) *Drugs in Prison*, March (available at http://www.centreforsocialjustice.org.uk/core/wp-content/uploads/2016/08/CSJJ3090_Drugs_in_Prison.pdf accessed 22 November 2016).

Daily Mail (2009) Police Paid Out £560,000 in Compensation for Raiding the Wrong Properties. *Daily Mail*, 28 December.

Daily Mail (2010) The Bionic-Arm of the Law: Police Unveil New Metal Detector Glove to Fight Knife Crime. *Daily Mail*, 31 March.

Davies M, Croall H and Tyrer J (2010) *Criminal Justice* (4th ed.), Harlow: Pearson Education Ltd.

DBS News (Disclosure and Barring Service) (2016) Met Police Update: Working Together to Reduce Backlogs, March, Royal Wootton Bassett (available at https://www.gov.uk/government/uploads/system/uploads/attachment_data/file/513260/DBS_News_March_2016_Final.pdf accessed 10 May 2017).

Delsol R and Shiner M (2006) Regulating Stop and Search: A Challenge for Police and Community Relations in England and Wales. *Critical Criminology*, 14(3): 241–263

DCLG (Department for Communities and Local Government) (2007) *Preventing Violent Extremism: Winning Hearts and Minds*, London: DCLG.

Department for Transport (2010) *Interim Code of Practice for the Acceptable Use of Advanced Imaging Technology (Body Scanners) in an Aviation Security Environment*, London: Department for Transport.

Department for Transport (2016a) *Security Scanners Implementation Information – Guidance*, London: DfT (available from https://www.gov.uk/government/publications/information-on-the-implementation-of-security-scanners accessed 23 August 2016).

Department for Transport (2016b) *Security Scanners Direction 2016* (available at https://www.gov.uk/government/uploads/system/uploads/attachment_data/file/573488/security-scanner-direction-2016.pdf accessed 2 February 2017).

Department of Health (2015) *Mental Health Act 1983: Code of Practice*, London: TSO.

Department of Health and Home Office (2014) *Review of the Operation of Sections 135 and 136 of the Mental Health Act 1983: Review Report and Recommendations*, London: Department of Health.

DETR (Department of the Environment, Transport and the Regions) (1999) *Proposed New Regulations on Number Plates*, (Covering Letter to Consultation Exercise), 5 August (available at https://web.archive.org/web/20011224185632/http://www.roads.dtlr.gov.uk/vehicle/consult/numberplates/letter.htm accessed 15 February 2017).

DHSS (Department of Health and Social Security) (1976) Non-Accidental Injury to Children: The Police and Case Conferences, (DHSS Circular 76 (26)), London.

DHSS (Department of Health and Social Security) (1978) Release of Prisoners Convicted of Offences Against Children in the Home (Circular LAC (78) 22), London.

Diplock Report (1981) *The Interception of Communications in Great Britain*, Cmnd. 8191, March, London: HMSO.

DoH (Department of Health) (1991) *Working Together Under the Children Act 1989 – A Guide to Arrangements for Inter-Agency Co-Operation for the Protection of Children from Abuse*, London: HMSO.

DoH (Department of Health) (2012) *"Striking the Balance" Practical Guidance on the Application of Caldicott Guardian Principles to Domestic Violence and MARACs (Multi Agency Risk Assessment Conferences)*, London (available at https://www.gov.uk/government/uploads/system/uploads/attachment_data/file/215064/dh_133594.pdf accessed 6 December 2016).

DoH (Department of Health) Home Office, Department for Communications and Local Government, Ministry of Justice and Department for Education (2015) Our Joint Commitment to Share Information Effectively for the Protection of Children, 3 March, London.

Dovey HO (1986) Why National Registration Had to Go. *Public Administration*, 64: 459.

Doyle J (2013) Theresa May Under Pressure over Tagging Controls After Terror Suspects Goes on the Run Leaving London Mosque in a Burka. *The Daily Mail*, 3 November.

DSOU (Don't Spy on Us) (2016) *Investigatory Powers Bill: How to Make It Fit-For-Purpose* (available from: https://www.dontspyonus.org.uk/blog/2016/02/26/investigatory-powers-bill-how-to-make-it-fit-for-purpose/).

DSOU (Don't Spy on Us) (2017) Web Site (available at: https://www.dontspyonus.org.uk/ last accessed 16 March 2017).

Durham R, Lawson R, Lord A and Baird V (2017) *Seeing Is Believing – The Northumbria Court Observers Panel. Report on 30 Rape Trials 2015–16*, Newcastle: Northumbria Police and Crime Commissioners Office.

Dyer C (2000) Privacy Violated by Gay Sex Laws. *The Guardian*, 1 August.

Dyer C (2003a) Law Lords Rule There Is No Right to Privacy. *The Guardian*, 17 October.

Dyer C (2003b) Court Blow for 'Name and Shame' Drive. *The Guardian*, 13 June.

Ellis D (2010) Stop and Search Disproportionality Discretion and Generalizations. *The Police Journal*, 83: 199–216.

Ellis T, Jenkins C and Smith P (2015). *Body-Worn Video: Evaluation of the Introduction of Personal Issue Body Worn Video Cameras (Operation Hyperion) on the Isle of Wight*, Portsmouth: University of Portsmouth (available at https://researchportal.port.ac.uk/portal/files/2197790/Operation_Hyperion_Final_Report_to_Hampshire_Constabulary.pdf accessed 26 February 2017).

Ellison M (2014) *The Stephen Lawrence Independent Review – Possible Corruption and the Role of Undercover Policing in the Stephen Lawrence Case*, HC 1094, London: TSO.

Ellison M and Morgan A (2015) *Review of Possible Miscarriages of Justice: Impact of Undisclosed Undercover Police Activity on the Safety of Convictions*, a Report to the Attorney General, July HC 291, London: TSO.

EU (European Union) (1995) Directive 95/46/EC of the European Parliament and of the Council of 24 October 1995 on the Protection of Individuals with Regard to the Processing of Personal Data and on the Free Movement of Such Data, *Official Journal L 281, 23/11/1995 P. 0031 – 0050*, Brussels.

EU (European Union) (2000) *Charter of Fundamental Rights of the European Union*, (2000/C 364/01), Brussels.

European Commission (2012) *What Are the Technologies Used in the Proposed Security Scanners?* (available at http://ec.europa.eu/health/scientific_committees/opinions_layman/security-scanners/en/l-3/3-technology.htm accessed 23 August 2016).

Evans N (2014) Rape Suspects Need Anonymity. *Spectator*, 17 May.

Evans R (2016) Protester, 91, Goes to European Court over Secret Police Files. *The Guardian*, 25 July.

Evans R and Lewis P (2011a) Undercover Officer Spied on Green Activists. *The Guardian*, 9 January.

Evans R and Lewis P (2011b) Activists Walk Free as Undercover Officer Prompts Collapse of Case. *The Guardian*, 10 January.

Evans R and Lewis P (2013a) *Undercover the True Story of Britain's Secret Police*, London: Faber and Faber Ltd.

Evans R and Lewis P (2013b) Police Spy: 'I Thought, How Would They Feel About Their Son's Name Being Used'. *The Guardian*, 3 February.

Evans R and Lewis P (2015) Scotland Yard Shut Down Undercover Police Unit Because It Broke Rules. *The Guardian*, 26 July.

Evans R, Lewis P and Dodd V (2011) Revealed: Second Undercover Police Officer Who Posed as an Activist. *The Guardian*, 13 January.

Feldman D (1994) Secrecy, Dignity or Autonomy? Views of Privacy as a Civil Liberty. *Current Legal Problems*, 47(2): 41–71.

Fenton S (2016) The Women Forced to Give Birth in Front of Prison Guards. *The Independent*, 25 May.

Fido J (1977) The Charity Organisation Society and Social Casework in London 1869–1900, in Donajgrodski AP (ed.) *Social Control in Nineteenth Century Britain*, London: Croom Helm.

Finnigan L (2016) Man Ordered to Give Police 24-Hour Notice Before Sex Has Order Lifted. *Daily Telegraph*, 23 September.

Fitch K (2006) *Megan's Law: Does it Protect Children (2)*, London: NSPCC.

Fitzgerald P and Leopold M (1987) *Stranger on the Line*, London: Bodley Head.

Fitzgerald M (1999) *Report into Stop and Search*, London: Metropolitan Police Service.

Ford R (2004) Beware Rise of Big Brother State, Warns Data Watchdog. *The Times*, 16 August.

Forrester K (2013) Merseyside Police Apologise After Armed Officers Raid Family Home in Liverpool by Mistake'. *Liverpool Echo*, 7 May (available at http://www.liverpoolecho.co.uk/news/liverpool-news/merseyside-police-apologise-after-armed-3337814 accessed 23 August 2016).

FRA (Fundamental Rights Agency) (2010) *The Use of Body Scanners: 10 Questions and Answers*, Luxembourg: European Union Agency for Fundamental Rights, Vienna, Austria (available at http://fra.europa.eu/en/opinion/2011/use-body-scanners-10-questions-and-answers accessed 27 February 2017).

Franklin B and Murphy D (1991) Local Rags with a Reputation in Tatters. *The Independent*, 30 October.

Franklin B and Petley J (1996) Killing the Age of Innocence: Newspaper Reporting of the Death of James Bulger, in Pilcher and Wagg.

G4S (2017) Voice Verification (available at http://www.g4s.uk.com/en-GB/What%20we%20do/Services/Care%20and%20justice%20services/Electronic%20monitoring/Voice%20verification/ accessed 19 March 2017).

Gannon T, Wood J, Afroditi PA, Vasquesz E and Fraser I (2012) *The Evaluation of the Mandatory Polygraph Pilot*, University of Kent Ministry of Justice Research Series 14, Canterbury: University of Kent.

Gannon T, Wood J, Afroditi PA, Vasquesz E and Fraser I (2014) An Evaluation of Mandatory Polygraph Testing for Sexual Offenders in the United Kingdom. *Sex Abuse: A Journal of Research and Treatment*, 26(2): 178–203.

Gardiner Report (1972) *Living It Down: The Problem of Old Convictions*, Justice, NACRO, and the Howard League, London: A Stephens Publication.

Garfinkel S (2000) *Database Nation: The Death of Privacy in the 21st Century*, Sebastopol, CA: O'Reilly.

Garton Ash T (2016a) *Free Speech: Ten Principles for a Connected World*, London: Atlantic Books.

Garton Ash, T (2016b) Safe Spaces Are Not the Only Threat to Free Speech. *The Guardian*, 16 September.

Gayle D (2012) Are You One of the 20,000 People Wrongly Branded a Criminal? Police Blunders Give Thousands Records for Crimes They Have Not Committed – Official Figures Downplay the Scale of the Problem. *Mail Online*, 28 December (available at: http://www.dailymail.co.uk/news/article-2095303/Police-blunders-thousands-records-crimes-committed.html accessed 9 November 2016).

Gayle D (2015) Transgender Prisoner at HMP Bristol 'Being Sexually Harassed'. *The Guardian*, 20 November.

Gearson J and Rosemont H (2015) CONTEST as Strategy: Reassessing Britain's Counterterrorism Approach. *Studies in Conflict & Terrorism*, 38(12): 1038–1064.

Goldman L (2006) The Constitutional Right to Privacy. *Denver University Law Review*, 84: 601–605.

Gov.uk (2009) Prison, Probation and Rehabilitation: Public Protection Manual (available at https://www.gov.uk/government/collections/prison-probation-and-rehabilitation-public-protection-manual accessed 21 April 2017).

Gov.uk (2013) DBS Filtering Guide (available at https://www.gov.uk/government/publications/dbs-filtering-guidance/dbs-filtering-guide accessed 17 April 2017).

Gov.uk (2015a) *Police Powers to Stop and Search: Your Rights* (available at https://www.gov.uk/police-powers-to-stop-and-search-your-rights accessed 23 August 2016).

Gov.uk (2015b) *Your Rights at the Airport*, London (available at https://www.gov.uk/airport-rights accessed 23 August 2016).

Gov.uk (2016) *Being Arrested: Your Rights*, London (available at https://www.gov.uk/arrested-your-rights/how-long-you-can-be-held-in-custody accessed 23 August 2016).

Gov.uk (2017a) *Rules for Passport Photos*, London (available at https://www.gov.uk/photos-for-passports accessed 20 March 2017).

Gov.uk (2017b) *Apply for a Gender Recognition Certificate*, London (Available at https://www.gov.uk/apply-gender-recognition-certificate/overview accessed 8 May 2017).

Gov.uk (2017c) DBS Checks (Previously CRB Checks) (available at https://www.gov.uk/disclosure-barring-service-check/overview accessed 8 May 2017).

Greenfield SH (2014) 'The Missing Video Presumption', *Simple Justice: A Criminal Defence Blog* (available from http://blog.simplejustice.us/2014/03/30/the-missing-video-presumption/ accessed 23 August 2016).

Greenslade R (2016) New Police Guidelines Reinforce Controls on Journalistic Contacts. *The Guardian*, 25 May.

Greenwald G, Poitras L and MacAskill E (2013) Edward Snowden: US Surveillance 'Not Something I'm Willing to Live Under'. *The Guardian*, 8 July.

Grey A (1992) *Quest for Justice; Towards Homosexual Emancipation*, London: Sinclair-Stevenson.

Grossmith L, Owens C, Finn W, Mann D, Davies T and Baika L (2015). *Police, Camera, Evidence: London's Cluster Randomised Controlled Trial of Body Worn Video*, London: College of Policing and the Mayor's Office for Policing and Crime (MOPAC).

Groves N and Thomas T (2014) *Domestic Violence and Criminal Justice*, Abingdon: Routledge.

Grubin D (2006) *Polygraph Pilot Study: Final Report*, London: Home Office.

Grundy S (1990) Fast and Friendly. *Police Review*, 2 June.

Halford A and Barnes T (1993) *No Way Up the Greasy Pole: The Fight for Equality*, London: Constable.

Halifax Evening Courier (2008) Menace to Be Set Free: But We Can't Show You What He Looks Like, 27 September (available at: http://www.halifaxcourier.co.uk/news/menace-to-be-set-free-1-1918605 accessed 2 February 2017).

Halifax Evening Courier (Letters) (2008) Showing His Pic Would Not Help, 3 October (available at http://www.halifaxcourier.co.uk/news/letters/showing-his-pic-would-not-help-1-1918974 accessed 21 July 2016).

Hall K (2011) Police National Database Launched Containing Details of 15 Million UK Citizens. *Computer Weekly*, 22 June.

Halliday J (2011) Sun and Mirror Fined for Contempt of Court in Christopher Jefferies Articles. *The Guardian*, 29 July.

Halliday J (2016) Almost 4,000 People Referred to UK De-Radicalisation Scheme Last Year. *The Guardian*, 20 March.

Halliday J and Mason R (2015) Pritchard Calls for Rape Anonymity Laws to Be Reviewed After Case Dropped. *The Guardian*, 6 January.

Hamilton M and Sims P (2016) Johnson in the Perm-ier League: Footie paedo Has Landed 'Cushy' Job Inside as a BARBER. *The Sun*, 23 May.

Haskins Report (1999) *Review of Fit Person Criteria: A Review of the Criteria Used to Judge People's Suitability for Certain Occupations*, Better Regulation Task Force, May, London: Cabinet Office.

Heilbron Committee (1975) Report of the Advisory Group on the Law on Rape, Cmnd. 6352, London: HMSO.

Herbert I (2005) Mother Says Boy, 10, with Asbo is 'Cheeky' and in Bad Company. *The Independent*, 10 February.

Hirsch A (2011) Mark Kennedy and the Strange Case of Undercover Sex. *The Guardian*, 13 January.

HM Prison Service (2007) Mandatory Drug Testing (Order Number 3601), London.

HMG (HM Government) (2006a) *Countering International Errorism: The United Kingdom's Strategy*, July 2006, Cm 6888, London.

HMG (HM Government) (2006b) *Information Sharing Vision Statement*, DCA 47/06, September, London.

HMG (HM Government) (2010a) *The Coalition: Our Programme for Government*, May, London: Cabinet Office.

HMG (HM Government) (2010b) *Securing Britain in an Age of Uncertainty: The Strategic Defence and Security Review*, Cmnd. 7948, London.

HMG (HM Government) (2011) *Prevent Strategy*, June, Cm 8092, London.

HMG (HM Government) (2015) *Channel Duty Guidance: Protecting Vulnerable People from Being Drawn into Terrorism*, London.

HMG (HM Government) (2016a) *CONTEST – The United Kingdom's Strategy for Countering Terrorism: Annual Report for 2015*, July 2016, Cm 9310, London.

HMG (HM Government) (2016b) *The Government Response to the Annual Report on the Operation of the Terrorism Acts in 2014 by the Independent Reviewer of Terrorism Legislation*, Cm 9357, November, London: Home Office.

HMIC (HM Inspectorate of Constabulary) (2000) *On the Record: Thematic Inspection Report on Police Crime Recording, the Police National Computer, and Phoenix Intelligence System Data Quality*, July, London.

HMIC (HM Inspectorate of Constabulary) (2002) *Police National Computer Data Quality and Timeliness (Second Report)*, London: Home Office.

HMIC (HM Inspectorate of Constabulary) (2012) *A Review of National Police Units Which Provide Intelligence on Criminality Associated with Protest*, February, London.

HMIC (HM Inspectorate of Constabulary) (2013a) *Stop and Search Powers: Are the Police Using Them Effectively and Fairly?* (available at: http://www.justice-inspectorates.gov.uk/hmic/media/stop-and-search-powers-20130709.pdf last accessed 23 August 2016).

HMIC (HM Inspectorate of Constabulary) (2013b) *A Review of Progress Made Against the Recommendations in HMIC's 2012 Report on the National Police Units Which Provide Intelligence on Criminality Associated with Protest*, June, London.

HMIC (HM Inspectorate of Constabulary) (2014) *A Inspection of Undercover Policing in England and Wales*, October, London.

HMIC (HM Inspectorate of Constabulary) (2015) *Building the Picture: An Inspection of Police Information Management*, July, London.

HMIC (HM Inspectorate of Constabulary) (2016a) *PEEL: Police Legitimacy 2015: A National Overview*, London: HMIC.

HMIC (HM Inspectorate of Constabulary) (2016b) Non-police Organisations' Use of the Police National Computer (Press Release) 10 May.

HMIP (HM Inspectorate of Prisons) (2015) Report by HM Inspectorate of Prisons, Prison Communications Inquiry by HM Chief Inspector of Prisons, July, London.

Hollingsworth M and Norton-Taylor R (1988) *Blacklist: The Inside Story of Political Vetting*, London: The Hogarth Press.

Home Office (1938) *Report of the Departmental Committee on Detective Work and Procedure*, Vol. 3 Chapter 5, London: HMSO.

Home Office (1964) Children and Young Persons Act 1963: Parts 1 and 11 (Circular No. 22/1964), London.

Home Office (1969) Police National Computer (Circular no. 152/1969), London.

Home Office (1980) *The Interception of Communications in Great Britain*, Cmnd. 7873, April, London: HMSO.

Home Office (1981) *The Interception of Communications in Great Britain*, Cmnd. 8191, March, London: HMSO.

Home Office (1984) *Guidelines on the Use of Equipment in Police Surveillance Operations*, London.

Home Office (1985) The Interception of Communications in the United Kingdom, Cmnd. 9438, June, London: HMSO.

Home Office (1989) Press Access to Court Lists and to the Register of Decisions in Magistrates Courts (Circular 80/1989), London.

Home Office (1991) *The National Collection of Criminal Records: Report of an Efficiency Scrutiny*, London.

Home Office (1993) Disclosure of Criminal Records for Employment Vetting Purposes: A Consultation Paper by the Home Office, Cm 2319, September, London: HMSO.

Home Office (1995a) DNA Database Goes Live (Press Release) 10 April, London.

Home Office (1995b) *Phoenix – Putting You in the Picture*, London.

Home Office (1996) *On the Record: The Government's Proposals for Access to Criminal Records for Employment and Related Purposes in England and Wales*, Cm 3308, London: HMSO.

Home Office (1998) *Speaking Up for Justice: Report of an Interdepartmental Working Group on the treatment of Vulnerable or Intimidated Witnesses in the Criminal Justice System*, June, London.

Home Office (1999a) Prime Minister Announces Hi-Tech Drive Against Crime (Press Release) 28 September.

Home Office (1999b) *Interception of Communications: A Consultation Paper*, Cm 4368, June.

Home Office (2000) *Regulation of Investigatory Powers Act 2000 – Explanatory Notes.*

Home Office (2002) *Breaking the Circle: A Review of the Rehabilitation of Offenders Act 1974*, July, London: TSO.

Home Office (2003) *Breaking the Circle: A Summary of the Views of Consultees and the Government's Response to the Report of the Review of the Rehabilitation of Offenders Act 1974*, April, London.

Home Office (2004) One Step Ahead: A 21st Century Strategy to Detect Organised Crime, Cm 6167, March, London.

Home Office (2005a) *Code of Practice on the Management of Police Information*, July, Wyboston: National Centre for Policing Excellence.

Home Office (2005b) *Code of Practice – The Police National Computer*, National Centre for Policing Excellence, January, Wyboston.

Home Office (2006a) Sir Lawrence Byford Report into the Police Handling of the Yorkshire Ripper Case (available at https://www.gov.uk/government/publications/sir-lawrence-byford-report-into-the-police-handling-of-the-yorkshire-ripper-case accessed 28 January 2017).

Home Office (2006b) Green Light for National Police Database (Press Release) 19 April.

Home Office (2006c) Electronic Monitoring on Bail for Adults: Procedures (Circular No. 25/2006), London.

Home Office (2007a) *Guidance for the Police Use of Body-Worn Video Devices, Police and Crime Standards Directorate*, London: Home Office.

Home Office (2007b) Talking CCTV Brings Voice of Authority to the Street (Press Release) 4 April.

Home Office (2007c) *Plymouth Head Camera Project – Body-Worn Video Recording System (Head Cameras): National Pilot, Final Report, April 2007*, London: Home Office.

Home Office (2007d) *Power of Search and Entry to Risk Assess Sex Offenders Subject to the Notification Requirements* (Circular No. 17/2007) London.

Home Office (2008) Government Responds to Casey Report (Press Release) 18 June, London.

Home Office (2009) Local Communities to Be Informed of Sentences (Press Release) 3 December, London.

Home Office (2010) Operation of Police Powers Under the Terrorism Act 2000 and Subsequent Legislation: Arrests, Outcomes and Stops & Searches, Great Britain 2009/10, Home Office Statistical Bulletin, 28 October, London.

Home Office (2010) The Child Sex Offender (CSO) Disclosure Scheme (Circular No. 007/2010), London.

Home Office (2012a) Police Officer Misconduct, Unsatisfactory Performance and Attendance Management Procedures – Guidance, Version 2, November.

Home Office (2012b) *The Government's Alcohol Strategy*, Cm 8336, March, London.

Home Office (2012c) *Guidance on Review of Indefinite Notification Requirements Issued Under Section 91F of the Sexual Offences Act 2003*, London.

Home Office (2013a) Home Secretary Launches Consultation into Stop and Search (Press Release) 2 July, London.

Home Office (2013b) PACE Code of Practice B *Police Powers to Search Premises and to Seize and Retain Property Found on Premises and Persons*, London.

Home Office (2013c) *Protection of Freedoms Act 2012: How DNA and Fingerprint Evidence Is Protected in Law*, London: Home Office.

Home Office (2013d) *Surveillance Camera Code of Practice*, June, London: TSO.

Home Office (2013e) *Using Conditional Cautions with Sobriety Requirements*, London: Home Office.

Home Office (2013f) Clare's Law to Become a National Scheme (Press Release) 25 November, London.

Home Office (2014a) *Police Powers of Stop and Search Summary of Consultation Responses and Conclusions*, London: Home Office.

Home Office (2014b) *Best Use of Stop and Search Scheme*, London: Home Office/College of Policing.

Home Office (2014c) *Covert Surveillance and Property Interference*, Code of Practice, December, London: TSO.

Home Office (2014d) *Data Retention and Investigatory Powers Act 2014*, London: Guidance.

Home Office (2014e) *Covert Human Intelligence Sources – Code of Practice*, December, London: TSO.

Home Office (2014f) *Guidance on ANPR Performance Assessment and Optimisation,* March, Publication No. 8/14, London.

Home Office (2014g) *Post-Legislative Scrutiny of the Counter-Terrorism Act 2008*, Memorandum to the Home Affairs Committee, Cm 8834, March, London.

Home Office (2014h) *Multi Agency Working and Information Sharing Project – Final Report*, July, London.

Home Office (2015a) PACE Code of Practice A *Exercise by Police Officers of Statutory Powers to Search a Person or a Vehicle Without First Making an Arrest and the Need for a Police Officer to Make a Record of a Stop or Encounter*, London.

Home Office (2015b) *Police Powers and Procedures England and Wales Year Ending 31 March 2015*, London: Home Office.

Home Office (2015c) *National DNA Database Strategy Board Annual Report 2014/15*, London: Home Office.

Home Office (2015d) Home Secretary Announces Statutory Inquiry into Undercover Policing (Press Release) 12 March, London.

Home Office (2015e) *Police Officer Misconduct, Unsatisfactory Performance and Attendance Management Procedures* Guidance Version 4, May.

Home Office (2015f) Review of the Retention and Use of Biometric Material Provided by the Protection of Freedoms Act 2012 (Home Office Response to Biometrics Commissioner Annual Report – available at https://www.gov.uk/government/news/publication-of-the-governments-response-to-the-biometrics-commissioners-first-annual-report accessed 27 September 2015).

Home Office (2015g) *Anti-Social Behaviour, Crime and Policing Act 2014: Reform of Anti-Social Behaviour Powers – Statutory Guidance for Frontline Professionals*, July, London.

Home Office (2015h) *Code of Practice for Examining Officers and Review Officers Under Schedule 7 to the Terrorism Act 2000*, 25 March, London: TSO.

Home Office (2016a) RIPA Codes (available at: https://www.gov.uk/government/collections/ripa-codes#current-codes-of-practice accessed 16 March 2017).

Home Office (2016b) Investigatory Powers Bill Receives Royal Assent (Press Release) 29 October, London.

Home Office (2016c) *Investigatory Powers Bill: Government Response to Pre-Legislative Scrutiny*, Cm 9219, March, London.

Home Office (2016d) *Guidance on Part 2 of the Sexual Offences Act 2003*, November, London: Public Protection Unit.

Home Office (2017a) PACE Code of Practice C *Requirements for the Detention, Treatment and Questioning of Suspects Not Related to Terrorism in Police Custody by Police Officers. Includes the Requirement to Explain a Person's Rights While Detained*, London.

Home Office (2017b) PACE Code of Practice D *Main methods Used by the Police to Identify People in Connection with the Investigation of Offences and the Keeping of Accurate and Reliable Criminal Records*, London.

Home Office (2017c) PACE Code of Practice H *Requirements for the Detention, Treatment and Questioning of Suspects Related to Terrorism in Police Custody by Police Officers. Includes the Requirement to Explain a Person's Rights While Detained in Connection with Terrorism*, London.

Home Office/Department of Health (1992) *Memorandum of Good Practice*, London: HMSO.

Home Office, ACPO and PA Consulting Group (2004) *Driving Crime Down: Denying Criminals the Use of the Road*, October, London: TSO.

Home Office, College of Policing, ACPO, Scottish Police Authority, Ministry of Justice (2013) *ViSOR Standards Version 3.1*, London.

Home Office, Department of Health, Department for Communities and Local Government, Ministry of Justice and Department for Education (2015) *Our Joint Commitment to Share Information Effectively for the Protection of Children* (Letter 3 March) (available at https://www.gov.uk/government/uploads/system/uploads/attachment_data/file/408843/info_sharing_letterv5.pdf accessed 12 February 2017).

Hope C (2008) Local Authorities Launched 10,000 Snooping Operations Last Year. *The Telegraph*, 22 July.

Hopkins N (2013) UK Gathering Secret Intelligence Via Covert NSA Operation. *The Guardian*, 7 June.

Hopkins N and Watt N (2013) Prism: Ministers Challenged over GCHQ's Access to Covert US Operation. *The Guardian*, 7 June.

Horne A and Berman G (2012) Pre-Charge Detention in Terrorism Cases, House of Commons Library.

House of Commons (1990) *Criminal Records* Home Affairs Committee, (3rd Report Session 1989–90), HC 285, April, London.

House of Commons (2001) *Criminal Records Bureau* Home Affairs Committee, (2nd Report Session 2000–2001), HC227, March, London.

House of Commons (2003) *Privacy and Media Intrusion* Culture, Media and Sport Select Committee (5th Report of Session 2002–3), Vol. 1 HC 458-1, May, London.

House of Commons (2008) *A Surveillance Society?* Home Affairs Committee (5th Report of Session 2007–08), HC 58-I, May, London.

House of Commons (2013) *Blacklisting in Employment: Addressing the Crimes of the Past; Moving Towards Best Practice* Scottish Affairs Committee (6th Report of Session 2013–4), HC 543, March, London.

House of Commons (2014) *Police, the Media, and High-Profile Criminal Investigations* Home Affairs Committee (5th Report of Session 2014–15), HC629, October, London.

House of Commons (2015a) *Privacy and Security: A Modern and Transparent Legal Framework* Intelligence and Security Committee, HC 1075, March, London.

House of Commons (2015b) *Policing and Mental Health* Home Affairs Committee (11th Report of Session 2014–15), HC 202 February, London.

House of Commons (2015c) *Police Bail*, Home Affairs Committee (17th Report of Session 2014–5), HC 962, March, London.

House of Commons (2015d) *Current and Future Use of Biometric Data and Technologies* Science and Technology Committee, (6th Report of Session 2014–5), HC 734, February, London.

House of Commons (2015e) *Transgender Equality Inquiry*, Women and Equalities Committee (1st Report of Session 2015–16), HC 390, October, London.

House of Commons (2016a) *Investigatory Powers Bill: Technology Issues* Science and Technology Committee (3rd Report of Session 2015–16), HC 573, January, London.

House of Commons (2016b) *Support for Ex-offenders*, Works and Pensions Committee (5th Report of Session 2016–7), HC 58, 19 December.

House of Lords (2009) *Surveillance: Citizens and the State* Select Committee on the Constitution (2nd Report of Session 2008–9), HL Paper 18–1, February, London: TSO.

House of Lords/House of Commons (2010) *Counter Terrorism Policy and Human Rights (Sixteenth Report): Annual Renewal of Control Orders Legislation 2010*, Joint Committee on Human Rights (9th Report of Session 2009–10), HL Paper 64/HC 395, February, London.

House of Lords/House of Commons (2012) *Draft Communications Data Bill*, Joint Committee on the Draft Communications Data Bill (Session 2012–13), HL Paper 79/HC 479, December, London.

House of Lords/House of Commons (2014) *Post-Legislative Scrutiny: Terrorism Prevention and Investigation Measures Act 2011*, Joint Committee on Human Rights, HL Paper 113/HC 1014, London.

House of Lords/House of Commons (2016) *Draft Investigatory Powers Bill – Report*, Joint Committee on the Draft Investigatory Powers Bill HL Paper 93/HC 651, February, London.

Hurrell K (2013) *An Experimental Analysis of Examinations and Detentions Under Schedule 7 of the Terrorism Act 2000*, Briefing Paper 8, Manchester: Equality and Human Rights Commission.

IATA (International Air Transport Association) (2015) *IATA Global Passenger Survey* (available at http://www.iata.org/publications/Pages/global-passenger-survey.aspx accessed 23 August 2016).

ICC (Interception of Communications Commissioner) (2015) *Half-Yearly Report of the Interception of Communications Commissioner*, HC 308, July, London.

ICO (Information Commissioner's Office) (2006) *What Price Privacy? The Unlawful Trade in Confidential Personal Information*, Wilmslow: ICO.

ICO (Information Commissioner's Office) (2007) Police Told to Delete Old Criminal Conviction Records (Press Release) 1 November, Wilmslow.

ICO (Information Commissioner's Office) (2011) *Data Sharing Code of Practice*, May, Wilmslow.

ICO (Information Commissioner's Office) (2014) *Conducting Privacy Impact Assessment: Code of Practice*, Wilmslow.

ICO (Information Commissioner's Office) (2015) *In the Picture: A Data Protection Code of Practice for Surveillance Cameras and Personal Information*, 21 May, Wilmslow.

ICO (Information Commissioner's Office) (2016) Police Force Fined for Passing on Personal Details in Domestic Abuse Case (Press Release) 21 April.

Ignatieff M (1978) *A Just Measure of Pain*, New York: Random House.

Ignatieff M (2002) Human Rights, the Laws of War, and Terrorism. *Social Research*, 69(4): 1143–1164.

Investigatory Powers Tribunal (2015) *Caroline Lucas Judgement* (available at: https://www.judiciary.gov.uk/judgments/investigatory-powers-tribunal-caroline-lucas-othrs-v-the-security-service-and-othrs/ accessed 6 December 2016).

IPCC (Independent Police Complaints Commission) (2010) *Independent Investigation into the Use of ANPR in Durham, Cleveland and North Yorkshire from 23–26 October 2009* London (available at https://www.ipcc.gov.uk/sites/default/files/Documents/investigation_commissioner_reports/ANPR%20Report%20to%20publish_1.pdf accessed 14 March 2017).

IPCC (Independent Police Complaints Commission) (2011a) *Learning the Lessons – Case 13, Bulletin 15*, London: IPCC (available from https://www.ipcc.gov.uk/sites/default/files/Documents/case13_bulletin15.pdf accessed 23 August 2016).

IPCC (Independent Police Complaints Commission) (2011b) *Investigation into West Yorkshire Police Contact with Martin Middleton* IPCC Reference: 2004/004576 Independent Investigation Commissioner's Report.

IPCC (Independent Police Complaints Commission) (2013) Officers to Face Misconduct Charges After IPCC Upholds Clubber's Strip Search Appeal (Press Release) 30 July.

James A (2013) *Examining Intelligence-Led Policing: Developments in Research, Policy and Practice*, Palgrave Macmillan.

James Z and Southern R (2007) *Plymouth Head Camera Project: Public Relations Evaluation*, Plymouth: SRRU.

Jeffreys-Jones R (2017) *We Know All About You: The Story of Surveillance in Britain and America*, Oxford: Oxford University Press.

Johnston P (2006) Your Life in Their Lens. *Daily Telegraph*, 2 November.

Jones S (2010) Rape Case Anonymity for Defendants Would Be an Insult to Victims. *The Guardian*, 20 May.

Jones SG (2012) *Hunting in the Shadows: The Pursuit of al Qa'ida Since 9/11*. New York: W.W. Norton.

Justice (1970) *Privacy and the Law*, London.

Justice (2011) *Freedom from Suspicion: Surveillance Reform for a Digital Age*, October, London.

Kambo H (2016) The Commons Have Failed to Hold the Government to Account on Sweeping New Surveillance Powers, *Privacy International*, (Press Statement) (available at: https://www.privacyinternational.org/node/874 accessed 6 December 2016).

Kane P (1988) The Murderer Age 12. *Daily Mirror*, 26 October.

Karn J (2013) *Policing and Crime Reduction The Evidence and Its Implications for Practice*, London: The Police Foundation.

Katsakou C and Priebe S (2007). Patients' Experiences of Involuntary Hospital Admission and Treatment: A Review of Qualitative Studies. *Epidemiologia e Psichiatria Sociale*, 16(2): 172–178.

Katz CM, Choate DE, Ready JR and Nuno L (2014) *Evaluating the Impact of Officer Worn Body Cameras in the Phoenix Police Department*, Arizona State University: Center for Violence Prevention and Community Safety.

Kelsey T (1992) Man Bitter at Being Barred from Town's Pubs. *The Independent*, 13 February.

Kent J (1986) *The English Village Constable 1580–1642*, Oxford: Clarendon Press.

Kimball P (1983) *The File*, London: George Allen & Unwin.

Knapper D (2016) Staffordshire Police to Install Metal Detector Arches in 'Crime Hotspots' to Stamp Out Knife Crime. *The Sentinel*, 29 June (available at http://www.stokesentinel.co.uk/staffordshire-police-to-install-metal-detectors-in-crime-hotspots-to-stamp-out-knife-crime/story-29456035-detail/story.html#a7iOfL3AUrua6QMf.99 accessed 23 August 2016).

Krol C (2015) Watch: World's First 4K Camera Drone Unveiled at CES. *Daily Telegraph*, 8 January.

Lacquer W (1987) *The Age of Terrorism*, Boston: Little, Brown and Co.

Lacquer W (2000), *The New Terrorism: Fanaticism and the Arms of Mass Destruction*, London: Oxford University Press.

Laib M and Wolkenstein L (2016a) Factors Predicting Explicit and Implicit Attitudes Towards Body Scanners. *Review of Social Sciences* 1(5): 18–33.

Laib M and Wolkenstein L (2016b) Does the Use of Body Scanners Discriminate Overweight Flight Passengers? The Effect of Body Scanners on Body Image. *International Journal of Business and Social Research*, 6(5): 1–16.

Laville S (2015) Woman Strip-Searched and Left Naked Wins Damages from Met Police. *The Guardian*, 14 June.

Laville S (2016) The Ched Evans Trial Showed How Rape Complainants Are Still Put in the Dock. *The Guardian*, 14 October.

Law Commission (2010) *Simplification of Criminal Law: Public Nuisance and Outraging Public Decency – Consultation Paper No. 193*, London: Law Commission.

Law Commission (2016) *Reforming Misconduct in Public Office: Consultation Paper No. 229*, September, London: Law Commission.

Leveson Report (2012) *An Inquiry into the Culture, Practices and Ethics of the Press*, HC 779, London: TSO.

Lewis J (2011) Hundreds of Police Officers Caught Illegally Accessing Criminal Records Computer. *Daily Telegraph*, 20 August.

Lewis P (2008) Straw Launches High-Visibility Community Punishment. *The Guardian*, 2 December.

Lewis P (2010a) Surveillance Cameras in Birmingham Track Muslims Every Move. *The Guardian*, 4 June.

Lewis P (2010b) Birmingham Stops Camera Surveillance in Muslim Areas. *The Guardian*, 17 June.

Lewis P (2010c) CCTV in the Sky: Police Plan to Use Military-Style Spy Drones. *The Guardian*, 23 January.

Lexis (2016) *Inferences from Silence* (available at: http://lexisweb.co.uk/sub-topics/inferences-from-silence accessed 23 August 2016).

Liberty (2003) Liberty Wins Key CCTV Privacy Case (Press Release) 28 January (available at https://www.liberty-human-rights.org.uk/news/press-releases/liberty-wins-key-cctv-privacy-case accessed 15 February 2017).

Liberty (2010a) Liberty Demands Removal of Unlawful Birmingham Surveillance Cameras (Press Release) 18 October.

Liberty (2010b) Terrorism Pre-charge Detention: Comparative Law Study. Liberty (available at: https://www.liberty-human-rights.org.uk/sites/default/files/comparative-law-study-2010-pre-charge-detention.pdf accessed 3 February 2017).

Liberty (2010c) The Story of Cerie Bullivant (available at: https://www.liberty-human-rights.org.uk/sites/default/files/control-orders-case-study-cerie-bullivant.pdf accessed 2 February 2017).

Liberty (2013) Victory for Human Rights as Court of Appeal Rules Blanket Disclosure of Criminal Records Disproportionate (Press Release) 29 January.

Liberty (2015a) Intelligence Sharing Between UK and USA Was Unlawful, Tribunal Rules (Press Release) 6 February.

Liberty (2015b) Liberty Responds to Police Photo Database Revelations' (Press Release) 4 February.

Liberty (2016a) *DNA Retention*, London: Liberty.

Liberty (2016b) Liberty Responds to the Snoopers' Charter Becoming Law After Receiving Royal Assent (Press Release) 29 November, London.

Liberty (2016c) Overview of Terrorism Legislation (available at: https://www.liberty-human-rights.org.uk/human-rights/countering-terrorism/overview-terrorism-legislation accessed 13 January 2017).

Liberty (2016d) *Section 44 Terrorism Act*, London: Liberty (available at: https://www.liberty-human-rights.org.uk/human-rights/justice-and-fair-trials/stop-and-search/section-44-terrorism-act accessed 23 August 2016).

Liberty (2016e) *Schedule 7* (available at https://www.liberty-human-rights.org. uk/human-rights/countering-terrorism/schedule-7 accessed 9 February 2017).

Liberty (2016f) TPIMs (available at: https://www.liberty-human-rights.org.uk/human-rights/countering-terrorism/tpims accessed 27 January 2017).

Liberty (2016g) Counter-Extremism (available at https://www.liberty-human-rights.org.uk/unsafe-unfair accessed 10 February 2017).

Liberty (2016h) *Show Me Yours…* (available at: https://www.youtube.com/watc h?v=szN7DlmMLYg&feature=share accessed 14 May 2017).

Lillington C (2016) Coventry Cops Accused of 'Trespassing' After Tweeting Snaps in People's Homes in Anti-Burglary Stunt. *Coventry Telegraph*, 26 January (available at http://www.coventrytelegraph.net/news/coventry-news/coventry-cops-accused-trespassing-after-10788373 accessed 23 August 2016).

Lindop Report (1978) *Report of the Committee on Data Protection*, Cmnd. 7341, London: HMSO.

Lippert R (2009) Signs of the Surveillant Assemblage: Privacy, Regulation, Urban CCTV and Governmentality. *Social and Legal Studies*, 18(4): 505–522.

Lippert RK and Newell BC (2016) Debate Introduction: The Privacy and Surveillance Implications of Police Body Cameras. *Surveillance & Society*, 14(1): 113–116.

Little C (2015) The 'Mosquito' and the Transformation of British Public Space. *Journal of Youth Studies*, 18(2): 167–182.

Logan W (2009) *Knowledge as Power: Criminal Registration and Community Notification Laws in America*, California: Stanford University Press.

Lyon D (1994) *The Electronic Eye*, Cambridge: Polity Press.

Lyon D (2006) *Theorizing Surveillance: The Panopticon and Beyond*, Cullompton: Willan Publishing.

Lyon D (2015) *Surveillance After Snowden*, Cambridge: Polity Press.

MacAskill E, Borger J, Hopkins N, Davies N and Ball J (2013) GCHQ Taps Fibre-Optic Cables for Secret Access to World's Communications. *The Guardian*, 21 June.

MacAskill E (2016) 'Extreme Surveillance' Becomes UK Law with Barely a Whimper. *The Guardian*, 19 November.

Madgwick D and Smythe T (1974) *The Invasion of Privacy*, London: Pitman Publishing.

Mair G and Nee C (1990) *Electronic Monitoring: The Trials and Their Results*, Home Office Research Study 120, London: HMSO.

Mair G and Mortimer E (1996) *Curfew Orders with Electronic Monitoring*. Research Study No. 163, London: Home Office.

Malik S (2013) Terror Suspect's Disappearance Sparks Criticism of Control-Order Regime. *The Guardian*, 1 January.

Manzoor S (2016) You Look Familiar: On Patrol with the Met's Super-Recognisers. *The Guardian*, 5 November.

Marks A (2007) Drug Detection Dogs and the Growth of Olfactory Surveillance: Beyond the Rule of Law. *Surveillance and Society*, 4(3): 257–271.

Marshall D and Thomas T (2015a) The Disclosure of Police-Held 'Non-conviction Information' to Employers. *International Journal of Police Science and Management*, December, 17(4): 237–245.

Marshall D and Thomas T (2015b) Polygraphs and Sex Offenders: The Truth Is Out There, *Probation Journal.*

Mason R (2016) Female Labour MPs Call for Legal Change Following Ched Evans Re-trial. *The Guardian*, 23 October.

Mason S (2011) *A Common Sense Approach: A Review of The Criminal Records Regime in England and Wales – Report on Phase 2,* December, London: Home Office.

Mathieson S (2007) Worried About Being Watched? You Already Are. *The Guardian*, 15 February.

Mathieson S (2011) Open Up the Number Plate Recognition Camera System. *The Guardian*, 17 May.

McCandless R, Feist A, Allan J and Morgan N (2016) *Do Initiatives Involving Substantial Increases in Stop and Search Reduce Crime? Assessing the Impact of Operation BLUNT 2,* London: Home Office.

McCartney C (2006) *Forensic Identification and Criminal Justice: Forensic Science, Justice and Risk,* Cullompton: Willan Publishing.

McLynn F (1989) *Crime and Punishment: Eighteenth Century,* London, England: Routledge.

McTague T (2016) Investigatory Powers Bill: Theresa May Accused of Rushing Snoopers' Charter into Law to Avoid Scrutiny. *Independent,* 27 February.

Metropolitan Police Authority (2005) *Operation Blunt,* London: MPA (available at http://policeauthority.org/metropolitan/committees/mpa/2005/050526/10/index.html accessed 23 August 2016).

Metropolitan Police Authority (2008) *Equality and Diversity of Operation Blunt 2,* London: MPA (available at http://policeauthority.org/metropolitan/committees/x-eodb/2008/080925/07/index.html accessed 23 August 2016).

MIB (Motor Insurance Bureau) (2016) Chief Executive's Blog – Vnuk – The Unintended Consequences of a Farmyard Misfortune, April (available at https://www.mib.org.uk/about-mib/chief-executives-blog/vnuk-the-unintended-consequences-of-a-farmyard-misfortune/ accessed 3 March 2017).

Micklethwaite J (2016) Porn-Sniffing Dog Trained for Fightback Against X-rated Material in US State. *Evening Standard*, 28 June (available at http://www. standard.co.uk/news/world/pornsniffing-dog-trained-for-fightback-against-xrated-material-in-us-state-a3282521.html accessed 23 August 2016).

Middlesbrough Council (2017) Security and Surveillance (available at https:// www.middlesbrough.gov.uk/environment-and-public-protection/crime-and-emergencies/security-and-surveillance accessed 3 March 2017).

Miller S (2009) *Terrorism and Counterterrorism: Ethics and Liberal Democracy*, Malden, MA: Blackwell.

Milne S (2004) *The Enemy Within: The Secret War Against the Miners*, 3rd ed., London: Verso Books.

Mironmenko O (2011) Body Scanners Versus Privacy and Data Protection. *Computer Law and Security Review*, 27(3): 232–244.

Mitchener-Nissen T, Bowers K and Chetty K (2011) Public Attitudes to Airport Security: The Case of Whole Body Scanners. *Security Journal*, 25(3): 229–243.

MoJ (Ministry of Justice) (2008a) *Disrupting the Supply of Illicit Drugs into Prisons: A Report for the Director General of National Offender Management Service by David Blakey*, May.

MoJ (Ministry of Justice) (2008b) Offenders to Wear High-Visibility Jackets on 'Payback' (Press Release) 1 December.

MoJ (Ministry of Justice) (2010) *Providing Anonymity for Those Accused of Rape: An Assessment of Evidence*, Research Series 20/10 November, London.

MoJ (Ministry of Justice), Home Office and Attorney General's Office (2011) Publicising Sentencing Outcomes Guidance for Public Authorities on Publicising Information (Including Via the Internet) About Individual Sentencing Outcomes Within the Current Legal Framework, June, London.

MoJ (Ministry of Justice) (2012) Punishment and Reform: Effective Community Sentences, Government Response, October, London.

MoJ (Ministry of Justice), National Probation Service, HM Prison Service and Association of Chief Police Officers (2012) MAPPA Guidance 2012 Version 4, National Offender Management Service, Offender Management and Public Protection Group, London.

MoJ (Ministry of Justice) (2012a) Getting it Right for Victims and Witnesses (ref. CP3/2012) Cm 8288, January, London.

MoJ (Ministry of Justice) (2012b) Getting it Right for Victims and Witnesses: The Government's Response Cm 8397, July, London.

MoJ (Ministry of Justice) (2014) *New Guidance on the Rehabilitation of Offenders Act 1974* (available at https://www.gov.uk/government/publications/new-guidance-on-the-rehabilitation-of-offenders-act-1974 accessed 10 February 2017).

MoJ (2014b) First Victims Spared Harrowing Court Room Under Pre-Recorded Evidence Pilot (Press Release) 28 April, London.

MoJ (Ministry of Justice) (2016a) *Process Evaluation of Pre-recorded Cross Examination Pilot (Section 28)*, London: Ministry of Justice Analytical Services.

MoJ (Ministry of Justice) (2016b) Review of the Youth Justice System in England and Wales (Taylor Report), Cm 9298, December, London.

MoJ (Ministry of Justice) (2016c) *Prison Safety and Reform*, Cm 9350, November, London.

MoJ (Ministry of Justice) (2016d), *Review on the Care and Management of Transgender Offenders*, November, London.

MoJ (Ministry of Justice) (2016e) *Official Statistics – Prisoner Transgender Statistics, March/April 2016 England and Wales* – 9 November, London.

MoJ (Ministry of Justice) (2016f) 'Sobriety Tags' Rolled Out Across London (Press Release) 25 February, London.

MoJ (Ministry of Justice) (2016g) *Multi-Agency Public Protection Arrangements Annual Report 2015/16* Statistical Bulletin, London.

MoJ (Ministry of Justice) (2017) Greater Protection for Rape Victims and Children at Risk of Grooming (Press Release) 19 March (available at https://www.gov.uk/government/news/greater-protection-for-rape-victims-and-children-at-risk-of-grooming accessed 19 March 2017).

MoJ (Ministry of Justice), Home Office and Attorney General's Office (2009) *Engaging Communities in Criminal Justice*, April, Cm 7583, London.

MoJ (Ministry of Justice), NOMS, and HM Prison Service (2017) *Prison Population Figures: 2017*, May (available at https://www.gov.uk/government/statistics/prison-population-figures-2017 accessed 8 May 2017).

Morgan T (2015) Scotland Yard's Multi-Million Pound Apology to Seven Women Deceived into Relationships with Officers. *Daily Telegraph*, 20 November.

Morgan M (2004) The Origins of New Terrorism. *Parameters*, Spring Edition: 29–43.

Morris S (2003) Vetting Failures Let Caretaker Slip Through Net. *The Guardian*, 18 December.

Moskvitch K (2015) The New Tech Changing Airport Security. *BBC Worldwide*, 19 May (available at http://www.bbc.com/future/story/20150519-how-airport-security-is-changing accessed 23 August 2016).

Mowery K, Wustrow E, Wypych T, Singleton C, Comfort C, Rescorla E, Checkoway S, Halderman JA and Shacham, H. (2014) Security Analysis of a Full-Body Scanner, *Proceedings of the 23rd USENIX Security Symposium, August 2014* (available from https://www.radsec.org/secure1000-sec14.pdf last accessed 23 August 2016).

MPS (Metropolitan Police Service) (2006) *Operation Blunt Knife-Enabled Crime – Knife Amnesty Impact on Knife-Enabled Offences*, London: MPS (available at http://news.bbc.co.uk/1/shared/bsp/hi/pdfs/06_12_06_%20 knife_amnesty.pdf accessed 23 August 2016).

MPS (Metropolitan Police Service) (2015a) *Special Demonstration Squad Tradecraft Manual, Freedom of Information Request*, June (available at http:// www.met.police.uk/foi/pdfs/priorities_and_how_we_are_doing/corporate/ operation_herne_sds_tradecraft_manual.pdf accessed 6 December 2016).

MPS (Metropolitan Police Service) (2015b) Claimants in Civil Cases Receive MPS Apology (Press Release) 20 November.

MPS (Metropolitan Police Service) (2015c) *Privacy Impact Assessment of the Deployment of Body Worn Video, Freedom of Information Request*, London: MPS (available at http://www.met.police.uk/foi/pdfs/disclosure_2015/february_2015/2015010000985.pdf accessed 23 August 2016).

NACRO (National Association for the Care and Rehabilitation of Offenders) (2002) *Policing Local Communities: The Tottenham Experiment*, London: NACRO.

NAPO (National Association of Probation Officers) (2008) High Visibility Vests – Threats, Abuse, Boycotts and Legal Issues (Press Release) 30 December, London.

Nash M (2006) *Public Protection and the Criminal Justice Process*, Oxford: Oxford University Press.

National Centre for Policing Excellence (2005) *Code of Practice: National Intelligence Model*, London: Home Office.

NCA (National Crime Agency) (2015) Introduction to Suspicious Activity Reports (SARs), April (available at http://www.nationalcrimeagency.gov.uk/ publications/suspicious-activity-reports-sars/550-introduction-to-suspicious-activity-reports-sars-1/file accessed 14 February 2017).

NCA (National Crime Agency) (2016) *National Strategic Assessment of Serious and Organised Crime 2016*, 9 September, London.

NCA (National Crime Agency) (2017) UK Protected Persons Service (available at http://www.nationalcrimeagency.gov.uk/about-us/what-we-do/specialist-capabilities/uk-protected-persons-service accessed 12 March 2017).

NOMS (National Offender Management Service) (2011) *Care and Management of Transsexual Prisoners* (Reference PSI 7/2011), London.

NOMS (National Offender Management Service) (2012a) *MAPPA Guidance 2012 Version 4*, London: Ministry of Justice.

NOMS (National Offender Management Service) (2012b) *Certified Prisoner Accommodation* (Reference PSI 17/2012), London.

NOMS (National Offender Management Service) (2014a) *Mother and Baby Units* (Reference PSI 49/2014), London.

NOMS (National Offender Management Service) (2014b) *Community Payback High Visibility Tabards* (Reference PI 12/2014), London.

NOMS (National Offender Management Service) (2016a) *Searching of the Person* (Reference PSI 07/2016), London.

NOMS (National Offender Management Service) (2016b) *Cells, Area and Vehicle Searching* (Reference PSI 09/2016).

NOMS (National Offender Management Service) (2016c) *The Interception of Communications in Prisons and Security Measures* (Reference PSI 04/2016).

NOMS (National Offender Management Service) (2016d) *The Care and Management of Transgender Offenders* (Reference PSI 17/2016), London.

NOMS (National Offender Management Service) (2016e) Determining Pre Sentence Reports – Sentencing Within the New Framework (Reference PI 04/2016), London.

Norris C and Armstrong G (1999) *The Maximum Surveillance Society: The Rise of CCTV*, Oxford: Berg.

Northamptonshire Police (8 December 2014) *Northamptonshire Sobriety Bracelets Pilot Project: Update Northamptonshire*: Northamptonshire Police (https://www.northants.police.uk/#!/News/24735).

Northrop Grumman (ND) Integrated Identification Services – IDENT 1 (available at http://www.northropgrumman.com/Capabilities/Identification SystemsSolutions/IDENT1/Documents/Ident1-USversion.pdf accessed 28 January 2017).

NPIA (National Policing Improvement Agency) (2010a) *Code of Practice on the Operation and Use of the Police National Database*, March, Home Office (available at https://www.gov.uk/government/publications/code-of-practice-on-the-operation-and-use-of-the-police-national-database accessed 5 May 2010).

NPIA (National Policing Improvement Agency) (2010b) Guidance on Protecting the Public: Managing Sexual Offenders and Violent Offenders 2010 (version 2) (available at http://library.college.police.uk/docs/acpo/Guidance-Protecting-the-Public-2010.pdf accessed 5 May 2017).

NPCC (National Police Chief's Council) (2013) A UK Wide Witness Protection Scheme Has Been Launched (Press Release) October 7.

NPCC (National Police Chief's Council) (2015) Automated Number Plate Recognition (ANPR) (Press Release) 14 December.

NPCC (National Police Chief's Council) (2016a) Freedom of Information Request Reference Number: 000026/16, March 7 (available from: http://

www.npcc.police.uk/Publication/NPCC%20FOI/CT/02616 ChannelReferrals.pdf last accessed 20 February 2017).

NPCC (National Police Chief's Council) (2016b) *Automatic Number Plate Recognition (ANPR) – Factsheet*, April (available at http://www.npcc.police. uk/documents/ANPR%20Factsheet.pdf accessed 14 February 2017).

NPCC (National Police Chief's Council), Home Office and National DNA Database (2017) *National DNA Database Strategy Board Annual Report 2015–16*, February, London (available at: https://www.gov.uk/government/ uploads/system/uploads/attachment_data/file/594185/58714_Un-Num_ Nat_DNA_DB_Accessible.pdf accessed 20 March 2017).

NPS (National Probation Service) (2005) *Visible Unpaid Work* (Reference PC 66/2005).

NSW (New South Wales) Ombudsman (2006) *Review of the Police Powers (Drug Detection Dogs) Act 2001*, Sydney: NSWO.

NSWCCL (New South Wales Council for Civil Liberties) (2006) *Police Sniffer Dogs* (available from: http://www.nswccl.org.au/police_sniffer_dogs last accessed 23 August 2016).

Nyst C (2014) The Government Is Trying to Create a Surveillance State. *The Telegraph*, 17 July.

O'Leary B and McGarry J (2016) *The Politics of Antagonism: Understanding Northern Ireland*, London: Bloomsbury.

O'Neill E (2011) Fingerprint Evidence 'Based on Opinion Rather than Fact'. *The Guardian*, 14 December.

O'Toole T, Jones SH, DeHanas DN and Modood T (2013) Prevent After Terror: Why Local Context Still Matters, publicspirit.org/University of Bristol (available at: http://www.publicspirit.org.uk/themes/the-legacy-and-the-future-of-prevent/ accessed 20 February 2017).

OCJR (Office for Criminal Justice Reform) (2009) *Publicising Sentence Outcomes: Guidance for Public Authorities on Publishing Information (Including Via the Internet) About Individual Sentencing Outcomes Within the Current Legal Framework*, December, London.

Office of the Biometrics Commissioner (2014) *Annual Report 2014 Commissioner for the Retention and Use of Biometric material*, November, London: Office of the Biometrics Commissioner.

Office of the Children's Commissioner (2008) 3,500 Ultra-Sonic Dispersal Devises Told to Buzz Off (Press Release) 12 February, London.

Omand D (2005) Countering International Terrorism: The Use of Strategy. *Survival*, 47(4): 107–116.

Orr-Munro T (2001) Quest for data. *Police Review*, 22 March.

Orwell (1949) *Nineteen Eighty Four*, London: Secker and Warburg.

Owen P (2009) Police Force Admits Errors over Intimate Body Search Figures. *The Guardian*, 18 August.

Owens C, Mann D and McKenna R (2014) *The Essex BWV Trial: The Impact of BWV on Criminal Justice Outcomes of Domestic Abuse Incidents*, London: College of Policing.

PA (Press Association) (2012) Karen Matthews 'Released from Prison'. *The Guardian*, 5 April.

Palmer SH (1988) *Police and Protest in England and Ireland 1780–1850*, Cambridge: Cambridge University Press.

Pantazis C and Pemberton S (2009) From the "Old" to the "New" Suspect Communities: Examining the Impact of Recent UK Counter-Terrorist Legislation. *British Journal of Criminology*, 49: 646–666.

Papademetriou T (2014) European Union: ECJ Invalidates Data Retention Directive, *The Law Library of Congress, Global Legal Research Center* (available at: https://www.loc.gov/law/help/eu-data-retention-directive/eu.php accessed 6 December 2016).

Peachey P (2016) How the Police's Body-Worn Camera Technology Is Changing the Justice System. *The Independent*, 1 March.

Pegg D and Evans R (2016) Controversial Snooping Technology 'Used by at Least Seven Police Forces'. *The Guardian*, 10 October.

Pepper M and Dawson P (2016) *Alcohol Abstinence Monitoring Requirement: A Process Review of the Proof of Concept Pilot*, London: MOPAC.

Phelps JM, Strype J, Le Bellu S, Lahlou S and Aandal J (2016) Experiential Learning and Simulation-Based Training in Norwegian Police Education: Examining Body-Worn Video as a Tool to Encourage Reflection. *Policing: A Journal of Policy and Practice*, 10(3): 1–16.

Phillips Report (1981) Royal Commission on Criminal Procedure, Cmnd. 8092, London: Her Majesty's Stationary Office.

Pigot Report (1989) Report of the Advisory Group on Video Evidence Home Office, London.

Pilcher J and Wagg S (eds.) (1996) *Thatcher's Children*, London: Falmer.

Pilkington E (1993) Boys Guilty of Bulger Murder – Detention Without Limit for 'Unparalleled Evil'. *The Guardian*, 25 November.

Pithers M (1992) Five Years' Custody for Girl, 12, Who Killed Baby. *The Guardian*, 30 April.

Plotnikoff J and Woolfson R (2009) *Measuring Up? Evaluating Implementation of Government commitments to Young Witnesses in Criminal Proceedings*, The Nuffield, London: Foundation/NSPCC.

Police Ombudsman's Office (2012) *Search Police Cells with Metal Detectors: Police Ombudsman*, Belfast: Police Ombudsman's Office (available from https://www.policeombudsman.org/Media-Releases/2014/Search-police-cells-with-metal-detectors-Police-Om#sthash.qW4IL42D.dpuf last accessed 23 August 2016).

Ponsford D (2009) Sex Killer Wins Pictures Ban After Sunday Life Legal Battle. *Press Gazette*, 8 January (available at http://www.pressgazette.co.uk/sex-killer-wins-pictures-ban-after-sunday-life-legal-battle/ accessed 26 February 2017).

Porter B (1987) *The Origins of the Vigilant State*, London: Macmillan.

Porter B (1989) *Plots and Paranoia: A History of Political Espionage in Britain 1790–1988*, London: Routledge.

Privacy International (2015) *Bulk Personal Datasets Challenge* (available from: https://privacyinternational.org/node/843 last accessed 6 December 2016).

Privy Council (2008) *Review of Intercept as Evidence – Report to the Prime Minister and Home Secretary*, 30 Jan, Cm 7324, London: The Stationery Office.

Probation Instruction (2013) 'Mandatory Use of ViSOR' (Ref. 03/2013).

Pubwatch (2017) FAQ (available at http://www.nationalpubwatch.org.uk/faq/#faq-1459 accessed 11 February 2017).

Quinton P (2011) The Formation of Suspicions: Police Stop and Search Practices in England and Wales. *Policing and Society*, 21(4).

Quinton P (2015) Race Disproportionality and Officer Decision-Making, in Desol R and Shiner, M (eds.) *Stop and Search – the Anatomy of a Police Power*, London: Palgrave Macmillan.

Ragazzi F (2016) Suspect Community or Suspect Category? The Impact of Counter-Terrorism as 'Policed Multiculturalism'. *Journal of Ethnic and Migration Studies*, 42(5): 724–741.

Ramsbotham D (2005) *Prison Gate – the Shocking State of Britain's Prisons and the Need for Visionary Change*, London: The Free Press.

Robins J (2013) The Right of Silence and Undermining Legal Representation at the Police Station. *The Justice Gap* (available at: http://thejusticegap.com/2013/04/the-right-of-silence-and-undermining-legal-representation-at-the-police-station/ accessed 23 August 2016).

Robins J (2016) More than Half of Local Newspapers Don't Have a Court Reporter. *The Justice Gap* (available at http://thejusticegap.com/2016/10/half-local-newspapers-dont-court-reporter/ accessed 19 March 2017).

Robinson M (2013) Police Forces Pay £25million to Informants and Nearly Half Is Spent by London's Met. *Daily Mail*, 18 June.

Rosenfeld R and Fornango R (2014) The Impact of Police Stops on Precinct Robbery and Burglary Rates in New York City, 2003–2010. *Justice Quarterly*, 31(1): 96–122.

Rosenfeld R, Deckard MJ and Blackburn E (2014) The Effects of Directed Patrol and Self-Initiated Enforcement on Firearms Violence: A Randomized Controlled Study of Hot Spot Policing. *Criminology*, 52(3): 428–449.

Rozenberg J (2005) Maxine Carr Gets Anonymity for the Rest of Her Life. *Daily Telegraph*, 25 February.

Rule J (1973) *Private Lives and Public Surveillance*, London: Allen Lane.

Rusbridger A, Gibson J and MacAskill E (2015) Edward Snowden: NSA Reform in the US IS Only the Beginning. *The Guardian*, 22 May.

RUSI (Royal United Services Institute) (2015) *A Democratic Licence to Operate: Report of the Independent Surveillance Review*, 13 July, London.

Russell B (2008) 'Community Payback' Vests Spark Rebellion by Probation Officers. *The Independent*, 30 December.

Russell J (1998) *Phoenix Data Quality*, Police Research Group, Special Interest Series: Paper 11, London: Home Office.

Sabur R (2017) Police Investigate Allegations Criminals 'Bribed Security Staff' to Fit Their Electronic Tags Loosely to Evade Curfews. *Daily Telegraph*, 4 February.

Sageman M (2014) The Stagnation in Terrorism Research. *Terrorism and Political Violence*, 26: 565–580.

Sample I (2016) Synthetic Cannabis 'Having a Devastating Impact in UK Prisons'. *The Guardian*, 1 May.

Savirimuthu, J (2012) *Online Child Safety: Law, Technology and Governance*, p. 376, England: Palgrave Macmillan.

Scarman Report (1982) *The Brixton Disorders 10–12 April 1981*, Cmnd. 8427, London: HMSO.

SCC (Surveillance Camera Commissioner) (2015) Surveillance Camera Commissioners Speech to the ANPR National User Group, (Delivered 18 November 2015), London: SCC (available at https://www.gov.uk/government/speeches/surveillance-camera-commissioners-speech-to-the-anpr-national-user-group-2015 accessed 3 March 2017).

SCC (Surveillance Camera Commissioner) (2016) *Surveillance Camera Commissioner Annual Report 2015/16*, London: TSO.

SCC (2017) Surveillance Camera Commissioner (available at https://www.gov.uk/government/organisations/surveillance-camera-commissioner).

SCYJ (Standing Committee on Youth Justice) (2015) *SCYJ Guide to the New Anti-Social Behaviour Powers*, February, London.

Scheerhout J (2014) Businessman's Fury After Police Smashed Door Down in Raid, Found Nothing, and Won't Pay for Damage. *Manchester Evening News*, 21 September (available at http://www.manchestereveningnews.co.uk/news/greater-manchester-news/businessmans-fury-after-police-smashed-7805095 accessed 23 August 2016).

Seamark M and Sims P (2009) Child Killer Mary Bell Becomes a Grandmother at 51: But All I Have Left Is Grief, Says Victim's Mother. *Mail Online*, 9 January (available at http://www.dailymail.co.uk/news/article-1110123/Child-killer-Mary-Bell-grandmother-51-But-I-left-grief-says-victims-mother.html#ixzz4YGwZ15KN accessed 10 February 2017).

Sengoopta C (2003) *Imprint of the Raj: How Fingerprinting Was Born in Colonial India*, London: Pan Books.

Sereny G (1998) *Cries Unheard: The Story of Mary Bell*, London: Macmillan.

SEU (Social Exclusion Unit) (2002) *Reducing Re-offending by Ex-Prisoners*, London: Office of the Deputy Prime Minister.

Sharpe S (2002) Covert Surveillance and the Use of Informants, in McConville M and G Wilson (eds.) *The Handbook of the Criminal Justice Process*, Oxford University Press.

Shepherd J (2010) Family Win School Catchment Spying Case. *The Guardian*, 2 August.

Shute S (2007) *Satellite Tracking of Offenders: A Study of the Pilots in England and Wales Research Summary No. 4*, Ministry of Justice.

Siddique H (2013) Cameras Offer Protection for Police and Public but Raise Privacy Concerns. *The Guardian*, 23 October.

Smith D and Chamberlain P (2015) *Blacklisted: The Secret War Between Big Business and Union Activists*, Oxford: New Internationalists Publications Ltd.

Smyth L (2008) Sex Killer Ken Callaghan Could Be Permitted to Work with Women. *Belfast Telegraph*, 11 September.

Sparrow A (2017) WhatsApp Must Be Accessible to Authorities, Says Amber Rudd. *The Guardian*, 26 March.

Spencer JR (1997) Bugging and Burglary by the Police. *Cambridge Law Journal*, 56(1): 6–8.

Sprenger P (1999) Sun on Privacy: 'Get Over It'. *Wired*, 26 January (available at http://archive.wired.com/politics/law/news/1999/01/17538 accessed 26 February 2017).

SRA (Solicitors Regulation Authority) (2016) *Handbook* (Version 18), 1 November, London.

Stephen JF (1973) *A History of the Criminal Law of England*, New York: Franklin.

Stohl M (2008a) Old Myths, New Fantasies and the Enduring Realities of Terrorism. *Critical Studies on Terrorism*, 1(1): 5–16.

Stohl M (2008b) The Global War on Terror and State Terrorism. *Perspectives on Terrorism*, 2(9): 4–10.

Stone R (2014) *Textbook on Civil Liberties* (10th ed.), Oxford: Oxford University Press.

Straw J (2008) Tough Consequences. *News of the World*, 28 December.

STV (2009) Police Launch New Metal Detectors in Fight Against Knives. *STV News*, 23 October (available at http://stv.tv/news/scotland/132224-police-launch-new-metal-detectors-in-fight-against-knives/ accessed 23 August 2016).

Surrey Police (2016) Police Acquire Four New Drones to Protect Public and Investigate Crime (Press Release) 8 April (available at https://surrey.police.uk/news/police-acquire-four-new-drones-to-protect-public-and-investigate-crime-1/ accessed 14 March 2017).

Sweney M (2009) Irish Court Stops Paper Printing Photos of Murderer. *The Guardian*, 7 January.

Taylor N (2002) State Surveillance and the Right to Privacy. *Surveillance & Society* 1(1): 66–85.

Taylor S (2015) *Investigation into Links Between Special Demonstration Squad and Home Office*, London: Home Office.

Telegraph (2013) Police Body Cameras Would Be 'Distressing' for Public. *Daily Telegraph*, 15 November.

Tempest M (2006) MPs Back Ban on 'Glorification' of Terrorism'. *The Guardian*, 15 February.

Thames Valley Police (2010) *Project Champion Review*, 30 September (available at http://www.statewatch.org/news/2010/oct/uk-project-champion-police-report.pdf accessed 15 February 2017).

Thomas P (2012) *Responding to the Threat of Violent Extremism*, London: Bloomsbury Academic.

Thomas T (2001) The National Collection of Criminal Records: A Question of Data Quality. *Criminal Law Review*, 886–896.

Thomas T (2005) The Continuing Story of the ASBO. *Youth and Policy* 87(Spring): 5–14.

Thomas T (2007) *Criminal Records: A Database for the Criminal Justice System and Beyond*, Basingstoke: Palgrave Macmillan.

Thomas T (2008) Children and Fingerprinting: Sleepwalking into a Surveillance Society. *Childright*, April No. 245: 22–24.

Thomas T (with Thompson D) (2010) Making Offenders Visible. *Howard Journal of Criminal Justice*, 49(4): 340–348.

Thomas T (2011) *The Registration and Monitoring of Sex Offenders: A Comparative Study*, London: Routledge.

Thomas T and Thompson D (2010) Making Offenders Visible. *Howard Journal of Criminal Justice*, 49(4): 340–348.

Thompson E (1968), *The Making of the English Working Class*, Harmondsworth: Penguin.

Thompson E (1977) *Whigs and Hunters: The Origin of the Black Act*, Harmondsworth: Penguin.

Travis A (2009) Right to Privacy Broken by a Quarter of UK's Public Databases, Says Report. *The Guardian*, 23 March.

Travis A (2010a) Two Women Barred from Flight to Pakistan for Refusing Full-Body Scan. *The Guardian*, 3 March.

Travis A (2010b) 'Big Brother' Traffic Cameras Must Be Regulated, Orders Home Secretary. *The Guardian*, 4 July.

Travis A (2014) G4S Agrees to Repay £109m for Overcharging on Tagging Contracts. *The Guardian*, 12 March.

Travis A (2016) UK Security Agencies Unlawfully Collected Data for 17 Years, Court Rules. *The Guardian*, 17 October.

UCPI (Undercover Policing Inquiry) (2016) Official Website (available at https://www.ucpi.org.uk/ accessed 16 March 2017).

UN (United Nations) (1948) *Universal Declaration of Human Rights*, New York: United Nations.

UN (United Nations) (1989) *Convention on the Rights of the Child*, New York: United Nations.

UN (United Nations) (1990) *Standard Minimum Rules for Non-custodial Measures (The 'Tokyo Rules')* Resolution 45/110 of the General Assembly, 14 December, New York.

UNCRC (UN Committee on the Rights of the Child) (2008) *'Concluding Observations: United Kingdom of Great Britain and Northern Ireland'*, Forty-Ninth Session Consideration of Reports Submitted by States Parties Under Article 44 of the Convention 20 October (Ref. CRC/C/GBR/CO/4).

UNHRC (UN Human Rights Committee) (2008) *Consideration of Reports Submitted by States Parties Under Article 40 of the Covenant. Concluding Observations of the Human Rights Committee, United Kingdom of Great Britain and Northern Ireland, International Covenant on Civil and Political Rights.* CCPR/C/GBR/CO/6, Geneva: United Nations.

Unlock (2017) The Calculator (available at http://www.disclosurecalculator.org.uk/go accessed 13 March 2017).

Van Bueren G and Woolley S (2010) *Stop and Think*. London: Equality and Human Rights Commission.

Van Buskirk E (2010) Report: Facebook CEO Mark Zuckerberg Doesn't Believe in Privacy. *Wired*, 28 April.

Versi M (2016) Prevent Is Failing. Any Effective Strategy Must Include Muslim Communities. *The Guardian*, 20 October.

Vehicles (Crime) Act 2001 – 129.

Vincent D (1998) *The Culture of Secrecy: Britain 1832–1998*, Oxford: Oxford University Press.

Vincent D (2016) *Privacy: A Short History*, Cambridge: Polity Press.

Vine J (2011) *Inspection of Gatwick Airport North Terminal – April–September 2011*, London: ICI Inspector.

Wacks R (1989) *Personal Information*, Oxford: Clarendon Press.

Wainwright M (2008) How the Shannon Matthews Kidnap Plot Fell Apart. *The Guardian*, 4 December.

Wainwright M (2009) Brothers Back in Court over Quarry Attack. *The Guardian*, 15 April.

Walker P (2017) Two UK Schools Trial Use of Police-Style Bodycams for Teachers. *The Guardian*, 8 February.

Walsh JI and Piazza JA (2010) Why Respecting Physical Integrity Rights Reduces Terrorism. *Comparative Political Studies*, 43(5): 551–577.

Ward L (2007) 3,300 Sales and Rising – Ultrasonic Answer to Teenage Gangs Sets Alarm Bells Ringing. *The Guardian*, 17 March.

Warman M (2012) Talking CCTV Cameras to Be Turned Off. *Daily Telegraph*, 6 February.

Warren S and L Brandeis (1890) The Right to Privacy. *Harvard Law Review*, 4(193) 15 December.

Watson D (2006) Yob Shamed … on the Back of a Bus. *Daily Express*, 15 July.

Watt N (2000) 3m Face DNA Tests in Blair Crime Initiative. *The Guardian*, 1 September.

Watt N (2008a) Brown Abandons 42-Day Detention After Lords Defeat. *The Guardian*, 13 October.

Watt N (2008b) My Little Children Were Detained Because of a Toy Gun. Prevent Has Gone Too Far. *The Guardian*, 1 February.

Watts S (1991) Police Computer Could Be Threat to Civil Rights. *The Independent*, 18 December.

Weale S (2017) London University Tells Students Their Emails May Be Monitored. *The Guardian*, 20 January.

Weaver M (2015) Warning of Backlash over Car Number Plate Camera Network. *The Guardian*, 27 November.

Weaver M (2017a) Home Office Refuses to Enforce Privacy Code on NHS Staff Using Video. *The Guardian*, 18 January.

Weaver M (2017b) G4S Filmed Asylum Seekers in Their Homes Without Consent. *The Guardian*, 24 January.

Weisburd D, Wooditch A, Weisburd S and Yang S-M. (2016) Do Stop, Question, and Frisk Practices Deter Crime? *Criminology and Public Policy*, 15(1): 31–56, February 2016.

Welsh B and Farrington D (2007) *Closed-Circuit Television Surveillance and Crime Prevention – A Systematic Review*, Report Prepared for The Swedish National Council for Crime Prevention, Stockholm (available at: http://www.crim.cam.ac.uk/people/academic_research/david_farrington/cctvsw.pdf accessed 21 March 2017).

West Yorkshire Police (2016) Body Worn Cameras Increase Safety 'Focus' (Press Release) 8 August.

West Yorkshire Police (2017a) 'Caught on Camera' (available at https://www.westyorkshire.police.uk/camera-alerts/caught-on-camera accessed 17 February 2017).

West Yorkshire Police (2017b) 'In the Dock' – Web Site (available at https://www.westyorkshire.police.uk/camera-alerts/in-the-dock accessed 11 February 2017).

Westin A (1967) *Privacy and Freedom*, London: Bodley Head.

Weston A (2016) New High-Tech System Trialled at Altcourse to Combat Prison 'Throwovers'. *Liverpool Echo*, 6 December (available at http://www.liverpoolecho.co.uk/news/liverpool-news/new-high-tech-system-trialled-12277721?utm_content=buffer06b9c&utm_medium=social&utm_source=twitter.com&utm_campaign=buffer accessed 18 March 2017).

Whitehead T (2010) Venables Protected by Rare Identity Ban. *Daily Telegraph*, 4 March.

Whitehead T (2012) Thousands Wrongly Labelled as Criminals. *Daily Telegraph*, 2 February.

Whitfield D (1997) *Tackling the Tag: The Electronic Monitoring of Offenders*, Winchester: Waterside Press.

Whitfield D (2011) *The Magic Bracelet: Technology and Offender Supervision*.

Williams C, Patterson J and Taylor J (2009) Police Filming English Streets in 1935: The Limits of Mediated Identification. *Surveillance & Society*, 6(1): 3–9.

Wilson R and Adams I (2006) *Special Branch: A History: 1883–2006*, London: Biteback Publishing.

Wolff S and McCall Smith A (2000) Child Homicide and the Law: Implications of the Judgement of the European Court of Human Rights in the Case of the Children Who Killed James Bulger. *Child Psychology and Psychiatry Review*, 5(3): 133–138.

Wolfenden Report (1957) *Report of the Departmental Committee on Homosexual Offences and Prostitution in Great Britain*, Cmnd. 247, London: HMSO.

Wright P (1987) *Spycatcher*, New York: Viking.

Wright S (2009) Drivers Who Break Law Warned by Police. *Telegraph and Argus*, 14 December (available at http://www.thetelegraphandargus.co.uk/news/local/localbrad/4791523._Ring_of_steel__on_roads_extended/ accessed 21 March 2017).

Wynn Davies P (1997) Halford Triumphs over Workplace Phone Bugs. *Independent*, 25 June.

Yorkshire Post (2013) Landmark Register Victory for Child Sex Offender, 11 March (available at http://www.yorkshirepost.co.uk/news/landmark-register-victory-for-child-sex-offender-1-5485857 accessed 12 February 2017).

Yorkshire Evening Post (2015) Transgender Woman Should Never Have Been Sent to Leeds Prison Says Grieving Partner, 20 November (available at: http://www.yorkshireeveningpost.co.uk/news/transgender-woman-should-never-have-been-sent-to-leeds-prison-says-grieving-partner-1-7581859 accessed 21 November 2016).

Young A (1996) *Imagining Crime*, London: Sage Publishing.

Younger Report (1972) Report of the Committee on Privacy, Cmnd. 5012, London: HMSO.

Yourish K, Watkins D, Giratikanon T and Lee JC (2016) How Many People Have Been Killed in ISIS Attacks Around the World? *New York Times*, July 1.

Zamyatin Y (1993) *We*, Harmondsworth: Penguin.

Cases

Adamson v UK (1999) Application 22293/98 **222**.

A.D.T. v. the United Kingdom (Application No. 35765/97) judgment Strasbourg 31 July 2000 **33**.

A v Secretary of State for the Home Department [2004] UKHL 56 **197**.

A v United Kingdom (2009) 49 EHRR 29 **203**.

Appeal No: EA/2012/0171 Southampton City Council v. The Information Commissioner 19 February 2013 First-Tier Tribunal **128**.

Attorney General v Greater Manchester Newspapers Ltd [2001] All ER (D) 32 (Dec) **215**.

Bouchacourt v. France (Application No. 5335/06) 2009 **224**.

Callaghan v Independent News and Media Ltd [2009] NIQB 1 **214**.

Campbell v Mirror Group Newspaper [2004] UKHL 22 **36**.

Campbell Christie v United Kingdom (Application No. 21482/93) European Commission of Human Rights (27 June 1994) **75**.

*Carter v Metropolitan Police Commissioner [1975] 1 WLR 507.***55**.

Chief Constable of Humberside Police and Ors v The Information Commissioner and Anor [2009] EWCA Civ 1079 **115**.

*David Lewis v Director of Public Prosecutions [2004] EWHC 3081 (Admin).***55**.

*Davies v Merseyside Police & Anor [2015] EWCA Civ 114 (19 February 2015).***49**.

Davis and Watson v Secretary of State for the Home Department [2015] EWHC 2092 (Admin) **82**.

Digital Rights Ireland (C-293/12) and Seitlinger and Others (C-594/12) ECJ (Grand Chamber) 8 April 2014 **81, 209**.

Douglas v Hello! Ltd. [2007] UKHL 21 **36**.

*Entick v Carrington (1765) 19 State Tr 1029.***58**.

F and Angus Aubrey Thompson v. *Secretary of State for the Justice [2008] EWHC 3170* **223**.

Foka v. Turkey, No. 28940/09, §§ 74-79, 24 June 2008. **44**.

Folgerø and Others v. Norway (Application No. 15472/02) ECHR 29 June 2007 **199**.

G v Commissioner of Police for the Metropolis [2011] EWHC 331 (Admin) **61**.

Gardel v France (Application 16428/05) 2009 **224**.

Gillan and Quinton v UK (Application No. 4158/05) European Court of Human Rights (12 Jan 2010) **45, 195, 208**.

Guardian News and Media Ltd. and ors. v R and Erol Incedol [2016] EWCA Crim 11 **152**.

Halford v. United Kingdom [1997] ECHR 32 (25 June 1997) **76**.

Hancock v Baker (1800) 2 Bos and P 260. **61**.

Harriot v DPP [2005] EWHC 965 (Admin). **55**.

Hellewell -v- Chief Constable of Derbyshire QBD (Gazette 15-Feb-95, Times 13-Jan-95, [1995] 1 WLR 804, [1995] 4 All ER 473 **219**.

Kaye v Robertson [1991] FSR 62 **11, 12**.

Klass v Germany (1978) 2 EHRR 214 **34, 74**.

Knox v Anderton [1982] 76 Cr App R 156. **55**.

Malone v UK (1984) 7 EHRR 14 **34, 74**.

Massey v UK (2003) Application 14399/02 **222**.

Matthews v United Kingdom (Application No. 28576/95) European Commission of Human Rights (16 October 1996) **75**.

Maxine Carr v News Group Newspapers Limited & others [2005] EWHC 971 (QB) **216**.

MB v France (Application No. 22115/06) (2009) 224.

*Mohidin & Anor v Commissioner of the Police of the Metropolis & Ors [2015] EWHC 2740 (QB) (02 October 2015).*49.

Olsson v. Sweden, [1988] ECHR 2 200.

P and Others v. Secretary of State for the Home Department, and the Secretary of State for Justice [2017] EWCA Civ 321 117.

Peck v UK (2003) 36 EHRR 41 127.

PJS v News Group Newspapers Ltd. [2016] EWCA Civ 100 37.

Pretty v United Kingdom (2002) 35 EHRR 1 13.

Privacy International v. (1) Secretary of State for Foreign and Commonwealth Affairs, *(2) Secretary of State for the Home Department, (3) Government Communications Headquarters, (4) Security Service, (5) Secret Intelligence Service – Investigatory Powers Tribunal case No. IPT/15/110/CH [2016]* **83, 86**.

R (Catt) and R (T) v Commissioner of Police of the Metropolis [2015] UKSC 9 **117**.

R (Forbes) v Secretary of State for the Home Department [2006] EWCA Civ. 962 **223**.

R (Gillan) v Commissioner of Police for the Metropolis [2006] UKHL. 42.

R v A (No2) [2001] UKHL 25 147.

R v Beckles [2005] 1 WLR 2829, **65**.

R v Blackwell [2006] EWCA Crim 2185 160.

R v Bogdal [2008] EWCA Crim 1. 55.

R v. Chief Constable of North Wales Police, ex p. Thorpe (1998) The Times, 23 March 217.

R v Chief Constable of North Wales ex p Thorpe [1999] QB396). **217**.

R v Davis [2008] UKHL 36 149.

R v Edwards (1978) 67 Cr App R 228. 55.

R (Ellis) v Chief Constable of Essex Police [2003] EWHC 1321 (Admin) 220.

R v Gul [2013] 3 WLR 1207, [2013] UKSC 64 192.

R v Hamilton [2007] EWCA Crim 2062, [2008] QB 224 para 21 (CA) 34.

R v Hoare and Pierce [2004] EWCA Crim 784 65.

R v Khan [1996] 3 WLR 162 at 175 76.

R v. Morgan ([1975] 2 All ER 347 159.

R v Secretary of State for the Home Department, ex parte Daly [2001] UKHL 26 **170**.

R v Secretary of State for the Home Department, ex p Tremayne (1996) Unreported, 2 May 1996 **171**.

R (Wood) v Metropolitan Police Commissioner (2009) EWCA Civ 414 **123**.

R (Miranda) v Secretary of State for the Home Department and Commissioner for the Metropolitan Police [2016] EWCA 6 **193**.

R (RMC and FJ) v Metropolitan Police Service [2012] EWHC 1681 **120, 122**.

R (on the application of Christopher Prothero) v Secretary of State for the Home Department [2013] EWHC 2830 (Admin) **222**.

R (on the application of F (by his litigation friend F)) and Thompson (FC) (Respondents) v. Secretary of State for the Home Department (Appellant) [2010] UKSC 17 **223, 224**.

R, on the application of Mohamed Irfan v The Secretary of State for the Home Department [2012] EWCA Civ 1471 **205**.

R (on the application of P and A) v Secretary of State for Justice, Secretary of State for Home Department and Chief Constable of Thames Valley Police [2016] EWHC 89 (Admin) **117**.

R (R on the application of T and Another) v Secretary of State for the Home Department and Another [2014] UKSC 35 **116**.

R (on the application of Wang Yam) (Appellant)) v Central Criminal Court and another, (Respondents) [2015] UKSC 76 **151**.

R v Roberts [2003] EWCA Crim 2753. **55**.

R (Stanley, Marshall and Kelly) v Metropolitan Police Commissioner [2004] EWHC 2229 (Admin), **218**.

R (T) v Greater Manchester Chief Constable (CA) [2013] EWCA Civ 25 **229**.

re Gallagher [2003] NIQB **223**.

Rice v Connolly [1966] 2 QB 414. **42**.

Roberts, R (on the application of) v The Commissioner of the Metropolitan Police [2012] EWHC 1977 (Admin) (17 July 2012). **46**.

Roberts, R (on the application of) v The Commissioner of Police of the Metropolis & Ors [2014] EWCA Civ 69 (04 February 2014). **46**.

S. and Marper v. The United Kingdom – 30562/04 [2008] ECHR 1581. **35, 63, 103, 199**.

Secretary of State for the Home Department v JJ [2007] UKHL 45, [2007] 3 WLR 642 **203**.

Secretary of State for the Home Department v GG [2009] EWCA Civ 786 **203**.

Secretary of State for the Home Department v AF [2009] UKHL 28 **203**.

Sessay, R (on the application of) v South London & Maudsley NHS Foundation Trust & Anor [2011] EWHC 2617 (QB). **55**.

Storck v Germany 16 September 2005 ECHR Application No. 61603/00 **190**.

T v. UK, No. 24724/94, 16 December 1999 **157**.

Wainwright v UK European Court of Human Rights (Fourth Section) Application No. 12350/04, Strasbourg 26 September 2006 **177, 178**.

Venables and Thompson v NG Newspapers Ltd., [2001] 1 WLR 1038 **215**.
Willcock v Muckle [1952] 1 KB 367 **27**.
X, A Woman Formerly Known As Mary Bell -and-Y v Stephen O'Brien -and- News Group Newspapers Ltd. -and- Mgn Ltd. [2003] EWHC 1101 (QB) 21 May 2003 **215**.

Statutes

Anti-Social Behaviour, Crime and Policing Act 2014 – 150, 158.
Anti-Terrorism, Crime and Security Act 2001 – 80, 204.
Coroners and Justice Act 2009 – 66, 146, 150.
Counter Terrorism Act 2008 – 204.
Crime (Sentences) Act 1997 – 155.
Crime and Disorder Act 1998 – 38, 157, 182, 218, 220.
Crime and Security Act 2010 – 174.
Criminal Evidence (Witness Anonymity) Act 2008 – 149–150.
Criminal Justice Act 1948 – 25.
Criminal Justice Act 1967 – 25.
Criminal Justice Act 1988 – 143–144, 159.
Criminal Justice Act 1991 – 144, 187.
Criminal Justice Act 2003 – 43, 102, 105–106, 162, 183, 189, 202, 227.
Criminal Justice and Courts Act 2015 – 111.
Criminal Justice and Courts Services Act 2000 – 226.
Criminal Justice and Public Order Act 1994 – 43–47, 64, 144, 155, 171, 187.
Data Protection Act 1984 – 32, 113.
Data Protection Act 1998 – 32, 36, 96, 101, 115, 124, 127, 136.
Gender Recognition Act 2004 – 180.
Habitual Criminal Act 1869 – 24.
Human Rights Act 1998 – 13, 29, 36–37, 59, 76, 96, 101, 172, 210, 233.
Interception of Communications Act 1985 – 35–36, 70, 74–77, 87.
Investigatory Powers Act 2016 – 8, 17, 36, 70–72, 80, 83–87, 209, 232, 235.
Licensed Premises (Exclusion of Certain Persons) Act 1980 – 219.
Mental Health Act 1983 – 11, 54–57, 162.
Misuse of Drugs Act 1971 – 31, 43.
Offender Management Act 2007 – 65, 174, 230.
Official Secrets Act 1989 – 111.
Police Act 1996 – 101, 108, 111.

Police Act 1997 – 76–77, 87, 101, 116, 229.
Police Reform Act 2002 – 108, 111.
Police and Criminal Evidence Act 1984 – 25, 41–44, 49, 58, 60, 87, 102, 119–120, 141.
Protection of Freedoms Act 2012 – 63, 103–104, 121, 124, 127, 136, 195.
Regulation of Investigatory Powers Act 2000 – 17, 36, 70, 76–79, 83, 88, 131, 175.
Rehabilitation of Offenders Act 1974 – 18, 116, 211–213.
Sexual Offences Act 1967 – 33.
Sexual Offences Act 2003 – 33, 61, 106, 160, 222–224, 228.
Sexual Offences (Amendment) Act 1976 – 147, 159–160.
Sexual Offences (Amendment) Act 1992 – 159.
Telecommunications Act 1984 – 83.
Terrorism Act 2000 – 43, 45, 192, 194–196, 202.
Terrorism Act 2006 – 62, 192, 195, 201–202.
Youth Justice and Criminal Evidence Act 1999 – 144–147, 155–156, 161.
Violent Crime Reduction Act 2006 – 61.

Index

A

Adamson v UK (1999) Application 22293/98, 252

A.D.T. v. the United Kingdom (application no. 35765/97) judgment Strasbourg 31 July 2000, 29

Anti-social Behaviour, Crime and Policing Act 2014, 166, 175

Anti-social Behaviour Order (ASBO), 165, 174, 175, 258

Anti-Terrorism, Crime and Security Act 2001, 84, 230

Appeal No: EA/2012/0171 Southampton City Council v. The Information Commissioner 19 February 2013 First-Tier Tribunal, 138

Approved Mental Health Professional, 55, 56

arrest, 10, 41, 43, 55, 63, 64, 69, 108, 139, 227

A v Secretary of State for the Home Department [2004] UKHL 56, 222

Association of Chief Police Officers (ACPO), 67, 68, 96, 115, 121, 122, 130, 141, 142

Attorney General v Greater Manchester Newspapers Ltd [2001] All ER (D) 32 (Dec), 244

Audio Recording of Police Interviews, 40

A v United Kingdom (2009) 49 EHRR 29, 230

Australia, 19, 251

Automatic Number Plate Recognition (ANPR), 2, 107, 127, 134, 138–45

National ANPR Data Centre (NADC), 141, 142, 144

© The Author(s) 2017

D. Marshall, T. Thomas, *Privacy and Criminal Justice*,

https://doi.org/10.1007/978-3-319-64912-2

B

Bentham, Jeremy, 17, 23
Big Brother Watch (BBW), 9, 83,
    84, 86, 116, 117, 131, 132,
    138, 139, 146, 147
blacklisting, 117
body scanners, 53–4
Body-Worn Video (BWV), 145–7
*Bouchacourt v. France (Application no.
    5335/06) 2009*, 254
Brandeis, Louis, 4, 21
branding, 16
bugging. *See* electronic surveillance
    devices
Bulger, Jamie, 134, 172, 173, 244

C

*Callaghan v Independent News and
    Media Ltd [2009] NIQB 1*,
    243
Cambridgeshire police, 106
*Campbell Christie v United Kingdom
    (application No. 21482/93)
    European Commission of Human
    Rights (27 June 1994)*, 78
*Campbell v Mirror Group Newspaper
    [2004] UKHL 22*, 34
*Carter v Metropolitan Police
    Commissioner [1975] 1 WLR
    507*, 56
Charter of Fundamental Rights of
    the European Union, 25
CCTV. *See* Closed Circuit Television
    (CCTV)
*Chief Constable of Humberside Police
    and Ors v The Information
    Commissioner and Anor [2009]
    EWCA Civ 1079*, 123

Child Sex Offender Disclosure
    Scheme (CSOD), 256
civil liberties, 5, 56, 148, 228
Cleveland police, 140
Closed Circuit Television (CCTV),
    2, 8, 11, 65, 127, 133–8, 146,
    148, 159, 191
Commissioner for the Retention and
    Use of Biometric Material,
    109, 110, 131
communication service providers,
    84, 88
community notification, 256
community payback, 12, 206–9, 249
Control Orders, 223, 228–30, 232,
    234
Coroners and Justice Act 2009, 68,
    161, 165
Council of Europe, 28, 33, 150, 207
Counter Terrorism Act 2008, 228
Counter-terrorism Strategy
    (CONTEST), 223–5
courts, 153–81
    intermediaries, 160
    Pre-Sentence Reports, 179–81
    special measures, 159, 160, 181
    video links, 158
Covert Human Intelligence Sources,
    71, 82, 83, 93, 98, 99
Crime and Disorder Act 1998, 35,
    174, 205, 246, 249
Crime and Security Act 2010, 195
crime prevention, 1, 11, 23, 43, 63,
    92, 245–50, 254, 257, 262,
    265
Crime (Sentences) Act 1997, 171
Criminal Evidence (Witness
    Anonymity) Act 2008, 165
Criminal Justice Act 1948, 20

Criminal Justice Act 1967, 20
Criminal Justice Act 1988, 158, 176
Criminal Justice Act 1991, 158
Criminal Justice Act 2003, 42, 108,
    111, 112, 206, 213, 228, 257,
    258
Criminal Justice and Courts Act
    2015, 118
Criminal Justice and Courts Services
    Act 2000, 257
Criminal Justice and Public Order
    Act 1994, 41–7, 158, 172,
    191, 211
Criminal Record Office (CRO), 20,
    104, 108
Criminal Records Bureau (CRB),
    114

D

data protection, 9, 28, 29, 33, 35,
    53, 92, 102, 107, 118, 120–2,
    134, 136, 146
Data Protection Act 1984, 28, 121
Data Protection Act 1998, 29, 33,
    102, 107, 122, 134, 136, 146
data retention, 84, 85, 121, 122,
    144, 236
*David Lewis v Director of Public
    Prosecutions [2004] EWHC
    3081 (Admin)*, 56
*Davies v Merseyside Police & Anor
    [2015] EWCA Civ 114 (19
    February 2015)*, 49
*Davis and Watson v Secretary of State
    for the Home Department
    [2015] EWHC 2092 (Admin)*,
    86

Derbyshire Constabulary, 97, 247
detention, treatment and
    questioning, 40, 63
Devon and Cornwall Constabulary,
    145
*Digital Rights Ireland (C-293/12) and
    Seitlinger and Others
    (C-594/12) ECJ (Grand
    Chamber) 8 April 2014*, 86,
    236
Disclosure and Barring Service
    (DBS), 124, 260, 266
DNA, 11, 32, 64, 65, 102, 108, 125,
    128, 129, 214, 220
    National DNA Database, 32, 35,
    64, 109, 110
Don't Spy on Us, 86, 90
*Douglas v Hello! Ltd. [2007] UKHL
    21*, 34
Driver and Vehicle Licensing Agency
    (DVLA), 103
drones. *See* Unmanned Aerial
    Vehicles (UAVs)
drugs, 27, 42, 43, 47, 49–51, 64, 79,
    188, 190, 191, 195, 199
    drug detection dogs, 50
Durham Constabulary, 27, 140

E

electronic monitoring, 156, 209–12
    Alcohol Abstinence and
    Monitoring Requirement
    (AAMR), 212, 213
    sobriety tags, 212–14
    voice verification, 212
electronic surveillance devices, 80
employment screening, 125

Entinck v Carrington (1765) 19 State
    Tr 1029, 58
European Court of Human Rights
    (ECHR), 6, 25, 32, 43, 44, 77,
    110, 125, 136, 173, 198, 199,
    220, 225, 230

F

F and Angus Aubrey Thompson v.
    Secretary of State for the Justice
    [2008] EWHC 3170, 253
facial recognition technology, 130
Female Genital Mutilation (FGM),
    178
fingerprints, 20, 64, 102, 103, 108,
    109, 116, 128, 252
Foka v. Turkey, no. 28940/09, §§
    74-79, 24 June 2008, 43
Folgerø and Others v. Norway
    (Application no. 15472/02)
    ECHR 29 June 2007, 225
France, 18

G

G v Commissioner of Police for the
    Metropolis [2011] EWHC 331
    (Admin), 62
Gardel v France (Application
    16428/05) 2009, 254
Gender Recognition Act 2004, 203
Germany, 10, 23, 31, 77, 214,
    228
Gillan and Quinton v UK (application
    no. 4158/05) European Court of
    Human Rights (12 Jan 2010),
    44, 220, 235

Government Communications
    Headquarters, 87, 91
Greater Manchester Police, 63
Guardian News and Media Ltd.
    and ors. v R and Erol
    Incedol [2016] EWCA Crim
    11, 167

H

Habitual Criminal Act 1869, 20
Halford v. United Kingdom
    [1997] ECHR 32 (25 June
    1997), 79
Handcock v Baker (1800) 2 Bos and
    P 260, 62
Harriot v DPP [2005] EWHC 965
    (Admin), 55
Hellewell -v- Chief Constable of
    Derbyshire QBD (Gazette
    15-Feb-95, Times 13-Jan-95,
    [1995] 1WLR 804, [1995] 4
    All ER 473, 248
Home Office, 20, 40, 46, 55, 74, 79,
    81, 92, 93, 98, 99, 104, 105,
    107, 113, 114, 119, 123, 128,
    130, 135, 142, 146, 150, 158,
    159, 165, 175, 176, 199, 205,
    210, 247, 253, 254, 256, 259,
    260, 264
Home Office Large Major Enquiry
    System (HOLMES), 113
Home Office Police Scientific
    Development Branch, 138
Human Rights Act 1998, 6, 25, 33,
    34, 60, 80, 102, 107, 193,
    236, 265
Humberside Police, 106, 123

I

identification, 40, 102, 108, 171,
    243
identity cards, 23, 36
informants, 11, 16, 18, 71, 76, 99
Information Commissioner, 3, 36,
    123, 137, 138
information privacy, 6–10, 26, 32,
    33, 147, 231, 236, 241, 267
Information Tribunal, 123
Interception of Communications Act
    1985, 73, 78, 92
Interception of Communications
    Commissioner, 32, 78
intimate searches, 49–50
Investigatory Powers Act 2016, 11, 33,
    73–5, 87–91, 235, 264, 267
Investigatory Powers Tribunal, 83,
    87, 91
Italy, 72

J

juries, 167, 168

K

Kaye v Robertson [1991] FSR 62, 4
Kent police, 148
*Klass v Germany (1978) 2 EHRR
    214*, 31
*Knox v Anderton [1982] 76 Cr App R
    156*, 56

L

Law Enforcement Data System
    (LEDS), 107
Leicestershire police, 130

liberty (campaign group), 44, 64,
    87–90, 123, 125, 130, 134,
    136, 140, 141, 216, 219, 220,
    228, 230, 232, 236, 260, 264
Licensed Premises (Exclusion of
    Certain Persons) Act 1980, 248
Luddites, 17

M

Malone v UK (1984) 7 EHRR 14, 31
*Massey v UK (2003) Application
    14399/02*, 252
*Matthews v United Kingdom
    (application no. 28576/95)
    European Commission of
    Human Rights (16 October
    1996)*, 78
*Maxine Carr v News Group
    Newspapers Limited & others
    [2005] EWHC 971 (QB)*, 245
Mazzini, Guiseppe, 16, 72
*MB v France (Application no.
    22115/06) (2009)*, 254
McKie, Shirley, 116
media, 33, 34, 60, 69, 84, 89, 96,
    167, 169, 171, 175, 177, 180,
    187, 243, 267
Mental Health Act 1983, 4, 55–8, 180
Merseyside police, 49, 60, 63, 79
Metropolitan Police, 21, 44, 45, 48,
    49, 52, 56, 59, 74, 93–6, 99,
    108, 116, 129, 145, 148, 217,
    247
Misuse of Drugs Act 1971, 27, 42
*Mohidin & Anor v Commissioner of
    the Police of the Metropolis &
    Ors [2015] EWHC 2740 (QB)
    (02 October 2015)*, 49

Mosquito, 149, 150
Motor Insurance Database, 103, 140
Multi-Agency Public Protection
    Arrangements (MAPPA), 111,
    257, 258

N

National Crime Agency (NCA), 156,
    166, 189
    NCA Financial Intelligence Unit,
    155
National Domestic Extremism Unit,
    96
National Intelligence Model (NIM),
    107
National Police Chiefs' Council
    (NPCC), 110, 143, 144, 148,
    166, 226
National Prison Intelligence
    Coordination Centre, 189
National Probation Service, 206, 213
National Public Order Intelligence
    Unit, 95, 98
National Security Agency, 86, 87
National Special Branch Intelligence
    System, 111, 125
North Yorkshire Police, 140
Northamptonshire Police, 213
Northumbria Police, 123

O

Offender Management Act 2007, 67,
    195, 260
Official Secrets Act 1989, 117–18
Olsson v. Sweden, [1988] ECHR 2,
    226
Orwell, George, 3, 23, 173

P

*P and Others v. Secretary of State for
    the Home Department, and the
    Secretary of State for Justice
    [2017] EWCA Civ 321)*, 125
Panopticon, 17, 23
Parole Conditions, 260–1
Payne, Sarah, 256
    Sarah's Law (*see* Child Sex
    Offender Disclosure Scheme
    (CSOD))
Peck v UK (2003) 36 EHRR 41, 136
Peck, Geoffrey, 136
pitchford enquiry, 98, 99
*PJS v News Group Newspapers Ltd.
    [2016] EWCA Civ 100*, 34
Police Act 1996, 115, 118
Police Act 1997, 80, 92, 107, 124,
    260
Police and Criminal Evidence Act
    1984, 20, 40–3, 59, 61, 92,
    108, 128, 155
police–*passim*, 155
    custody suites, 48, 51, 65, 128
    police cautions, 43, 46, 63, 93–5,
    99, 104, 121–3, 212, 213,
    260, 266
    police intelligence, 11, 20, 27,
    103, 105, 106, 111, 118, 119,
    133, 147, 265 (*see also*
    NPIOU, NSBIS)
    police national computer, 101–4,
    106, 107, 109, 114, 115, 125,
    144, 156, 240, 260
    police national database, 11, 35,
    102, 103, 105–7, 129, 132,
    144
Police Reform Act 2002, 115, 118
polygraphs, 67, 260

Post Office, 16, 72
press. *See* media
Pretty v United Kingdom (2002) 35
    EHRR 1, 6
prisons
    Certified Normal
        Accommodation (CNA),
        185
    contact with family and friends,
        195–200
    Covert Communications Data
        Capture (CCDC), 197
    Dedicated Search Teams (DSTs),
        191
    Home Detention Curfew (HDC),
        205
    Local Security Strategy (LSS),
        184, 197
    mandatory drugs tests (MDT),
        11, 184, 191–4
    Mother and Baby Units (MBUs),
        200–2
    National Security Framework
        (NSF), 184, 190
    National Prison Intelligence
        Coordination Centre, 189
    Operational Capacity, 185, 186
    overcrowding, 11, 184–7
    pregnant women in prison, 200–1
    Prison Rules, 187, 191, 192,
        194–6, 201, 202
    searches in prisons, 11, 184,
        187–200
    trans-gender prisoners, 202–4
privacy–passim
    definition, 3–7, 29, 32, 33, 76,
        268
    history, 13–38
    public attitudes toward, 9

Privacy International, 87, 90, 91,
    197
Privacy International v. (1) Secretary
    of State for Foreign and
    Commonwealth Affairs(2)
    Secretary of State for the Home
    Department, (3) Government
    Communications Headquarters,
    (4) Security Service, (5) Secret
    Intelligence Service -
    Investigatory Powers Tribunal
    case no. IPT/15/110/CH
    [2016], 91
privileged information, 80, 155, 195
Protection of Freedoms Act 2012,
    64, 109, 110, 129, 134, 137,
    147, 220
public protection, 36, 111, 123, 189,
    195, 205, 206, 239, 245,
    250–9, 266

R

R v A (No2) [2001] UKHL 25, 163
R v Beckles [2005] 1 WLR 2829, 67
R v Blackwell [2006] EWCA Crim
    2185, 177
R v Bogdal [2008] EWCA Crim 1, 56
R (Catt) and R (T) v Commissioner of
    Police of the Metropolis [2015]
    UKSC 9, 125
R v Chief Constable of North Wales ex
    p Thorpe [1999] QB396), 246
R v. Chief Constable of North Wales
    Police, ex p. Thorpe (1998) The
    Times, 23 March, 246
R v Davis [2008] UKHL 36, 164
R v Edwards (1978) 67 Cr App R
    228, 55

re Gallagher [2003] NIQB, 253
registration of sex offenders, 251–4
registration of terrorists, 230–1
Regulation of Investigatory Powers
    Act 2000, 11, 73, 79, 81–4,
    87, 92, 141, 196
rehabilitation, 12, 19, 124, 206
    anonymity, 241
Rehabilitation of Offenders Act
    1974, 12, 124, 240, 241
*R (Ellis) v Chief Constable of Essex
    Police [2003] EWHC 1321
    (Admin)*, 249
*R (Forbes) v Secretary of State for the
    Home Department [2006]
    EWCA Civ. 962*, 252
*R (Gillan) v Commissioner of Police for
    the Metropolis [2006] UKHL*, 41
*R v Gul [2013] 3 WLR 1207, [2013]
    UKSC 64*, 217
*R v Hamilton [2007] EWCA Crim
    2062, [2008] QB 224 para 21
    (CA)*, 30
*R v Hoare and Pierce [2004] EWCA
    Crim 784*, 67
Rice v Connolly [1966] 2 QB 414, 41
R v Khan [1996] 3 WLR 162 at 175,
    80
*R (Miranda) v Secretary of State for
    the Home Department and
    Commissioner for the
    Metropolitan Police [2016]
    EWCA 6*, 217
R v. Morgan ([1975] 2 All ER 347, 176
*Roberts, R (on the application of) v
    The Commissioner of Police of
    the Metropolis & Ors [2014]
    EWCA Civ 69 (04 February
    2014)*, 45

*Roberts, R (on the application of) v
    The Commissioner of the
    Metropolitan Police [2012]
    EWHC 1977 (Admin) (17 July
    2012)*, 45
*R (on the application of Christopher
    Prothero) v Secretary of State for
    the Home Department [2013]
    EWHC 2830 (Admin)*, 252
*R (on the application of F (by his
    litigation friend F)) and
    Thompson (FC) (Respondents) v.
    Secretary of State for the Home
    Department (Appellant) [2010]
    UKSC 17*, 253
*R, on the application of Mohamed
    Irfan v The Secretary of State for
    the Home Department [2012]
    EWCA Civ 1471*, 231
*R (on the application of P and A) v
    Secretary of State for Justice,
    Secretary of State for Home
    Department and Chief
    Constable of Thames Valley
    Police [2016] EWHC 89
    (Admin))*, 125
*R (on the application of Wang Yam)
    (Appellant) v Central Criminal
    Court and another, (Respondents)
    [2015] UKSC 76*, 167
*R v Roberts [2003] EWCA Crim
    2753*, 55
*R (R on the application of T and
    Another) v Secretary of State for
    the Home Department and
    Another [2014] UKSC 35*, 124
*R (RMC and FJ) v Metropolitan
    Police Service [2012] EWHC
    1681*, 129, 131

R v Secretary of State for the Home Department, ex p Tremayne (1996) Unreported, 2 May 1996, 192

R v Secretary of State for the Home Department, ex parte Daly [2001] UKHL 26, 190

R (Stanley, Marshall and Kelly) v Metropolitan Police Commissioner [2004] EWHC 2229 (Admin), 247

R (T) v Greater Manchester Chief Constable (CA) [2013] EWCA Civ 25, 260

Rule, James, 26

R (Wood) v Metropolitan Police Commissioner (2009) EWCA Civ 414, 132

S

S. and Marper v. The United Kingdom - 30562/04 [2008] ECHR 1581, 32, 64, 225

S and Marper v UK 48 EHRR 1169 2008 ECHR 1581, 109

Sarah's Law, 256

searching premises, 40, 58–63

Secretary of State for the Home Department v AF [2009] UKHL 28, 229

Secretary of State for the Home Department v GG [2009] EWCA Civ 786, 229

Secretary of State for the Home Department v JJ [2007] UKHL 45, [2007] 3 WLR 642, 229

security services, 20, 31, 32, 75, 78, 83, 84, 86, 91, 235

Sessay, R (on the application of) v South London & Maudsley NHS Foundation Trust & Anor [2011] EWHC 2617 (QB), 56

Sexual Harm Prevention Order (SHPO), 177, 258

Sexual Offences (Amendment) Act 1976, 162, 176, 177

Sexual Offences (Amendment) Act 1992, 176

Sexual Offences Act 1967, 29

Sexual Offences Act 2003, 29, 62, 112, 177, 251, 253, 254, 258, 259

Sexual Risk Order (SRO), 177, 258, 259

sniffer dogs. *See* drug detection dogs

Snowden, Edward, 37, 86–9, 100, 217, 263, 267

soft information. *See* police intelligence

Special Branch, 20, 93, 97, 111, 117, 125

special demonstration squad, 93–5, 97

Special Duties Section, 95

Staffordshire police, 123

Stephen Lawrence family, 97

stop and question, 40–1

stop and search, 10, 27, 39, 41–8, 52, 219, 220, 235

Storck v Germany 16 September 2005 ECHR Application no. 61603/00, 214

strip searches, 10, 47–9, 51, 53, 187, 189, 198

super-recogniser programme, 149

Surveillance Camera Commissioner (SCC), 107, 134, 137, 138, 143

T

Telecommunications Act 1984, 87
telephone tapping, 10, 27, 31, 36,
    71, 74–7, 82, 87, 184, 195,
    220, 235
terrorism, 215–37
Terrorism Act 2000, 42, 44, 216,
    219, 220, 222, 227, 228
Terrorism Act 2006, 64, 216, 220,
    226–8
Thames Valley Police, 106, 125, 141
*T v. UK, No. 24724/94, 16 December
    1999*, 170

U

undercover police, 11, 92, 94, 96, 97
United Nations (UN), 207, 227
    UN Convention on the Rights of
        the Child 1989, 174
    UN Universal Declaration of
        Human Rights 1948, 5, 24
Unmanned Aerial Vehicles (UAV's),
    147
USA, 4, 8, 26, 37, 87, 212, 215,
    222, 228, 251, 254–6
USSR, 10

V

*Venables and Thompson v NG
    Newspapers Ltd., [2001] 1 WLR
    1038*, 244
Violent Crime Reduction Act 2006,
    62
ViSOR, 11, 111–13, 231
visual recording of police interviews,
    40, 158, 159

W

*Wainwright v. UK European Court of
    Human Rights (Fourth Section)
    Application No. 12350/04,
    Strasbourg 26 September 2006*,
    199
Warren, Samuel, 4, 21
Watergate affair, 27
West Midlands police, 119, 140, 141
West Yorkshire Police, 69, 113, 134,
    139, 145, 243, 250
Westin, Alan, 26
Willcock v Muckle [1952] 1 KB 367,
    23
Wilson Doctrine, 75, 88, 91
witnesses, 11, 61, 153, 157
    intimidated and vulnerable, 159,
        160
    investigation anonymity orders, 68
    Witness Anonymity Orders, 163,
        165
    Witness Protection, 165, 166

X

*X, A Woman Formerly Known As Mary
    Bell -and-Y v Stephen O'Brien
    -and- News Group Newspapers
    Ltd. -and- Mgn Ltd. [2003]
    EWHC 1101 (QB) 21 May
    2003*, 244

Y

youth court, 168–70
    reporting restrictions, 170–3
Youth Justice and Criminal Evidence
    Act 1999, 159–63, 178